Behavioural Psychotherapy
A Handbook for Nurses

Behavioural Psychotherapy
A Handbook for Nurses

DAVE A. RICHARDS RMN ENBCC 650
Nurse Behaviour Therapist, Institute of Psychiatry, De Crespigny Park, Denmark Hill, London.

and

BOB McDONALD BSc, RMN ENBCC 650
Northwick Park Hospital, Watford Rd, Harrow, Middlesex

Heinemann Nursing

Heinemann Medical Books
An imprint of Heinemann Professional Publishing Ltd
Halley Court, Jordan Hill, Oxford OX2 8EJ

OXFORD   LONDON   SINGAPORE
NAIROBI   IBADAN   KINGSTON

First published in 1990

British Library Cataloguing in Publication Data
Richards, David A.
  Behavioural psychotherapy.
  1. Medicine. Behavioural psychotherapy
  I. Title   II. McDonald, Bob
  616.89142

ISBN 433 025263

Typeset by Lasertext Ltd, Stretford, Manchester
Printed and bound in Great Britain by
Biddles Ltd, Guildford and King's Lynn

Contents

Introduction

Our reasons for writing this book at this time, and aiming a text on behavioural psychotherapy at psychiatric nurses are fourfold.

- Firstly, behavioural psychotherapy has now become firmly established as an integral part of mental health provision and has advanced so much in recent years that it seemed necessary to produce a summary of the 'state of the art'.
- Secondly, there have been changes in the training syllabus for psychiatric nurses which have greatly increased the profile of behavioural approaches but there are still no specialized nursing texts which adequately cover the subject matter.
- Thirdly, many psychiatric nurses and particularly community psychiatric nurses, are attempting to apply behavioural approaches to clinical problems and, in our personal experience, have been demanding a book like this for some time.
- Fourthly, and perhaps most importantly, there is no text which brings a nursing perspective to behavioural psychotherapy and treats nurses as experts and potential experts in the field.

We have not, however, written a treatment manual. We firmly believe that behavioural psychotherapy, like any other skill, cannot be learned from a book but must be taught interpersonally and supervised by experienced clinicians. We intend this book, however, to be useful both during supervised training and as a reference to the practitioner.

We have split the book into four parts.

- The first deals with the theoretical model which behavioural psychotherapists use. We have tried to break with tradition and present learning theory in a way which makes it more applicable to everyday life than to the laboratory. We then look at how behavioural psychotherapy has developed in its relatively brief history and trace the role of psychiatric nursing in that history.
- The second part deals with interviewing, assessment, planning,

evaluation and implementation. We have designed these chapters to be explicit guides to good practice and have endeavoured to supply enough detail for them to be used as such.

- The third part describes our treatment approach to generalized anxiety problems, phobias, obsessions and compulsions and sexual diversity and dissatisfaction. We chose these because, although they do not represent the full range of problems which people bring to behavioural psychotherapy, they are the more common and illustrate well the approach.

- The fourth part looks to the future, both in terms of how we see behavioural psychotherapy developing and how we see the future of nursing within that. We also discuss some of the innovative problems and approaches being tackled by nurse behavioural psychotherapists right now. We expect that by the time this is read, some will seem familiar and others, perhaps forgotten. Such are the risks of predicting future directions in a fast-moving field which is still in its adolescence as opposed to the stability found in longer established psychotherapeutic approaches.

We have consciously taken a stance on one of the issues debated in psychiatric nursing today. Some would argue that the use of all medical terminology is dehumanizing and 'labelling' and implies an acceptance by the writer of a medical model and approach to 'treatment'. We do not take this position. The use of agreed and objective terms for regularly occurring problems provides merely a starting point for the application of an individually tailored programme of care. Classificatory systems such as ICD and DSM III (which we have used in this book) are not the monopoly domain of the medical profession. Instead, they represent the results of an objective approach to the difficult but necessary task of ordering the complex world of mental health problems. As such, they are available and valuable to anyone who accepts the need for the creation of order out of chaos and, just as importantly, recognizes the need to communicate accurately with professionals from other backgrounds. As nursing becomes more research based, it is increasingly important that we can talk to the rest of the scientific community in a language which they understand and do not find alienating.

Finally, we should like to acknowledge our debt to the many friends and colleagues who have contributed over the years to the clinical and teaching work of the Psychological Treatment Unit at the Maudsley Hospital. Our experiences there have shaped us, this book and, we believe, the future direction of psychiatric nursing in this country.

Dave A. Richards
Bob McDonald

1990

Part 1

Chapter 1

The behavioural model

Misconceptions and issues

The way in which behavioural psychologists and therapists conceptualize their activities is probably one of the most misrepresented in the social sciences and it is, therefore, necessary to take a little time to describe what the model *is not* as well as what it is.

The main misconception is that 'behaviourism' is a psychological theory which denies the existence of thoughts and feelings. There was, and probably still is, a philosophical position which took this provocative stance. Thankfully, however, this is not a book about philosophy and we don't really have to worry about the strange positions philosophers get themselves into.

There was, in fact, an early psychologist, William James, who believed that thoughts and feelings were *byproducts* of behaviour (i.e. he accepted they existed but didn't think they were very important) but this view has not been seriously held for about 50 years now and it seems more useful to consider more current views.

Nowadays, the consensual view among those associated with the behavioural position is that behaviour, autonomic responses and thoughts and feelings are all important parameters of any human activity. They would say, however, that all three are linked (the jargon word is synergistic) and that an emphasis on behaviour is more productive because it is more easily measured and more directly modifiable.

Importantly, this does not attempt to deny either the existence or importance of emotional and cognitive responses but argues that these will inevitably be altered by attainable changes in behaviour. There is, in fact, a great deal of experimental and clinical evidence to support this stance.

Perhaps a rather trivial example will help make this line of argument a bit clearer. Let's suppose that someone is very afraid of spiders. This is fairly common for reasons which we'll touch on later in this section. In order to understand what is happening to this person, we need to classify their responses to spiders into three areas.

Behavioural
They might scream, run away, insist that someone else removes the offending beastie, or indulge in some more extreme and possibly dangerous strategy to avoid the arachnid.

Autonomic
This refers to the activity of the peripheral nervous system and we would expect to see changes in heart rate, blood pressure, respiration rate, sweat gland activity, EEG measures and a few other things when someone encounters something which makes them seriously afraid.

Cognitive
These are the thoughts, attitudes and feelings that the person has about the spider. They may see them as dangerous, ugly, nauseating and have the subjective experience of fear.

Now, in theory, because these three response systems are generally consistent with one another, we should be able to modify the fear response by changing any one of them. However, changing cognitions directly, which is what most psychotherapies attempt to do, is an extremely difficult and generally fruitless endeavour. This is not to say that it cannot be done; only that it has been attempted very frequently indeed with very few, if any, unequivocal successes.

Altering the autonomic responses associated with anxiety is generally attempted by the administration of drugs such as tranquillizers (these days, usually benzodiazepines) or β-blockers. These have not been shown to be effective and, certainly in the case of benzodiazepines, to have harmful long-term effects.

On purely practical and humanitarian grounds, therefore, we are forced to consider the possibility of behavioural intervention.

Happily, we have more reason to be hopeful of this producing the kind of change we are seeking. By methods which will be described in more detail in Chapter 9, it is possible to alter the behavioural component of the fear response to spiders. What happens next is remarkably consistent.

When the individual begins to voluntarily approach spiders, the next thing to happen is that the autonomic responses begin to diminish (e.g. heart rate returns towards baseline). Then, in time, attitudes and thinking begin to change (e.g. spiders are considered to be less ugly and dangerous).

The main point here, of course, is that deliberately altering behaviour does not simply result in a change in behaviour but that it produces enduring changes in the other two systems as well.

Approaches oriented towards an initial alteration of the other two systems fail consistently to achieve even remotely comparable effects. This may seem a rather pragmatic argument in favour of a behavioural approach but it is, of course, what behavioural theory would predict and we will, throughout this book, favour an approach which blends theoretical and pragmatic viewpoints.

The term 'behaviourism' is used rarely these days to describe the theoretical position of someone researching or practising behavioural interventions. It has been almost entirely superseded by 'learning theorist' which again emphasizes an integrated approach as well as acknowledging the influence of experimental psychology. There is, of course, room for confusion since 'behaviour therapy', 'behavioural therapy' and 'behavioural psychotherapy' continue to be in common use and seem too well established to be supplanted.

Some workers now prefer the term 'cognitive-behaviour therapy' and, although at first glance this might appear to be helpful in a semantic way, the problem is that it suggests a central role for cognitive change when this has not been clearly demonstrated. This is very much a live and continuing debate and it is hard to see how it can readily be resolved since it is extremely difficult to implement cognitive strategies of change which do not have, at the very least, *implicit* instructions to alter behaviour.

This is a very old problem in psychological therapies and even Sigmund Freud gave explicit instructions to his phobic patients that they should enter, and remain in, situations which evoked their fears on a regular basis. That, of course, we now know to be a potent treatment for even the most serious phobic problems (McDonald *et al.*, 1978).

The key concepts

It is not possible in a book of this size to give a fully argued and complete account of the concepts behavioural psychotherapists use to understand the origins of the disorders they treat and to provide an explanatory model of how treatments work. What follows is therefore a necessarily truncated consideration of the main principles.

There are two basic 'building blocks' associated with the behavioural tradition and these are *classical* and *instrumental* learning. Both are often described as conditioning theories and we should explain our strong preference for the term 'learning'. Firstly, 'conditioning' is etymologically unsound and derives from a mis-translation from Russian. Secondly, it has powerful overtones of something that one imposes on another organism.

While that may be a good description of what goes on in an animal laboratory, it seems a far from apt term for real life where serendipity is probably the most significant influence.

This is not so pedantic as it may sound. Our attitudes and understanding of concepts are necessarily influenced by the emotional tone we associate with them (via, of course, the process of classical learning) and 'learning' is a much more accurate term to describe the plasticity and adaptivity we need for survival in a complex environment.

It is also important to move instrumental and classical learning away from the laboratory and into the natural environment in order to give them ecological validity. Both learning theorists and, less forgiveably, behaviour therapists have been slow to do this and to communicate this to the public and other professional groups and have, therefore, contributed greatly to misconceptions about the field.

For example, classical and instrumental are often written about as though they were completely separate processes one of which is important in some situations and the other in others.

Therapeutic strategies have been developed which hinge on the laboratory-developed 'laws' of one of these forms of learning. However, this is to forget that it takes a great deal of ingenuity, even in a laboratory, to unequivocally demonstrate one form of learning in the absence of the other. Clearly, anything so elusive in the laboratory is a very unlikely event in the 'real world' and, therefore, any attempt to explain emotional responding using only one process is doomed to failure and confusion.

Classical Learning is that associated with I. P. Pavlov whose famous dogs learned to salivate at the sound of a tone which had been previously presented at the same time as meat powder on the tongue. The basic paradigm is very straightforward and is the event that occurs when a stimulus, through being paired with another stimulus, comes to produce a response which is similar to the one originally produced by the other stimulus. For example, if we direct a puff of air to someone's eye, they blink. If we sound a tone at the same time as the air-puff, the person will rapidly come to blink merely at the sound of the tone.

It is well established that inconsistent pairings of the two stimuli lead to less reliable learning and that, in general, learning gradually disappears if the pairings are discontinued.

It is a pity that Pavlov was a physiologist because, although he elaborated an important psychological idea, it has become almost entirely associated with physiological responding to the exclusion of other systems. While it is easy to demonstrate classical learning with autonomic responses, both cognitive and behavioural effects can also be readily produced and most everyday instances will involve all three.

Instrumental Learning or *Operant Conditioning* has, as a set of ideas, been around for a long time although its modern formulation is attributable to B. F. Skinner and his co-workers. The basic idea is that a response is altered in probability by its consequences. If an organism emits a behaviour which leads to either reward (such as food when it is hungry) or relief from discomfort (having an electric shock terminated) then it becomes much more likely to produce that behaviour in future. Alternatively, if a certain behaviour leads to discomfort or the deprivation of an expected reward, then that behaviour becomes less likely. In both these examples we would say that it had learnt a *contingency*.

One feature of instrumental learning, in contrast to classical, is that in general it is strengthened rather than weakened by inconsistent pairings. In other words, when a certain behaviour is followed unpredictably by reward or punishment then changes in its probability are more robust.

It must be said that there is a vast literature on both these forms of learning and any reader wishing to explore the detail of instrumental and classical learning (or conditioning) further can find an appropriate starting point in virtually any introductory psychology text. There you will find a lot of detail about schedules of reinforcement, habituation curves, frustrative non-reward and so on.

While this is an important area of study in its own right and may some day give rise to significant therapeutic advances, such detail would be distracting here because of the way in which the two forms of learning are considered in isolation with, therefore, very limited applicability to the kind of real life experiences we want to consider. All that we really need to know here is that classical and instrumental learning are separable in theory but effectively not in practice and that the principles briefly outlined above hold.

LEARNING AND EVERYDAY LIFE

What we would now like to do is to consider most of the important concepts used by behaviour psychotherapists to explain how their clients came to acquire their particular difficulty and how treatment approaches work.

Arousability

Often referred to by the technically correct but rather laden term 'neuroticism', every parent knows about the biological basis of this. Quite simply, we come into the world with autonomic nervous systems 'set' at different levels of responsivity and, if we happen to be at the extremes of the distribution, this is readily apparent from an early age. Like other biologically determined characteristics (e.g. height), most of us are in the middle of the range. Being at either extreme can be disadvantageous. Too little arousability can leave us with too little incentive to perform as well as we might and too much can render us prone to excessive worry and strain. We all know people who react markedly to the smallest thing and always have something to worry about and other people who are infuriatingly unbothered about what seems to others to be major dramas. Another disadvantage of being at the high arousability end of the spectrum is that we are then much more prone to develop and to fail to unlearn fears, phobias and depression.

Unpleasant events, psychological disorder and various physiological events (e.g. the amount of tea and coffee we drink, the functioning of our thyroid glands) influence our level of arousability but biology sets the baseline.

Avoidance and escape

A friend of ours recently went to the dentist for what was anticipated would be a routine and familiar treatment but which turned out to be an extremely painful experience. When he was due to return for the treatment to be completed a week later, he experienced a marked reluctance to do so, a dread of what was going to happen and the subjective and physical manifestations of anxiety which reached a peak while he was in the waiting room *even though he knew that the follow-up did not involve a painful procedure.*

This was clearly related to his experience of the week before and it may be worthwhile considering what might have produced this reaction. Clearly, simply learning a new physiological response by classical means could not possibly account for a response with such clear cognitive components and which, in any case, produced a physiological response not present in the original experience. So, his reluctance to go to the dental surgery might be understood as an instrumental response to the punishing effect of the previous visit, his negative thoughts a classically learned product of unpredicted pain and his heightened arousal a comprehensible effect of making himself do things he didn't want to do.

We're happy to say that he did not succumb to the temptation to stay away (*avoid*) or leave after he had arrived (*escape*) and that he can now visit his dentist with reasonable equanimity. However, if he had avoided or escaped this would almost certainly have had the effect of increasing his fear and he might now be quite committed to staying away from dentists and experience marked anxiety just thinking about it. The importance of these concepts are that they are central to our ideas about how situational anxieties such as phobias are developed and, more importantly, maintained.

Habituation

Shortly after his trip to the dentist, he went to visit his grandmother. She has a large pendulum clock in her sitting room which has a very loud 'tock'. When he arrived, he was unable to concentrate on her conversation because the noise of the clock was so distracting. She didn't seem to notice it. However, after a while he realized he had got used to it (*habituated*). Later in the afternoon, however, he suddenly realized that something was wrong – the clock had stopped!

Now, his grandmother hadn't noticed this although he became aware of it as soon as it had missed one 'tock'. The difference between them was that while she had become completely used to the noisy clock over the years (*chronically habituated*), he had to get used to it from scratch on each, infrequent, visit (*acute habituation*) and needed his brain to be doing something fairly active to suppress the noise. This is an important idea in explaining the process of change in fear reduction treatments.

Sensitization

This is a concept closely linked to habituation and refers to the mechanism by which emotion becomes associated with certain objects or events. It is necessary to explain how anxieties get worse over time, how some contacts with objects make one less fearful and why some more fearful, and how some behavioural treatments act, particularly those which seek to inhibit unwanted behaviours. We can see this operating most clearly in fears. Habituation, loss of fear, is the consequence of regular, prolonged and voluntary contact with a feared object or situation. Sensitization, on the other hand, is the increase in fear produced by erratic, short and involuntary contact and is why, each time we run away, we become a little more afraid.

Preparedness

Most of us have an illogical fear of something. If you ask a group of friends what they are afraid of, you are likely to find a few spider and snake phobics, someone who doesn't like underground train or plane travel and, perhaps, someone who is afraid of public speaking. You are very unlikely to find anyone who is seriously afraid of sheep, flies, scissors or bank managers. The important point about this is that there does seem to be a selectivity about the things we become afraid of and the commonest are:

- spiders and snakes
- being alone or among strangers
- being out in the open or enclosed
- heights
- the sight of blood.

There is much debate about whether these things are innate fears, objects and situations we are biologically more likely to become afraid of, or simply the kind of thing we are most likely to pay attention to. This is an interesting and important debate. Right now, we simply need to know that we are more ready to become fearful of some objects rather than others and that when we see someone with a complex cluster of fears, we should expect to find one of these core fears providing a thematic link.

The above are the main ideas which, together with the general processes of classical and instrumental learning, are used by behavioural psychotherapists to describe and understand the problems that clients bring to treatment and the *specific* processes involved in change. However, we should end this chapter as we began – by trying to debunk another myth. We are not arguing, as we are sometimes represented as doing, that the success of psychological treatment does not depend on a number of non-specific factors to do with the style of therapy and the relationship between therapist and therapee.

We would, however, argue strongly that the specific factors are an essential ingredient and that much of what we see practised in mental health relies too much on the non-specifics and is, therefore, less effective than it should be with the consequence that clients are denied their right to the most useful treatment available and their right to their maximum possible mental health.

REFERENCES

McDonald R., Sartory G., Grey S. J. et al. (1979). The effects of self-exposure instructions on agorophobic outpatients. *Behaviour Research and Therapy*, 17, 83–5.

Chapter 2

Development of behavioural psychotherapy

Pragmatic versus theoretical approaches

The connection between a theoretical model, such as the behavioural one described in the previous chapter, and the practical consequences of that theory are rarely clearcut. Except perhaps for the 'hard' sciences like physics and chemistry, practice in most fields of endeavour – the actual things that people do – can be understood from a number of possible perspectives.

This is certainly true in psychotherapy. When the debate between behavioural and analytic psychotherapists was at its height in the 1960s and early 1970s a number of papers were published from both camps which demonstrated that it was comparatively easy to reinterpret the procedures and effects of both treatments in terms of the opposing theory.

There is also dispute among behavioural psychotherapists about the importance of theory in their work. Some (e.g. Wolpe, 1976) have seen theory and practice as necessarily intertwined while the opposite view that behavioural psychotherapy has evolved in a purely pragmatic way has also been strongly argued (Marks, 1982). This may well be a fallacious argument. What the various proponents would appear to be saying is that theory has a greater or lesser importance to *themselves* in understanding and thinking about what *they* are doing in treatment and that they have a differing emphasis about the purpose of their work.

If a clinician is most concerned with achieving a satisfactory outcome in his patients in the shortest time possible then the pragmatic approach may well suffice. If, on the other hand, his emphasis is on using the outcome of clinical work to test and refine a theoretical model which he can then use to develop new therapeutic strategies then he will be inclined to perceive theory playing a larger part in his work.

An important point is, however, that both therapists may, to an independent observer, be doing exactly the same things with their patients. This chapter will take a neutral stance on this continuing debate. When theory has been important in producing developments, we shall acknowledge this and where pragmatism has been the progenitor we shall give this due credit. In this way, we hope that readers will be able to draw their own conclusions.

Historical precursors

There are a number of historical instances in which techniques closely resembling current or recent behavioural practices were used and which clearly predate behavioural therapy.

One approach which was very important in establishing behavioural psychotherapy was Systematic Desensitization (Wolpe, 1958) which is described in more detail below.

This essentially consists of repeatedly pairing relaxation with imagining anxiety-producing stimuli in an attempt to make these stimuli less fear-provoking. Approaches which now appear very similar to this were used in France in the 1890s to treat muscular tics and in Germany and the United States in the 1920s for the relief of a wide range of disorders. A non-clinical example of the use of repeated imagery to deal with anxiety can be found in Chapter 2 of '*Island*' by Aldous Huxley, a utopian novel written in the 1930s in which an entire population is skilled in what we would now call behavioural psychotherapy techniques.

Similar approaches to current behavioural approaches can also be found in Buddhist writings which appear to advocate relaxation and both imaginal and real-life exposure. This similarity between approaches derived from greatly differing theoretical and cultural roots is reviewed in detail by de Silva (1984). Relaxation, particularly the approach proposed by Jacobsen (1938), has been used in many countries continuously since then for both psychological and physical disorders.

Real-life exposure for fear reduction only became common practice in behavioural psychotherapy in the late 1960s but has clear precedents in the work of Jones (1924) where anxiety provoked by a rabbit was reduced by gradually moving the rabbit closer while the child, the famous Peter, was eating chocolate.

One can even find similarities in the work of Freud who wrote in 1919:

> 'one can hardly master a phobia if one waits till the patient lets the analysis influence him to give it up ... one only succeeds when one can induce them ... to go and to struggle with the anxiety while they make the attempt.'

Perhaps this is also a good example of the point made above that it is important to consider what a therapist is actually doing as well as the theory they consider they are implementing.

In the 1940s, approaches very similar to current treatments for anxiety disorders involving repeated approach in real life to situations which evoke anxiety were used for wartime stress victims and others.

Reinforcement techniques are now used extensively in a wide range of situations and for a considerable diversity of problems and have a number of precursors including Lancaster's (1805) educational system which used incentive to control classroom behaviour and was widely practised throughout the world in the nineteenth century.

The beginnings of behavioural psychotherapy

The first treatment approach which was overtly and unambiguously behavioural was that derived by Joseph Wolpe in South Africa. Wolpe was, and still is, interested in theory. He was influenced by the work of Pavlov on the 'conditioned reflex' and the possibility of using this to explain neurotic symptoms. He began in the early 1950s by researching on cats and attempting to produce fear reactions in them which could be seen as similar to human phobias. He then demonstrated that these could be eliminated by gradual reintroduction to the situation where the fear was learned at the same time as inducing the animal to eat. Wolpe's idea was that if fear is learned through classical learning then pairing a competing response, such as eating, with the stimuli which evoke the fear will have the effect of weakening and eventually eliminating the fear. What was required was that the strength of the competing response should be stronger than that of the fear response. He termed this process 'reciprocal inhibition'.

This line of reasoning led him to attempt to treat human fears. In order to keep the level of anxiety low, he asked his patients to create a 'hierarchy', typically of 20 to 30 items of ascending fearfulness and to imagine these rather than experience them in real life. As the 'reciprocal inhibitor', Wolpe used Jacobson's well established relaxation method. The treatment consisted of gradually working up the hierarchy of fear and briefly imagining each scene repeatedly until it could be imagined without anxiety. This, with a number of variants, turned out to be a successful treatment and Wolpe published a number of reports claiming a success rate of up to 80% with phobias. His influential book *'Psychotherapy by Reciprocal Inhibition'* was published in 1958 and helped to publicize this approach.

While these days this may seem a familiar and uncontroversial approach, it should be borne in mind that this was a revolutionary approach to psychotherapy which had, up till then, been almost entirely dominated by psychoanalysis (now more or less discredited as a therapeutic approach). Psychoanalysts had long claimed that any attempt to remove a 'symptom' in this way would inevitably lead to the appearance of new problems via a process termed 'symptom substitution'. This, of course, simply never happens (and psychoanalytic theory has now been modified to take account of this) but the view was held so widely in the past that it required considerable courage to begin this kind of treatment.

It was, in fact, the emergence of dissatisfaction with the psychoanalytic approach which sparked off parallel developments in the UK. In the early 1950s, Hans Eysenck began his rigorous scientific evaluation of analytic psychotherapy and argued powerfully that no case could be made for its effectiveness. At the same time, clinical psychologists, were becoming increasingly dissatisfied with their role as the administrators of psychometric tests and were attempting to find new ways of approaching clinical problems through general psychological principles. This combination of academic and clinical psychologists, both seeking alternatives to the hegemony of psychoanalysis, produced innovative treatment approaches based on the work of Pavlov and Hull. Case reports from students at the Maudsley during the 1950s came from individuals such as Hugh Gwynne Jones, Vic Meyer and Aubrey Yates who were later to become internationally known figures in the field of behaviour therapy (a term, by the way, which was effectively coined by Eysenck in 1959). In the early 1960s, a student of Wolpe's, Jack Rachman, arrived at the Maudsley bringing systematic desensitization with him. This fitted neatly with the developments at the Maudsley and this synergism provided the springboard for a continuing programme of clinical research. Psychiatry, by this time, had also joined in and Michael Gelder and Isaac Marks worked closely with psychologists to further refine and develop the techniques during the 1960s and 1970s. The 1960s also saw the first attempts to treat obsessional patients by behavioural means.

This was a very brave thing to do at the time. The perceived wisdom at the time was that one should never attempt to interfere with the rituals of obsessional patients because of the distress this would cause them. However, convinced that laboratory experiments with rats which showed that stereotyped avoidance behaviour could be extinguished by physically preventing the rats carrying out the avoidance behaviour, Meyer (1966) began treating obsessional patients by preventing them ritualizing. The patients were continuously accompanied during their waking hours and persuaded not to ritualize. Meyer termed his approach 'Atopretic Therapy' and, while the name never became popular, the basic approach of response prevention is now a central component of the treatment of obsessionals although these days patients take responsibility for this themselves rather than the therapist.

The period of extensive research undertaken by people like Isaac Marks and Jack Rachman during the 1970s, which also saw nurses taking a full part in behavioural psychotherapy for the first time, laid the foundations for the practice of behavioural psychotherapy we see in Britain today.

The development of behavioural approaches in the United States was rather different and did not take place over such a small time scale or only in one location. As early as 1928, Knight Dunlap was using an approach still recognizable today and called by him 'negative practice' which attempted to alter an undesirable habit by frequent repetition. This might be called satiation today, but the important point is that Dunlap derived his approach directly from the experimental psychology of the day.

Russian workers during the 1920s were the first to use aversion therapy for alcoholism and, again, this is particularly important because the workers involved (e.g. Kantorich, 1929) were explicitly basing their treatments on Pavlov's conditioning experiments.

This approach caught on in the United States (a rare example of East–West cross-fertilization in psychotherapy) and was practised widely from the 1930s to the 1960s and spread into Western Europe from the US.

Another man influenced by Pavlov was the largely unsung hero, Andrew Salter. His approach was called 'Conditioned Reflex Therapy' and his 1949 book of that title makes startling reading today. He anticipated the criticism of psychoanalysis and described a wide range of treatment approaches which emphasize real life practice and which are extremely close to what happens today. Salter really deserves to be considered the first Behaviour Therapist and it is a pity that his pioneering work was not directly continued.

Another strand which can be followed through until the present day is that of operant conditioning. B. F. Skinner began to write extensively about reinforcement effects in the 1940s and this formed the foundation of a rapid development of clinical applications during the 1950s and 1960s.

In the early 1950s, Ogden Lindsley attempted to use operant means to modify the symptoms of psychotic patients and Sidney Bijou applied similar approaches to the behaviour disorders of children. By the early 1960s, a range of problem behaviours such as tics, stuttering and thumb sucking were being modified in children. The next major development was the collaboration between Teodoro Ayllon and Nathan Azrin who pioneered the reinforcement system for institutions which came to be known as the 'Token Economy'. This has been widely used in many countries and is still an important part of the rehabilitation of institutionalized patients.

After these rather disconnected beginnings, it did not take long for behaviour therapy to develop an identity. The 1960s saw a great deal of information exchange across the Atlantic and 1963 saw the founding of the journal *'Behaviour Research and Therapy'* with Eysenck as the first editor. National and international organizations evolved and the number of publications increased rapidly. Because of the widespread acceptance and practice of behavioural approaches today, it is important to remind ourselves of its very short history and the fact that it is continuously and rapidly evolving so that any description of the field becomes quickly out of date.

There are controversies today, such as the importance of cognitive-behavioural approaches to depression and anxiety, which require the passage of a few more years before a definite conclusion can be drawn about their significance in the field.

Summary

Behavioural psychotherapy evolved in a piecemeal way, mainly through attempts by psychologists to apply the principles of experimental psychology to clinical situations. After the initial period, however, greater emphasis has been placed on pragmatism with treatment techniques being compared and contrasted and the most effective being preferred. It is probably not too much of an over-simplification to say that psychiatric researchers have favoured a pragmatic approach and psychologists a theory-based one. The position of the increasing number of nurses involved in behavioural psychotherapy will be discussed in Chapter 3.

REFERENCES

Jacobsen E. (1938). *Progressive Relaxation*. University of Chicago Press.

Jones M. C. (1924). A laboratory study of fear. *Pedagogical Seminary*, 31, 308–315.

Kantorich N. V. (1929). An attempt at curing alcoholism by associated reflexes. *Novoye Refleksologii nervoy i Fiziologi Sistemy*, 3, 436–445.

Lancaster J. (1805). *Improvements in Education, as it Respects the Industrious Classes of the Community*. Darton & Harvey, London.

Marks I. M. (1982). Is conditioning relevant to behaviour therapy? In: *Learning Theory Approaches to Psychiatry*, Boulougouris. J. Ed: New York: Wiley.

Meyer V. (1966). Modification of expectations in cases with obsessional rituals. *Behaviour Research & Therapy*, 4, 273–280.

Salter A. (1949). *Conditioned Reflex Therapy*. Strauss & Young, New York.

de Silva P. (1984). Buddhism and behaviour modification. *Behaviour Research & Therapy*, 22, 661–678.

Wolpe J. (1958). *Psychotherapy by Reciprocal Inhibition*. Stanford, California: Stanford University Press.

Wolpe J. (1976). Behaviour therapy and its malcontents. *Journal of Behaviour Therapy and Experimental Psychiatry*, 7, 109–116.

Chapter 3

Nursing and behavioural psychotherapy

Introduction

Nurses have had a role in behaviour therapy since the early days of its application to human problems. Our involvement mirrors the development of nursing itself, from instructed provider of care under the control of the medical profession to autonomous practitioner with full accountability for our actions. Within this wide spectrum, from the traditional role to the current view of nursing as visualized by many in the profession, there are numerous roles for nurses.

Derek Milne is a writer who is much concerned with the training of behaviour therapists and has reviewed the literature on the differing roles adopted by nurses in behaviour therapy (Milne, 1986). He identifies five levels of sophistication:

1   The applicator
2   The technician
3   The specialist
4   The generalist
5   The nurse therapist

Milne makes these distinctions by both the level of skill and the degree of training given. The applicator, for example, acts under the direct instruction of another professional and applies behavioural techniques under close supervision. This is the type of role nurses traditionally undertook in the past. The spectrum continues through technician and specialist where more training is given and the nurses still act as primary change agents, but with less supervision. Skilled in certain techniques, these nurses choose when and how to utilize them. The final two levels of sophistication, the generalist and in particular the nurse therapist, have a more extensive training which enables them to assess clients and then apply behavioural techniques to their problems. The nurse therapist in particular is expected to be autonomous and work with little or no supervision.

Historical perspectives

The first recorded example of nurses being specifically instructed in behavioural techniques came in 1959. Ayllon and Michael (1959) taught nurses to use basic operant skills in order to modify the behaviour of patients in a long stay psychiatric institution. Nurses were a natural choice since they made up the bulk of the staff concerned with the care of the institution's residents. We shall see how such considerations crop up again in the rationale for training other nurse therapists. However, the nurses were instructed in the application mode, were given very little training and were little involved in the generation of the treatment programmes.

There are many other examples of individual professionals, usually psychologists, experimenting with the training and supervision of nurses in behaviour therapy. Most of these examples, however, come from North America and it was not until the early 1970s that nursing's involvement with behaviour therapy in Great Britain took a more permanent turn.

The nurse therapist in behavioural psychotherapy

As we discussed in the last chapter, it became apparent in the late 1960s and early 1970s that there was emerging a strong research based discipline that could directly challenge the prevailing blind adherence to analytically based psychotherapy. Techniques were available that offered real hope to the thousands of people with so called 'neurotic' problems. There was, however, a snag. The availability of trained therapists was very low and it would be a long time before sufficient therapists could be trained in these new techniques.

At that time most, if not all, behavioural psychotherapy was carried out by psychiatrists and psychologists. Isaac Marks, a psychiatrist and researcher at the Maudsley Hospital in London proposed that nurses be trained to deliver behavioural psychotherapy. This idea in itself was not completely new, as we have seen. However, Marks suggested that nurses could be trained to act as *main* therapists working under little or no supervision. At the time this was a controversial suggestion. Few psychiatric nurses worked in the community where most of the work was to be carried out and even fewer nurses worked unsupervised. One of the most reactionary comments at the time was that it was like training lorry drivers to become airline pilots! We must remember that this was before the role of the community psychiatric nurse had been developed and established, so most doctors and psychologists had no expectations of nurses as independent practitioners.

Psychiatrists were primarily concerned that nurses would not be competent to take on such a role and that clinical standards would fall. Of course, like any professional group, there was probably an understandable desire to maintain a skill monopoly.

Clinical psychologists were, at that time, attempting to clarify their role in relation to psychiatry and were concerned that this incursion into 'their' territory would undermine these efforts. They felt, only partially correctly, that they had been responsible for innovating behavioural treatments and should, therefore, maintain control over the development of behaviour therapy.

Marks had good reasons for suggesting nurses be trained as behaviour therapists however, and these are detailed below.

1 Economics

Nurse training is shorter and cheaper in comparison with that received by psychiatrists and psychologists. Nurses do not need an expensive university education and their training is more service based than psychologists or psychiatrists. Although not specifically cited by Marks as a reason to train nurse therapists, nurses are also cheaper to employ. (Most nurses, of course, would argue that an equivalent responsibility demands an equivalent wage.) The most important point Marks was trying to make here was that he and others believed it was not necessary to have a highly detailed and academic *general* psychiatric or psychological training in order to become skilled in behavioural psychotherapy.

2 Numbers

There are many considerations that need to be looked at when designing training programmes. One of these is the availability of people on the ground already, available to be trained up. Nurses make up the largest group of mental health care workers in Britain. Training the numbers needed to fill the behaviour therapy gap would make little impact on the pattern of resources. This situation contrasts with, for example, Holland where there are more psychologists than jobs for them. In this case psychologists would have been the natural choice for training in behavioural psychotherapy. Thus, less distortion of the current workforce picture would occur if nurses were trained as behaviour therapists.

3 Nursing development

The argument was also put forward that training nurses as behaviour therapists, to assess, plan, implement and evaluate their work in a completely autonomous and largely unsupervised way was assisting the development of nursing. Clinical nurse specialists had appeared in other specialities such as intensive care, but the proposal to train nurse therapists was the first time psychiatric nurses had this opportunity. Although some people felt that this role was too great a departure from the traditional 'caring' role of the nurse, in practice the distinction between caring and treating is rather blurred even in the most traditional environment.

All these ideas had merit and together they made a strong case for training nurse therapists. One crucial question had to be answered, however, to quell the objections. Would nurses be as effective as other professionals in treating people with specified problems suitable for behavioural psychotherapy?

The first training course, therefore, was run for 3 years and the five nurses on the course were rigorously evaluated as to their performance. The final arbiter of competence is the level of improvement achieved by clients treated by the nurse therapists. Clinical outcomes were, therefore, rated during the first two years of the course and during the final year, which was a more autonomous placement away from the Maudsley. The clinical outcomes these nurses achieved with their clients were compared with the results from other professionals. Their results were found to be *at least as good as those obtained by other professional groups* studied previously (Marks *et al.*, 1977). The results of this study clearly showed that nurses could be trained to be effective therapists.

Apart from the very human benefits of decreased handicap and suffering for clients treated by the nurses on the course, Marks also calculated the cost-benefits to the country of employing nurses as behaviour therapists (Ginsberg and Marks, 1977). People treated by the nurses used fewer health care resources after treatment than before, leading after three years to a net saving of resources. This information is very important and is summarized in Table 3.1.

This research project paved the way for the establishment of a post-basic nurse training course of 18 months duration to train nurses as nurse therapists in behavioural psychotherapy. Currently this is run as the ENB 650 course at three centres in England. It provides a training that, in the words of one psychologist, 'puts to shame' the courses many trainee clinical psychologists receive (Hall, 1979). Nurse therapists have a reputation for clinical excellence and efficiency and are highly sought after in the UK.

Encouragingly, despite the lack of an effective clinical career structure (even with the recent grading review), most trained nurse therapists remain in the field as behaviour therapists, either practising themselves or combining this with teaching other nurses. It is the experience of most of them that the service they offer, once established, is heavily oversubscribed.

Table 3.1 Change in use of Health Resources

Resource	Year Before Treatment	Year After Treatment	% Change
Psychiatric In-patient	28.5 weeks	4.0 weeks	88%
Psychiatric Day-patient	81.0 weeks	67.0 weeks	17%
Non-psychiatric In-patient	15.3 weeks	10.0 weeks	35%
NHS GP	105.4 hours	43.8 hours	59%
NHS Specialist	77.1 hours	44.2 hours	43%
Non-NHS Psychiatrist	40.0 hours	4.8 hours	88%
Social Services	2.4 hours	0.0 hours	100%
Voluntary Organizations	11.6 hours	0.0 hours	100%

A table showing the change in use of health resources by 42 patients treated during the first experimental training course for nurse therapists. Figures given are totals for all 42 patients.

Nurse therapists in the community

A further study, also carried out by Marks, examined the role of nurse therapists in a primary care setting (Marks, 1985). The first study had not been a 'controlled' one, i.e. there was no direct comparison of nurses' results with outcomes obtained by other professionals. The comparisons that were made were done retrospectively by looking at the results of other studies published previously. This second study looked at the differences in outcome for clients treated by nurse therapists working in health centres compared to clients receiving routine general practice treatment. Suitable clients were randomly allocated to either the nurse therapist or the normal GP consultation.

The positive results from the first study were replicated in this study. Marks makes the following comment:

> 'It is concluded that nurse therapists giving behavioural psychotherapy in primary care improve the clinical status of suitably selected patients whose problems would not otherwise remit, that patients obtain treatment earlier and more conveniently in primary care settings and prefer it there, and that benefits to the community of such placements may exceed costs as treated patients slightly reduce their use of health care resources. Nurse therapists work effectively with the primary care team.' (Marks, 1985.)

It was again demonstrated, therefore, that nurse therapists trained in behaviour therapy could make a significant impact on health care both clinically and economically.

Other courses

At around the same time as the Maudsley experiment, two other courses in behaviour therapy were being set up. One, at the Hilda Lewis House, also in London, looked at training mental handicap nurses in behaviour modification and training techniques. This too developed into a national training course under the control of the ENB. The second course, however, reflected a rather different philosophy within behaviour therapy.

Philip Barker, a clinical nurse specialist in behaviour therapy at the Royal Dundee Liff Hospital in Scotland collaborated with psychologists in devising a training programme of six months duration to teach nurses behavioural skills. He believed that the clients considered by Marks and his co-workers to be suitable for behaviour therapy represented too narrow a range of disorders. Barker refers to his training as 'the dissemination of a radical, catholic model of behavioural psychotherapy' (Barker and Fraser, 1985). The Scottish course has continued to offer a basic grounding in behavioural techniques covering a wide range of client problems. In this respect it most clearly resembles the generalist level of training referred to by Milne (1986). It is a less cautious approach than that of Marks. Barker emphasizes in his books (e.g. Barker, 1982) that he believes the behavioural model to be universally applicable to most nursing situations. Although he refers to nurses as therapists, this is not in the same sense as the Maudsley nurse therapists. Instead, he takes a wider view of training and the Scottish course takes nurses from many different areas of psychiatric nursing. Rather than return to a predetermined specific role, nurses completing this course return to many different areas of nursing, skilled in behavioural techniques.

Unfortunately, this course has not been subject to the same type of rigorous evaluation as the Maudsley course. Nurses from this course have published successful case reports (a selection is found in Barker and Fraser, 1985) but economic and controlled outcome data have not been produced. Certainly, nurses from this course play a great role in promoting behaviour therapy amongst a wider population than the English nurse therapists. However, because of the lack of controlled or comparative data this particular application of behaviour therapy nurse training is open to the criticism that it is just another model of care, to be chosen at random from the many models available. There are many people who have a vested interest in misrepresenting behaviour therapy in this way, mostly the protagonists of other, unscientific theoretical models of care. We should add that the standard of case reports and the evaluation measures taken by nurses trained on the Scottish course put to shame those of other psychiatric nurse training courses.

Despite the above comments, Barker's ideas about behaviour therapy do not differ fundamentally from Mark's. He too believes in an essentially science-based, pragmatic discipline, constantly evaluating its own effectiveness and changing its practice according to new research evidence derived from the scientific method at the core of behaviour therapy. Clearly, this is more than 'just another nursing model'.

We could enlarge in much more detail about the many other

local training courses run by various professionals to equip nurses with behavioural change skills, but that is beyond the scope of this book. For those with a specialist interest in training, Derek Milne's book referred to earlier (Milne, 1986) gives a comprehensive review of the literature including his own training initiatives. We will take up the training debate further in the concluding chapter of this book.

Nurses' attitudes and behaviour therapy

During the initial study to determine the effectiveness of nurses as behaviour therapists, the trainees were given several questionnaires to assess their attitudes to nursing activities (Caine and Smaile, 1968, 1969). The nurses showed attitudes that reflected their beliefs that nurses should be active therapists and not just ward custodians. These are also attitudes found in samples of nurses working in therapeutic communities. At the end of the training period these attitudes were strengthened and 'in addition' the nurses were much more critical and uncertain of the value of dynamic psychotherapy and just talking to patients.

The similarity in attitudes between nurse therapists and therapeutic community nurses is striking. Initially the two systems seem poles apart. However, this has more to do with the rather negative image of behaviour therapy put forward by those who view it as a mechanical, over simplified and punitive discipline (e.g. MacMillan, 1979). The experience of nurse therapists is that it is just the opposite – client centred, humanistic and above all requiring the nurse to empathize with the client's problems.

Another nurse who experienced similar contradictory opinions when he started working as a nurse therapist was Kevin Gournay. He undertook a more wide ranging study of nursing attitudes with nurse therapists and two other groups of nurses (Gournay, 1986). He found that nurse therapists were the least conservative of the three groups and again makes the point that nurse therapists' attitudes are similar to those found in nurses working in 'liberal' regimes like therapeutic communities. Rather than believing in the mechanistic and autocratic approaches that have been falsely portrayed as 'behaviour therapy', nurse therapists believe in using individualized and negotiated treatment strategies with personalized interventions of a psychotherapeutic nature.

The image of behaviour therapy

The negative image of behaviour therapy referred to in the last section has been identified and reviewed by O'Leary (1984). The overriding message from this review, and the experience of many nurses working in the field, is that the *practice* of behaviour therapy is radically different from the image many other professionals have. We feel this image is based on out-of-date ideas and fails to take into account the research-based development of behavioural methods over the last 20 years. In Chapter 1 we described the behavioural model as it really is. In clinical practice it includes such concepts as holism, client-centred care, negotiation of therapeutic aims, etc. These ideas are not the preserve of any one ideology, although they are often portrayed as belonging exclusively to the dynamic therapies. The dissemination of images of simplicity and mechanistic care, however, benefits other therapeutic methods whose value has not been so rigorously evaluated as that of behaviour therapy.

In a world where the voice of consumerism is growing ever more strong (in our opinion quite rightly so) behaviour therapy's strong research-based method is unique among the psychological treatments. Behaviour therapy has been demonstrated to be the *treatment of choice* for some of the major mental health problems in our society. Since we now have a professional code of conduct (UKCC, 1987) that stresses accountability for our actions, we have a moral and professional responsibility to give our clients the treatment and care that has the best chance of success. For those mental health problems where behaviour therapy has been shown to be more effective than anything else, we must deliver the goods.

We would also do well to remember that behaviour therapy is not 'owned' by anybody despite the rather grandiose claims among some of the psychological fraternity that they are 'giving psychology away'. As nurses we are well placed to offer effective therapy to more people than any other profession. There is only one beneficiary of the increasing use of behavioural psychotherapy in nursing – the client.

Summary

We have discussed briefly the ways in which nurses have played a role in delivering behavioural treatments. We have quoted evidence that reveals that nurses can be highly effective therapists and can work in a community setting delivering behaviour therapy to those that can benefit from it. Nurses working in behaviour therapy show personal attitudes that fit closely with the humanistic ideals often prescribed for the nursing profession.

The remainder of this book will go on to describe treatments and a therapeutic method that offers the best hope for some of the most prevalent mental health problems in society. We will concentrate on the types of problems for which behavioural psychotherapy is known to be highly effective and for which there is strong research evidence to back us up. Many of these problems concern the various forms of excessive anxiety, which is *the most common* psychological difficulty in today's world, probably experienced by at least 10% of the population each year (Matthews, 1984). We do not agree with Barker and Fraser (1985) that this represents an extremely limited range of client problems. Quite the reverse; we consider that the wider application, by nurses, of the techniques described in this book could significantly improve the quality of life for a substantial number of people. In addition, Chapter 13 will consider the application of the behavioural model to a wider range of problems than is normally considered 'suitable'. We hope to facilitate the ideas that behavioural principles have a wide use, even where hard and fast evidence is still not available.

The techniques we will describe are a fundamental shift away from the traditional psychiatric nurses' strategy of altering the general 'milieu' of a social or ward system in the expectation that somehow change will result. The techniques are active, interactive and individually tailored to the client's specifically identified problem areas. Techniques on their own, however, are not enough and so in the next chapter we will start to deal with the process of delivering therapy and outline therapeutic principles that encompass the attitudes and values we have discussed in the work of Marks and Gournay.

REFERENCES

Ayllon T., Michael J. (1959). The psychiatric nurse as a behavioural engineer. *Journal of the Experimental Analysis of Behaviour*, 2, 323–34.
Barker P. J. (1982). *Behaviour Therapy Nursing*. Beckenham: Croom Helm.
Barker P. J., Fraser D. (eds.) (1985). *The Nurse as Therapist*. Beckenham: Croom Helm.

Caine T. M., Smaile D. J. (1968). Attitudes of psychiatric nurses to their role in treatment. *British Journal of Medical Psychology*, **41**, 193–7.

Caine T. M., Smaile D. J. (1969). The effects of personality and training on attitudes to treatment. *British Journal of Medical Psychology*, **42**, 277–82

Ginsberg G., Marks I. M. (1977). Costs and benefits of behavioural psychotherapy: a pilot study of neurotics treated by nurse therapists. *Psychological Medicine*, **7**, 685–700.

Gournay K. (1986). A pilot study of nurses' attitudes with relation to post-basic training, In *Psychiatric Nursing Research*, Brooking, J. J. ed. Chichester: Wiley and Sons.

Hall J. N. (1979). Nurse therapy and role change in the health care professions. *Bulletin of the British Psychological Society*, **32**, 71–73.

MacMillan P. (1979). 'Let the punishment fit the crime?'. Nursing Times, **75**, 1657–8.

Marks I. M., Hallam R. S., Connolly J., Philpott R. (1977). *Nursing in Behavioural Psychotherapy*. London: Royal College of Nursing.

Marks I. M. (1985). *Psychiatric Nurse Therapists in Primary Care*. London: Royal College of Nursing.

Mathews A. (1984). Anxiety and its management, In *Current Themes in Psychiatry*, Vol. 3, (Gaind R. N. ed.) New York: Medical and Scientific Books.

Milne D. (1986). *Training Behaviour Therapists*. Beckenham: Croom Helm.

O'Leary K. D. (1984). The image of behaviour therapy: It is time to take a stand. *Behaviour Therapy*, **15**, 219–-33.

UKCC Central Council for Nursing and Midwifery Health Visiting (1987) *Code of Professional Conduct for the Nurse, Midwife and Health Visitor*, London: UKCC.

Part 2

Chapter 4

Interviewing

Introduction

The essential prerequisite of any nursing intervention is an accurate assessment of the client's problems. Any treatment plan is only as good as the information it is based on. Behavioural techniques are powerful and it is important to give careful thought to their application and then use them appropriately. The aim of behavioural psychotherapy is to reduce distress and handicap. To wrongly apply behavioural techniques may directly increase distress by the use of the wrong technique, or indirectly prolong distress by the omission of the correct technique. We cannot stress too highly that the first stage in any treatment programme is the comprehensive and accurate assessment of both the client and his problem.

How we go about gathering information will affect what information we get. For most of the problems discussed in this book, interviews with clients and their families are the primary source of information. A high level of skill in interviewing will make information gathering both more accurate and facilitate the development of the rapport between client and nurse so essential for effective behavioural treatment.

In this chapter we will, therefore, discuss the *process* of assessment. To do this we will consider a pragmatic model of interviewing, i.e. one that is based on results and not theory. We will not look at clients from any standpoint other than that we will put no conditions on our positive regard for them and will not attempt to interpret the information they give us to fit a particular theoretical view of human nature. This pragmatic model will allow us to examine clients and their problems without clouding the issue with our own beliefs and values.

A PRAGMATIC INTERVIEW MODEL

An 'interview' is usually described as any situation where two or more people meet face to face to elicit information or a statement from one of the participants, the interviewee. In clinical practice the definition must include information gathering but interviews may also be used to deal with feelings and to foster new behaviours. Each interview is unique and we will use a mixture of skills designed to tackle these three areas.

Interviewing – basic concepts

The pragmatic approach to interviewing in which results, rather than theories, dictate how to proceed can be summarized as:

1 Consider the goals of the interview
2 Use relevant procedures to meet these goals
3 Monitor client's responses and BE FLEXIBLE.

Before considering goals and the use of relevant procedures we will look briefly at some of the factors which can have a bearing on the way the interview will proceed.

Influence

In all interviews, each party is influenced by the other. In a clinical situation, because of several reasons, the clinician will have a greater influence than the client. Such reasons will include:

- Expectations the client has of us and what we will do in the interview. Such expectations may come from the client's preconceived ideas about nurses or he may have been told by someone else to expect certain behaviours from us.
- The roles which both ourselves and the client play in the interview will greatly influence the behaviour of the client. Our role in the interview is to act as a professional provider of health care. The client may perceive his role as a passive recipient of care, to be given by somebody with knowledge and authority.
- Our status in relation to the client will also have an effect on the interview. Again, as a professional we are in a powerful position. The client is immediately at a disadvantage. He has to talk about himself whilst we engage in little self-disclosure.

On the other hand, nursing's status as a 'working class profession' may mean we have to work harder to establish our competence and expertise than would a therapist from another professional group.

- The sex of the interviewer and the client can make the client more or less willing to disclose relevant but personal information and will affect the establishment of our competency. Men in our society are often seen as more authoritative whilst women are perceived as more caring and understanding.

Table 4.1 The Pragmatic Interview Model

---

1. Consider goals
2. Use relevant procedures
3. Monitor responses
4. Be flexible

The four principles of interviewing.

The influence that these factors can have on an interview occurs before or at the early stages and, because they are initially outside our control, can be termed *inevitable influence*.

Inevitable influence has an impact on information gathering, emotion handling and the fostering of new behaviours. This influence, if used unintentionally or without thought, has the potential to be a destructive force in an interview. The negative aspects of inevitable influence can be minimized if we are aware of the potentially destructive characteristics of these factors and use procedures to counter this. Whilst we cannot change sex, we can use other strategies to turn this influence to the advantage of ourselves and the client. For example, the use of language which is congruent with the client's own will avoid the impression that we are either talking down to the client or being over simplistic.

Thus, one of the basic skills of interviewing is to recognize the presence of inevitable influence and to use this selectively, i.e. use *selective influence* to promote an effective exchange.

Expectation effects

As noted above, clients will have expectations of us, but they will also be influenced by what they think we expect of them. Clients

Table 4.2 Expectation Effects

The Client:	tries to cope
	is responsive
	is honest

These three beliefs we hold about our clients are central to effective interviewing.

will often try to live up to these expectations. By making it plain just what we expect, we can use selective influence for the benefit of the therapeutic process. It is therefore important that we demonstrate early on in the interview certain positive assumptions we hold about the client:

1   This person *tries to cope*.

We must convey to the client that we believe he tries to face up to his distress as best he can. We must show that we do not think he is having difficulties because he is simply not trying, but that his problem is genuine and he actually has resources to cope but currently needs advice/guidance/help to facilitate his coping.

2   This person is *responsive*.

We should always start an interview by regarding the client as a partner in therapy. The way we conduct the interview should tell the client that the expected relationship is not one where we set ourselves up to be the repository of truth, in the form of interpretation of the client's problems, which he must then accept and explore. Instead we should set up the expectation of a mutually cooperative practical working relationship. Problems will be tackled later together as a partnership so it is important that we make this expectation clear during the early stages of an initial interview. Techniques for doing this include getting the client to clarify his own problem and guiding him to suggest his own goals for treatment.

3   This person is *honest*.

We must convey to the client that we believe his account. Words such as 'manipulative' have no place in our interview model. In an interview we can demonstrate that we believe the client is not inventing or distorting symptoms and that what he is saying is the truth by using empathic statements and by being honest ourselves.

The point we are stressing here is that expectations have an effect on reality. If we can make it obvious to the client *what we believe and expect of him* it is highly likely he will actually act in this way. Tell someone they are honest and they are more likely to act in an honest way.

Matching goals and procedures

We have considered interviews to have three broad aims centred around the gathering of information, the handling of emotion and the development of new behaviours. We can choose specific procedures which are likely to produce specific effects and these should be related to the *goals* of the interview. Most interviews will have a mixture of different goals from the three broad categories. Different procedures will not lead to the same outcome. Therefore, it is very important that we identify the specific goals for the interview and choose procedures which are likely to meet those goals. Some examples are given below:

Information gathering
- sample goal – 'description of main problem'
- sample procedure – open ended questions

Handling emotion
- sample goal – 'reduce distress about problem'
- sample procedure – empathic statements

Encouraging new behaviour
- sample goal – 'reduce reassurance seeking from spouse'
- sample procedure – model appropriate response

Although goals are important to consider before an interview, they must not become so rigidly fixed that they inhibit the natural flow of an interview, becoming a rod for our own backs. For example, the time to use procedures to reduce distress is when the client is actually experiencing distress — something which may not be possible to predict. We should continually monitor the client's responses and *be flexible* in the procedures we use at any particular time. By monitoring the client's responses, the goals of the interview can be altered in response to the client's needs.

This pragmatic style of interviewing requires a disciplined and responsible approach. People who describe their clients as 'uncooperative' or 'poor historians' may well be describing themselves, because

interviewers get the cooperation they deserve.

Interviewing – general skills

Certain behaviours we use in an interview will facilitate the achievement of interview goals whether these goals are informational, emotional or behavioural. If we use these general skills we will promote cooperation between ourselves and the client. These skills are:

1 Planning
2 Introduction and orientation
3 Attention and continuity
4 Rapport and partnership
5 Flexibility
6 The ending

1 Planning
It is important in any interview to consider certain issues in advance and to prepare thoroughly for the interview. Issues that should be looked at are:

- Knowledge: what is known about this person and their previous behaviour in an interview? What is known about their presenting problems?

- Goals: the purpose of the interview will indicate what procedures should be employed to achieve these goals. We should be clear that we know what these goals are.

- Conditions: a very important consideration is where the interview will take place. This should be in a place where interruptions are at a minimum so that our full attention can be given to the client. Privacy is often an underrated quality. An interview conducted in the day room of a busy admission ward will yield less information than one held in a private room. Ideally the room should be quiet, not too hot or too cold and should have in it any facilities required. Attention should be paid to the type and placement of seats. How much time can be allowed for the interview should also be decided beforehand.

Table 4.3 Interviewing – Key
General Skills

1　Planning
2　Introductions and orientation
3　Attention and continuity
4　Rapport and partnership
5　Flexibility
6　Ending

---

2 Introduction and orientation

The first few minutes of an interview are crucial in setting the tone for the remainder of the time. Special care should be taken over introductions. People have been known to be halfway through an interview before realizing they are interviewing the wrong person! When meeting someone for the first time the identity of the client should be ascertained in full immediately, using both their names. We should introduce ourselves by name and role, trying not to use jargon-like titles that may have no meaning to the client. It is also useful to indicate to the client that he can sit down immediately and show him a seat.

Two other things should be clarified at the start of an interview – the purpose of the interview and the planned duration. The purpose should be clearly stated, if both participants in the interview start off by having the same ideas about the interview then it is more likely to lead to a successful conclusion. Specifying a time limit is a good way of setting limits to the interview and only in exceptional circumstances will there be unfinished business.

3 Attention and continuity

Clients will be more likely to give information freely or accept our suggestions if we show that we are paying attention to them and what they are saying. Such attention can be demonstrated verbally, by the appropriate response to what the client is saying, and non-verbally by the use of nods, facial expression, eye contact, etc. Ideally interruptions should be avoided in the selection of the interview venue, but any interruptions that do occur should be dealt with quickly, quietly and firmly. One skill that is very difficult to learn, but one that should be practised often, is the taking of notes. Memory is not enough, so note-taking must occur. The skill is to make this as non-intrusive as possible. Many interviewers develop shorthand styles or pick out key words to record; the important thing is practice. The interview will go very badly if we have our head down scribbling furiously all the time. The non-verbal signals this gives to the client are signs of inattention and a cold interrogating interview style.

4 Rapport and partnership

One of the aims in all interviews is the deliberate fostering of a partnership between ourselves and the client. Showing interest and concern in general will certainly do this but we should also comment on the *here and now* progress of the interview. If the client is giving long answers to questions and wandering off the point it is useful to politely tell him this, maybe by reminding him of the time limit to the interview. Likewise, for the client who is giving short curt answers, tactfully telling him this and suggesting a joint approach to any factor which is impeding progress should encourage partnership and make the interview run more smoothly.

5 Flexibility

The relationship between ourselves and a client in any interview is a complex one. We need to continually monitor the responses of the client and modify our own behaviour accordingly. A skilled interviewer is not one that sits stonily silent apart from when asking questions in order from a prepared list. We should not be afraid to change the running order in response to the client's behaviour. Avoid interrogation at all costs.

6 The ending

The ending is possibly one of the most important and most neglected of all interview skills. People will remember best the first and last parts of an interview, so it is vital to get them right. As the interview is coming to the end of its time we should notify the client well in advance and enlist his help in:

(a)   summarizing the key points of the interview
(b)   checking the next step is clearly agreed and understood
(c)   closing the interview on time.

Here again the concern is to facilitate partnership. By summarizing the key points of the interview we can check that both ourselves and the client have gained the same impression from the session and correct any misinterpretations either of us may have. By agreeing the next step we can both take away the same thing from the interview and minimize confusion. Having set a time limit it is sensible to stick to it except in very exceptional circumstances. Remember.

An interview which runs over time is not a successful one.

We will now consider in more detail the skills needed to elicit information, deal with emotion and foster new behaviours in an interview setting.

Interviewing – gathering information

Certain behaviours by an interviewer promote both the flow of the interview and the reliability of the information gained. What to ask will be covered later; this section is about how to get information reliably.

Table 4.4 Key Procedures for
Gathering Information

General skills
Non-verbal behaviour
Question usage – Free flow
               – Progressive focus
               – Clarification

---

1 General skills
The general interview skills explained in the last section must be used whatever the goal of the interview. Attention should be paid to planning, orientation, attention, rapport and ending.

2 Non-verbal behaviour
We should ensure we are communicating attention by appropriate use of eye contact, posture, gestures, nods, etc.

3 Question usage
Any question we ask the client should obey three golden rules:

1   the question is clearly put and is readily understood
2   single, not multiple, questions are used
3   questions are not leading and do not put words in the client's mouth.

The aim is for the process of gathering information to be smooth and progressive, unhindered by misunderstandings. The flow of questions can be regarded as resembling a funnel (Fig. 4.1). At the top, in the wide mouth of the funnel, are general open questions. These are used to get the client talking about his difficulties from his own point of view. An opening question such as, 'tell me about your main difficulties' allows the client free reign to decide the topic he feels needs discussing.

The next stage, as the funnel narrows, is to ask more specific questions but still keep them open. An example of this might be a client who has indicated that his sleep is an area of concern, so we might ask next, 'can you tell me some more about the problems you are having with your sleep?'. This focuses the interview to a specific area, but it is an area that the client has chosen, so we encourage the client to explore this in more depth.

As the funnel narrows further, closed questions can be used to clinch detail. Closed questions demand a specific answer, often yes or no, and we only need to use them to get specific facts on areas that the client has already described in detail. An example of a closed question would be, 'how often does this happen?', or, 'what time do you wake up in the morning?'. Overuse of this type

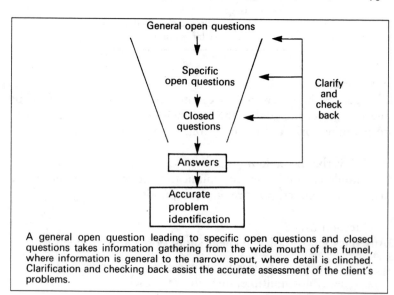

A general open question leading to specific open questions and closed questions takes information gathering from the wide mouth of the funnel, where information is general to the narrow spout, where detail is clinched. Clarification and checking back assist the accurate assessment of the client's problems.

Figure 4.1   Question Usage

of question early in an interview will mean that the direction of the interview will be dictated by ourselves and important information will be lost. However, closed questions are vital to assess the specific level of handicap the client is experiencing.

Finally, we should frequently check back with the client to clarify certain points of the interview. Feeding back of information may seem repetitive, but often facilitates the client divulging more information about the subject being discussed. Checking back also does just that, i.e. it allows both parties to agree that we have heard and understood the same information, and will assist in clarifying certain points that are not quite clear. This type of clarification and summarizing should be done frequently throughout the interview.

4 Facilitation

Although questioning will facilitate information gathering, encouraging statements such as, 'I'd like to hear more about that' will also assist the client in giving us more information. Again, non-verbal behaviour will help and nods, grunts, 'uh-hu's' and pauses will all facilitate information gathering if used appropriately.

5 Direction

As discussed earlier, we think it is important that we comment on the 'here and now' progress of the interview, firmly and politely directing the client's responses in a constructive direction. This is difficult and requires practice, but it is too easy to waste both the client's and our own time by allowing the interview to get out of control. Examples of the type of responses that may be helpful are:

> 'your answers are too brief, please try and say more.'
> 'your answers are too long, please be more selective.'
> 'you're moving off the subject, let's try and stick to your main problem.'

Equally important is that we remember to give the client positive feedback about the progress of the actual interview. We know from our own life experience that this is helpful. An example of this will illustrate the concept. If during a job interview we are told the answers we have given were helpful and just what was needed, we are likely to be even more confident and perform better. Positive feedback is a good way to enhance the flow of relevant information and help build rapport.

6 Summarizing

As part of the general skill of ending an interview, summarizing is important in order to check that understanding has been reached between ourselves and the client. The final summary is really an enlarged form of the clarification and checking back that has been going on throughout the interview. It may also be useful to summarize the emotional, as well as the informational content of the interview in order to draw all the strands of the interview together. The final summary will not be a period of talking *at* the client, but is an opportunity to come to a shared agreement on the content of the interview. A good tactic is to ask the client to summarize his view of the interview and to tell us what he has to do as a result of it. Summarizing is of particular importance because, as well as first impressions,

the last thing said is the best remembered.

Interviewing – handling emotion

The use of certain behaviours during an interview can help with distressing or disruptive emotions the client may express. During an interview a client may be telling us about his problems in greater depth than he has ever done before and this recall can provoke strong emotions. We need to pay attention to non-verbal cues especially. The most important question we must ask ourselves in any interview is: 'How might *I* feel in this situation?'.

When discussing their problems, clients may be expressing fears about the nature and severity of symptoms, may feel embarrassment, may feel anger and may feel depressed. Often

Table 4.5 Key Procedures for Handling Emotion

1	General skills
2	Non-verbal behaviour
3	Empathy
4	Limited self-disclosure
5	Reassurance
6	Avoidance of – Interpretation
	– Unhelpful responses

anxiety or panic is seen as an indication by the client that he is going 'mad'.

These feelings may not be communicated directly to us which is why sensitivity to non-verbal cues is so important. Our response to any expressed emotion will strongly influence the outcome of the interview.

Some important skills are discussed below. They are certainly not unique to an interview situation and should form part of the communication skills repertoire of any nurse.

1 General skills

2 Non-verbal behaviour

Although we will be using appropriate non-verbal behaviour to communicate attention and interest, specific behaviours can be employed to deal with specific emotions. Two examples of this are:

- To reduce distress — we can move closer, use warm tones, maybe touch the client to comfort him.

- To cool hostility — we can deal with a hostile client by adopting a submissive posture, i.e. moving away, sitting down, lowering our head. In this situation quiet, submissive tones and behaviour will be more likely to defuse the client's anger than a confrontational stance.

3 Empathic statements

Statements that are empathic indicate to the client that we recognize and accept the client's feelings. As a general principle when handling emotion, but especially when trying to convey empathy, it is best to use statements rather than questions. An example might be:

'I realize discussing this is very distressing to you.'

We are conveying our understanding and acceptance of the client's emotion. The use of the 'how might I feel in this situation?' question is essential to help us empathize with the client.

4 Limited self-disclosure

This technique can be used to alleviate distress, but it should be used with care since the client has not come to listen to our problems. A statement that discloses how we feel might be:

'I can remember feeling the same way when a similar thing happened to me'.

It is generally enough to show that we can understand the client's feelings, without going into details of our own emotions and risking the client feeling more vulnerable than before.

5 Reassurance

Clients will frequently ask for reassurance from us but we should be extremely careful how we give it. Bland and blanket statements like, 'everything will be fine' are most unhelpful and give a client no real information to help him cope better with his problems. In most cases it is unlikely the client feels any better for being reassured, and it may merely increase his dependence on us and encourage further reassurance seeking. Reassurance should be limited to:

(a) factually accurate, preferably conservative, predictions about the future.
   e.g. 'will I ever get better?'
   'most people with your problem do improve with time.'.
(b) events which are under our control.
   e.g. 'will I have to cope on my own?'
   'I will see you every week to give you my support.'.

6 Interpretation

We would only rarely advocate the use of interpretation. It is used to bring out feelings and ideas which are not being expressed or shown. The danger lies in these statements being perceived as judgemental, especially if we choose the wrong interpretation of the client's behaviour. An example might be:

'I think what you are really angry about is the lack of support you are getting from your wife.'

Such a statement could be seen as very offensive and as ourselves putting our own ideas into the client's mind. It is best to take feelings and statements at face value rather than make interpretations that must, in part at least, be a product of our own belief system. There are far better ways of understanding and clarifying emotion. Lastly, when dealing with a client's emotions avoid *unhelpful responses*. Examples of unhelpful responses are:

(a) Inappropriate probing – 'Why exactly do you feel this way?'
(b) Excessive reassurance – 'Everything will be OK.'
(c) Evasion – 'Please don't be upset.'
(d) Evaluative statements – 'Just think how your wife must feel.'
(e) Hostile statements – 'You're just being foolish.'

And remember,

don't make promises you can't keep.

Interviewing – changing behaviour

Certain behaviours by the interviewer will make it more likely that the client will carry out appropriate changes in his own behaviour. It has been demonstrated many times that simply giving advice is not an effective way of evoking behaviour change. An example of this from general medicine is that random checks have found 50% of medical out-patients do not take medication as prescribed by the doctor. Therefore, our behaviour, especially where we are advising new strategies for behaviour change, is crucial in promoting acceptance, cooperation and motivation in the client. We must remember that just because somebody is unwilling to accept our advice does not mean they are unmotivated.

Table 4.6 Key Skills for Changing Behaviour

1   General skills
2   Non-verbal behaviour
3   Image building
4   Rationale
5   Instruction
6   Modelling
7   Rehearsal
8   Attribution

1 General skills
Attention should be paid to planning, orientation, attention, rapport and ending.

2 Non-verbal behaviour
Non-verbal behaviour should be active, appropriate and varied to show attention and inspire confidence.

3 Image building
We talked earlier about the client's expectations of ourselves affecting his behaviour in an interview. It is unlikely a client will adopt a new behaviour on the recommendation of somebody who does not demonstrate expertise in his problem area. Most professionals try to foster an image of general prestige (often by their dress, by hanging diplomas and degrees from walls, etc.) but people are not fooled for long by inexpert or unclear advice. We would be far better to demonstrate *case-specific* expertise by having a thorough understanding of the client's problems and their affect on his life. Demonstrating that we understand his difficulties and informing him that we have seen other people with similar problems will all help to build the client's confidence in our skills and knowledge. The best way to convince a client we know what we are talking about is to have a thorough grasp of the subject first.

4 Rationale
When suggesting any new behaviour to a client the reasons for our giving this advice should be clear and reasonable. Clients are far more likely to adopt a new behaviour if they believe it has a rational basis and this basis can be understood. This means presenting the new course of action in a clear manner without jargon and confusing details. It also means being honest with the client, spelling out both the positive and negative consequences of the new behaviour and allowing him to choose on the basis of sound reasoning. It is unrealistic to expect a client to adopt a new behaviour unless he understands the rationale behind it.

5 Instruction
Once the rationale for a particular course of action has been established, any instructions given to the client to enable him to carry out the plan should be clearly understood. For any instruction to be effective it must first be understood at the time it is given and then remembered later. Therefore, instructions should be *simple, repeated and checked* to see if the client has understood. The best way to check this is to ask the client to repeat the

instructions back to us. Since people remember the first and last things of an interview best, it is useful to get the client to summarize their instructions right at the end of the interview.

6 Models
As stated earlier, merely telling people is not enough. Clients will be more likely to change their behaviour if they have a credible example to follow. Telling the client how other people coped in similar circumstances is useful, but even more powerful is to introduce the client to someone who actually is coping with a similar problem. This is one of the advantages of seeing people in groups. Clients can use each other as coping models, especially if the group contains people at different stages in therapy.

7 Rehearsal
One of the most useful techniques in influencing behaviour change is to rehearse the new behaviour in the interview setting before the client tries it out in real life. This almost invariably leads to an increased likelihood of the behaviour being practised after the interview. The rehearsal session needs to be successful to give the client the confidence to practise later, so the behaviour can be rehearsed slowly or the task can be split up into stages, each stage rehearsed separately. One very powerful rehearsal technique is to practice an actual behaviour in imagination first.

8 Attribution
Rather than give the client one set of instructions, it is better in some cases to give several options and ask the client to choose what he sees as the best one. People are more likely to adopt a new behaviour if they perceive themselves as having chosen it. If we put forward the advantages and disadvantages of each option but allow the client to choose, the client is more likely to adopt the chosen behaviour and identify the qualities he needs to bring about change as positive aspects of himself. Whenever helping people to change their behaviour,

> *telling people what to do is not enough.*

Summary

In this chapter we have looked at the *process* of interviewing. We have considered interviews to have three broad aims:

1 Gathering information
2 Dealing with emotion
3 Changing behaviour.

All interviews will have a combination of aims, but each interview will be unique and we need to be flexible in the behaviours we use. Some interview skills are general, others designed specifically to meet certain goals. The interview model presented is a *pragmatic* one that takes account of results and not theory, so that the most effective interchange between ourselves and the client can be facilitated. By careful planning, having clear goals, choosing appropriate procedures to meet these goals and above all:

monitoring the client's responses and being flexible,

we can achieve a high standard of interview skills. In the next chapter we will discuss the *content* of interviews, outlining a procedure that is designed to obtain comprehensive behavioural assessments of clients and their problems.

Chapter 5

Assessment – collecting the information

We stated at the beginning of the last chapter that assessment is essential to provide the data on which we will base our strategies for effective behavioural treatments. It is the basis for the problem identification and individual plan of care which will follow. Assessment also gives a baseline with which to compare a client's subsequent progress through therapy. One very important function of assessment is to facilitate the rapport and partnership between nurse and client that will lead to the mutual support and cooperation that is essential to the success of any treatment programme. Let us, therefore, look at assessment in more detail.

WHAT IS ASSESSMENT?

Assessment has been identified as a three stage process (Tierney, 1984):

1 Collecting information
2 Reviewing the information collected
3 Identifying problems from the data.

In this chapter we will explore the first stage of the process, that of data collection. Stages 2 and 3 will be considered in the following chapter.

The information required for a full assessment of clients and their problems can be gleaned from many sources but three key skills can be identified.

- Observing
- Interviewing
- Measuring.

   Assessment is not a once-only procedure but is an ongoing process of information gathering and reviewing of the client's problems. However, as well as using this global definition of assessment we often use the word 'assessment' to mean the first contact between nurse and client where the nurse is primarily concerned with gathering information so that the client can be helped to define his difficulties. The key skills required for this are observation and interviewing. Measurement can be used to identify problems but more usually follows when problems have already been identified or where clarification of a person's difficulties is needed. Because of this, and because measurement is such a key concept to behavioural treatment methods, we have devoted a separate chapter to measurement and associated issues.

   We have also approached this chapter on the basis of the nurse as prime therapist and the key person planning and implementing behavioural treatments. We accept that this will not always be the case, but this is no argument for not learning the relevant skills. The more skilled we become, the more opportunities there will be to practise these skills.

The first steps

Assessment starts before we even see the client. Referrals may be detailed or cursory, but any information we have access to before seeing the client should be used in drawing up the final picture. Apart from the referral information, more information can be obtained from other nursing colleagues who may have seen the client before, from members of other disciplines who may have had contact with the client or from any medical or psychiatric notes that may be available. This information should be gathered, but we should not make decisions about the client's problems until he has been interviewed and a full assessment carried out. It must be stressed that assessment information comprises a complex jigsaw that only reveals a true picture when the final piece is put into place. Prior assumptions can be very misleading and will prejudice the objectivity of the assessment.

```
┌─────────────────────────────────────────────┐
│  Collecting information ● Observation         │
│                        ● Interviewing         │
│                        ● Measurement          │
│  Reviewing the information collected          │
│  Identifying problems from the data           │
└─────────────────────────────────────────────┘
```

Figure 5.1   Assessment

Observation

Observation of clients is a skill we must all practise. Not only at assessment but throughout therapy we will be observing the client and making judgements on the basis of these observations. For example, when we first meet the client simple observations will give us an idea of how old the client is and his facial expression may indicate mood or emotion. The client's behaviour during an interview, his level of eye contact, speed and tone of speech, posture, gestures and other non-verbal behaviour should be observed and noted. We need to be careful in an assessment interview, as it is possible to pay so much attention to the questions we are asking that fundamental observations are inadvertently omitted. To combine interviewing, note-taking and observation can be a bit tricky at first, but regular practice will help us to feel comfortable.

When clients recount their difficulties it is often easy to see the obvious distress that their problems cause them by observing changes in tone of voice and non-verbal behaviour. However, it is not necessary in routine clinical practice to test out their account by asking them to demonstrate their difficulties and observing the result in some form of 'behavioural test'. A simple example of such a behavioural test would be to ask a client who fears dogs to approach a dog as close as he dares until his anxiety becomes unbearable and he cannot approach any closer. This was a form of assessment favoured in the early days of behaviour therapy. If we consider the client's account to be a product of our positive assumptions about him, i.e. that he is honest, responsive and tries to cope, then there is generally no need for such behavioural tests.

The assessment interview

Behavioural psychotherapy is a problem-oriented approach to people's difficulties so an assessment interview is best divided into:

1   Problem assessment
2   General assessment

On a practical note, the two parts are often undertaken on separate occasions since the whole process is rather lengthy. There is also little point in conducting a full general assessment if the presenting problem is not one which is amenable to a behavioural approach. If we are thinking of using such an approach we should be prepared to recognize when this is not appropriate.

1 The problem assessment

The aim in this part of the assessment is to define the client's problems as tightly as possible. It is not enough, for example, to know that someone is anxious in crowds. We need to know much more fine detail so that therapy can be an individually tailored in a client-centred process, rather than the blanket application of a battery of behavioural techniques. The problem assessment concentrates on the 'here and now' of the client's experience rather than a search for earlier, possibly obscure and unhelpful, causes of the presenting problems. Where causes are considered, this is in order to add further context to the person's current problems.

We must also be guided by the client's responses to our questions. The direction of the interview is determined by the priorities the client puts upon his various difficulties. We may ask highly specific questions, but those questions are in areas defined by the client.

Starting off — the five 'Ws'

We would normally start our enquiries, after introductions and orientation have been completed, using a simple question such as, 'Could you tell me, in your own words, about your main problem?'

We have, therefore, begun by using a general open question, putting the emphasis firmly on to the client to identify the areas of concern he is worried about. This is the first of the five 'Ws', i.e.

What is the problem?

Even if the referral letter or other notes are comprehensive, the client's own account of his problem will be the most important piece of information of all. We need to allow the client to give as much detail as he wants before moving on to get more information.

Next, we need to narrow down to more specific information in order to clinch details. Several other areas of questioning are crucial:

Where does the problem occur?

We must be specific in finding out the exact characteristics of situations in which the client is having difficulties. Taking a list and trying to find out what these situations have in common is a good strategy. It is also important to discover where the problem does *not* occur.

When does the problem occur?

Does the problem differ in intensity according to the time of day? Are some days easier than others? The important piece of information to determine here is if the problem is *predictable* whenever the client is presented with a specific situation or object. As we shall see later, this could be crucial in deciding if the problem is amenable to behavioural psychotherapy or not.

With whom is the problem better or worse?

Some people get enormous comfort from the presence of other people; others find this makes them worse. For some people strangers cause more problems than good friends; for others it is the opposite. The role of other people in the problem, therefore, should be rigorously assessed as it may be crucial both to our understanding of the client's difficulties and the organization of an effective treatment programme.

Why does the problem occur?

This may be the most difficult area to assess. Here we are trying to make sense of the problem and give some meaning to the client's actions. For people who complain of anxiety, particularly phobic anxiety, the *feared consequence* is particularly important to elicit. Why does the client avoid a particular situation? What

---

What is the problem?
Where does the problem occur/where not?
When does the problem happen/when not?
Why does the problem happen, the *feared consequence*?
With whom is the problem better or worse?

Figure 5.2 Questions which define the problem

does he fear would happen if he entered this situation? It is worth persevering with this line of questioning, despite the fact that many common fears are highly irrational and some people cannot identify their feared consequence.

The 'five Ws' should give us a fairly detailed description of the client's main problem. If the client identifies more than one problem area, then we can easily apply the same detailed assessment to each area. However, we can still obtain more detail on the client's problems by funnelling our questions further. We can now move to more specific closed questions to clinch this further detail.

1   *Frequency* – how often the problem occurs over a given time. This can help us to get a more objective idea of the level of handicap the problem is causing to the client, especially so for people with a compulsive behaviour like obsessive handwashing.

2   *Intensity* – how powerful the client's feelings are and whether they have changed over the recent past.

3   *Number* – how many times the behaviour is repeated. This is particularly important to ask about in people who have, for example, a compulsive urge to check. The frequency of daily checking may depend on the presence of certain cues and therefore be very variable, but checking may have to be repeated a specific number of times when these cues are present.

4   *Duration* – how long the problem behaviour lasts. What is the usual duration of symptoms of behaviour and what is the longest time the client has tolerated these symptoms before taking action to reduce them? In clients with phobic anxiety, investigation of this area will tell us how long the client's symptoms usually last and how long he has remained in difficult situations trying to ride out his feelings.

Frequency of the problem
Intensity of the problem when it occurs
Number of times the problem may occur or be repeated
Duration of time the experience of the problem lasts

Figure 5.3   Getting more detailed information

By this time we should have a reasonably precise idea of what the client's main problem is together with a lot of detail. We should know how often the problem occurs, how long it lasts, where it happens, how severe the experience is and the effect of other people on the problem. We may also have some idea why the client behaves as he does in response to the problem.

This amount of detail, however, is still not enough. We do not know enough about the actual experience the client goes through when the problem is manifesting itself. To find this out we need to use the *Behavioural Analysis*.

A behavioural analysis

There are three parts to a behavioural analysis:

Antecedents
Behaviour
Consequences

No problem or behaviour exists in isolation. There will always be events and experiences that precede it (antecedents) as there will be other events that follow it (consequences). Both the antecedents and the consequences of a behaviour will have an effect on the behaviour itself. Some antecedents and consequences will make the behaviour more likely to occur, whilst others will do the opposite. Let us take a simple example – crossing a road.

```
A – Antecedents
B – Behaviour
C – Consequences
```

Figure 5.4 The behavioural analysis

1 Antecedents
Before we can cross a road – the behaviour – we need certain conditions to apply, for example:

- a road
- ourselves
- a desire or need to cross the road
- the physical ability to get to the side of the road
- knowledge about traffic behaviour
- the ability to assess whether the road is clear or not

There are many more antecedents to such a simple action and we can group them together under several headings.

- *The Physical Environment*; where we are just prior to crossing the road (on the pavement).

- *The Social Environment*; who is around us, what they are doing, how they affect our actions (e.g. alone or with an elderly relative, crowds of people about).

- *Our Behaviour*; what we are doing just prior to crossing the road (e.g. standing watching the traffic).

- *Our Feelings*; what physical sensations precede the behaviour (e.g. tension, alertness, etc.).

- *Our Thoughts*; what we are thinking before we undertake the behaviour (e.g. apprehension about the traffic).

2 Behaviour

A similar breakdown can be used for the behaviour itself. The main analysis will be that we move one leg in front of the other in the generally accepted fashion in order to reach the other side of the road. During the crossing we will probably be looking around for cars as well as looking at our intended destination. Hopefully, we will be feeling alert and vigilant, and maybe a little apprehensive. If the road is busy and we are taking a risk we may run across the road. However, if we are with our elderly, favourite aunt we will probably be crossing at a pelican crossing, waiting for the lights to change, proceeding slowly and carefully.

3 Consequences

Whatever the consequences of the behaviour, we can analyse them in the same way as for antecedents. For example, we are now standing at the side of the road with our elderly aunt, feeling relieved we have got her across the road and looking forward to the cream tea she is about to buy us in the cafe we are standing outside. Thus, there are physical, social, behavioural, physiological and cognitive aspects to the consequence of crossing the road.

Whereas certain antecedents will act as cues for certain behaviours, consequences are more likely to be rewarding or punishing of the behaviour. Both antecedents and consequences determine whether the frequency of the behaviour increases or decreases. In the above example, we are probably more likely to cross the same road in the future if there is another cream tea on the other side (consequence) and we have our aunt with us (antecedent). Under these conditions the behaviour will increase.

The powerful effect that the consequences of our actions has on the probability that these actions will be repeated helps explain some of the puzzling aspects of many anxiety-related problems. If someone in a crowded shop suddenly becomes panicky, leaves the shop quickly and finds his anxiety reduces as soon as he is outside, he is less likely to go back into the shop. The consequence of his action, namely the reduction of his anxiety, has reinforced his behaviour and it will probably be repeated. If this avoidance spreads to other shops, however, then what started out as an effective coping mechanism can slowly lead to increasing restriction and handicap.

The three-systems analysis

Many of the clients for whom behavioural psychotherapy is a suitable approach have problems with anxiety. The three-systems model of emotional responses introduced in Chapter 1 and referred to throughout this book gives us a framework to properly assess an individual's experience of this most complicated of emotions. We shall see later just how vital this is when planning an individual's treatment. To recap, the three systems are:

1 Autonomic – the physiological symptoms of anxiety.
2 Behavioural – the behavioural effects of anxiety.
3 Cognitive – the thoughts experienced when anxious.

If we are to provide appropriate care to a person with anxiety problems we have to find out more about these three systems of anxiety and how important they are to the person. Each individual will experience different amounts of the autonomic, behavioural and cognitive effects of anxiety so careful questioning will tell us how these three systems vary in severity. We need to know:

1 What happens to the person physically when he is anxious or panicky, how does he feel, what happens to his body in identified anxiety-provoking situations?
2 What does the person do when he is anxious? Does he leave, avoid, check, seek reassurance or cancel out his anxiety in any other way?
3 What thoughts go through the person's mind when he is anxious? What does he actually think when in an anxiety-

provoking situation? What does he fear is happening to him?

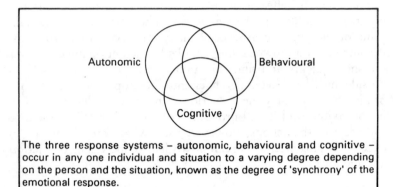

The three response systems – autonomic, behavioural and cognitive – occur in any one individual and situation to a varying degree depending on the person and the situation, known as the degree of 'synchrony' of the emotional response.

Figure 5.5   The three-systems analysis of emotion

The three-systems analysis gives us a blueprint for the future and is essential for correct identification of a client's problems and the subsequent selection of appropriate treatment strategies.

Other useful questions

Certain other areas need to be explored which 'flesh out' the detailed information we now have.

Onset and maintenance
We should ask about the person's first experience of the problem and how it has varied since then. A precise description of the first episode will tell us if the onset was traumatic or gradual, if the person was under great stress at the time and what emphasis he placed upon this experience then and now. The way the problem has varied over time should help us discover if the problem is unremitting or if it comes and goes. If the latter is true we should try to find out what influences the problem to get better or worse.

Modifying factors
It is worth asking specifically if there are things not covered earlier in the assessment that make the problem better or worse. Such things may include alcohol, drugs or the presence of other people.

> Onset and maintenance
> Modifying factors
> Handicap to life
> Why is help being sought now?
> What does the client want?
> Past treatment
> Drugs, alcohol and caffeine

Figure 5.6   Other useful questions

Handicap to life

What particular areas of the person's life does he feel are handicapped by his problems? There is a need here to be specific. The impact of anxiety or other problems may be focused in one particular area, for example, holding conversations with superiors at work, or they may be more global and affect most parts of a person's life. This question may help us understand some of the motivation behind the person seeking help.

Why now?

In order to clarify further the reasons why any one individual asks for professional help, simply asking, 'Why have you sought help now?' should go a long way. If a problem has been constant over a number of years it is a good idea to find this out, since it illuminates some of the motivational factors that drive a person to seek professional help. These reasons may be:

- individual: 'I have just had enough after all these years, I thought it would go away but it hasn't.'

- external: 'My wife says I need help.'

- because of the person's changing role in a social system: 'My children are at school now all day and I am becoming increasingly isolated.'

- or coincidental: 'I saw a programme on television about obsessions, I didn't know I could get help before.'

Each individual will have his own reasons for seeking help which may affect his determination to engage in treatment and see it through to the end. It is obvious that people are less likely to put a lot of effort into treatment if they are only there because somebody else thinks it is a good idea.

What the client wants

Hand in hand with the last question we should ask the client what he wants from therapy in general and ourselves in particular. This is a gentle way of introducing the idea of targets (which we will be specifying and measuring later). Even if two people had identical problems, their personal targets would be different. In order for our care to be based on the client's ideas of success rather than our own, we should pay particular attention to this issue. We are really asking the most fundamental question of all, 'What would you like to do in the future that you cannot do at the moment because of your problems?'

Past treatment

It is always very useful to assess what, if any, help the client has had for his problems. If we find that behavioural treatment has been tried before unsuccessfully we may want to question deeper to determine why this was so. The answers to this line of enquiry may determine whether we offer behavioural treatment again or not. Information about other treatments the client has tried and his attitude to them will give us an insight into his likely response to the idea of starting a behavioural programme.

Drugs, alcohol and caffeine

Drugs, legal and illegal, together with alcohol and caffeine all have a profound effect on people's behaviour whether it is in ordinary situations or during a behavioural treatment programme. It is vital that we assess a person's present and past consumption of these substances. When we come to review the information we have collected in the assessment we must know how many drugs are taken by the client, when they are taken, why they are taken, if they are prescribed, bought over the counter, borrowed from a friend or relative or obtained illegally.

The question of whether a person will admit to a total stranger on their first meeting that he takes illegal drugs is, of course, debatable. However, we must ask. By assuring the client of the absolute confidentiality of our interview we may get an accurate picture. We should also ask about over the counter drug use as well as prescribed drug use.

Alcohol consumption is another area of enquiry. Again we need to ask about total intake, frequency, type of drink, etc. This information may have a direct impact on the kind of treatment we offer the client.

A simple question to find out whether the client consumes large amounts of caffeine, found mainly in coffee but also tea, some painkillers, chocolate and soft drinks, takes little time and may turn out to be a vital aspect in a few people's problems. The effects of alcohol, drugs and caffeine are discussed in great detail in Chapter 6.

At this point we will have a lot of detailed information on the difficulties the client is having with his life. This part of the assessment has concentrated on the *client* and his specific problems and difficulties. We need also to gather information on the person's mental state, his family, personal, medical and psychiatric histories. This forms the basis of the general assessment, and gives us information on the person. It puts him in context and guards against us seeing him as 'the problem' alone.

General assessment

The amount of general assessment we undertake depends largely on the context in which we are seeing the client. The referral letter may contain much information about family, personal and other histories and it is only frustrating for the client to have the same information requested of him time after time by different people. It gives the feeling of non-communication between ourselves and the referrer. If we are working in a team much of the information may already have been found out, particularly in a hospital setting. Again it is unnecessary duplication to go over old ground. However, we should not assume that just because a GP or other agent refers a client to us he is aware of the client's background. Many referrers, especially GPs, do not have the time to take a full background history. It is better for us to err on the side of overdoing the background general assessment unless we are sure the referrer knows the full details already.

Mental state

The mental state examination is the name given to a series of questions directed at certain areas of a person's functioning that help us assess the presence or absence of serious mental illness. We have described it in this rather medical way since it is most often used by doctors in diagnosis. As nurses we do not usually undertake this role. However, we almost always make a subjective assessment of a client's mental health during our interactions with them. This mental state may change over the weeks that we see people.

It is our opinion that if nurses are to take on the role of 'main therapists' we must have knowledge of a more robust and objective way of assessing mental health than subjective assessment. We should be able to pick out signs of serious depression, delusions and hallucinations, problems with perceptions of reality and other indications that a person needs something other than behavioural psychotherapy. To pursue without this information would be negligent. It is not our purpose in this book to outline the main signs and symptoms of recognized 'mental illnesses'. However, for us to be certain that the person does not have a serious psychiatric problem needing medical help we must enquire along the following main areas of questioning:

- General appearance and behaviour – dress, manner, eye-contact, posture, abnormal gait or rigidity.
- Conversation – speed, content, form.
- Mood – consistency, sleep disturbance, appetite, energy, concentration difficulties, overwhelming guilt feelings, suicidal thoughts and/or plans, depression, elation, flattened mood.
- Abnormal experiences – delusions, hallucinations, ideas of reference.
- Dementia – memory impairment, orientation to place and time, concentration impairment.

A few general questions and observations in each area will indicate if there is further information to be gained by deeper questioning. However, we should always take a fairly detailed assessment of a person's mood as a matter of course, since mood has such a profound effect on a person's day-to-day functioning. Severe depression is also a potentially life-threatening problem and has an adverse effect on a lot of the techniques used in behavioural psychotherapy.

The rest of the assessment concerns information that puts the person's problems in the wider context of his life. We have presented this in the conventional order. We feel this is important in that communication of our findings to the referral agent is easier if we write letters to a standard format. A busy GP does not have the time to try to understand a new arrangement of information as well as trying to digest the content of our letters. We will, therefore, briefly mention the important areas in the order in which they are generally written in an assessment letter following the main problem description.

Past psychiatric problems and their treatment
A brief history of any previous contact with psychiatric or psychological services and the nature of the treatment given.

Past medical history
Any dates and brief descriptions of medical problems in the past up to the present day. Any current medical problem and its treatment.

Current social conditions
Where the client lives, with whom, what he does for a living, financial worries, how he spends his leisure hours.

Family history
A description of the client's family – parents, brothers and sisters, relationships in the family, any history of similar or other psychological problems in the family.

Personal history
A reasonably detailed personal history of the client's early home life, his schooling, his relationships with other family members and friends. Some information about his education, his working life, sexual development and relationships, marriage, children, etc., is all useful in getting a wider picture and may help identify other areas of difficulty.

This is the end of the general assessment. Each area may require more or less enquiry depending on the client's feelings and responses to our questioning. We should not treat the headings we have just described as either all essential or exhaustive. We need always to monitor the client's responses and be *flexible*.

Summary

We have now reached a point where we can gather all the information together and review it. We have extremely detailed data on the client's main problem or problems and how this fits in with his life now. We also know about his personal and family histories and whether he has any serious mental health problems that require us to ask for further help from a psychiatrist or the client's GP. We are, therefore, ready for the next stages of assessment – reviewing the information collected and planning a treatment strategy.

REFERENCE

Tierney A. (1984). *A Systematic Approach to Nursing Care: an introduction.* Milton Keynes: The Open University Centre for Continuing Education.

Chapter 6

Planning and evaluating therapy

Reviewing the information collected

In the previous two chapters we looked at the difficult process of gathering information on which to base an assessment. In this chapter we want to consider what to do with the information to make it clinically useful, and hopefully, therefore, to be able to offer the client an effective and appropriate treatment programme. Probably the key word here is 'appropriate'. How are we going to sort out the information we have collected in order to determine our next step? What are our priorities?

Whenever we receive information from the environment, we try to match this input with what we already know about the particular subject we are dealing with. This is equally true whether we are looking at a plate of food or assessing more complex pieces of human behaviour. Previous information and ideas, stored in memory, are compared with this new information and a course of action is then decided upon. Such stored information, structured in a way that makes sense to us, can be referred to as a model. The behavioural model, as described in this book, is the one we use to organize the assessment data. Equally, one could use the 'medical model', systems models, analytical models or any other model one chooses.

The advantage of using the behavioural model is that it uses *testable* principles to integrate the data collected. We have carried out a non-interpretive fact-gathering exercise and this must be complemented by research-based nursing actions. This contrasts strongly with the approach taken by the originators of most 'nursing models' (nursing models here refers to ideas about people which have been developed and published to assist in organizing nursing care (see Aggleton P. and Chalmers H., 1984). Here, ideas are generated which may feel theoretically very nice but are often interpretive and non-testable. The validity of organizing nursing care on the basis of such theoretical models has been questioned (Dylak P., 1986). In contrast, behavioural psychotherapy draws on a large body of research evidence to direct therapeutic actions.

The next question refers to what priorities we set when offering a package of therapy. In setting priorities in behavioural psychotherapy the responsibility rests with the client. It is better to reverse the usual client/therapist relationship, not to interpret and instead ask him what *his* priorities are. In fact the opening assessment question began this process, i.e. 'What is your main problem?' Later we asked the client to describe what effect his problems were having on his day-to-day life and what he wanted to change, i.e. 'What do you want from treatment?'

Again this is an example of the essentially pragmatic approach of behavioural psychotherapy. Only the client really knows what his problems are and only he can tell us what he needs our help for. Why go any further?

Suitability for behavioural psychotherapy

If we are going to use this client-centred method rather than therapist-centred treatment, it follows that we cannot use behavioural techniques no matter what the client's problem. Behavioural psychotherapy is not a panacea for all ills, nor are there always particular treatment techniques for particular problems. Some psychological and physical conditions are known to actively inhibit behavioural treatment. We need, therefore, to apply suitability criteria to a client's problem. This does not mean making a judgement about a *client* himself, but about the nature of his problem and whether it is likely to respond to behavioural techniques. Having obtained an accurate picture of a client's problem(s) and asked him to indicate what his handicaps are and what he would like to change, we can then decide if there is any role for a behavioural approach. The suitability criteria usually applied to presenting problems are detailed below.

1 The problem is expressed in terms of observable behaviour
Behavioural techniques are most likely to be useful if a person is complaining of a handicapping excess or deficit of behaviour. For

Table 6.1 Suitability for Behavioural
Psychotherapy

1 The problem is expressed as observable behaviour
2 The problem is current and predictable
3 Clear behavioural goals can be agreed
4 Client understands and agrees to treatment
5 No contra-indications to behavioural treatment

example, a client may be complaining of severe anxiety and panic. It is the effect this is having on his daily life and what he wants to change that is important. If this is expressed in terms of observable behaviour, e.g. anxiety leading to avoidance of feared objects and situations, then we should be able to help. This avoidance behaviour, as a result of the anxiety experienced in the feared situation, should be amenable to a behavioural intervention. Excesses of behaviour, such as compulsive handwashing or excessive checking, are also suitable. Another example is the client who has urges to expose his genitals in public. The urges may not themselves be problematic if the client can control them easily. However, if they result in deviant acts where the client is actually exposing himself, disturbing others and running the risk of imprisonment, then behavioural interventions are indicated.

2 The problem is current and predictable
If a problem usually occurs in certain places, with certain people or at certain times and is consistent in its presentation, then it is likely to be suitable for behavioural psychotherapy. The problem should, by and large, manifest itself in a predictable fashion. That is not to say that the problem cannot vary in intensity or severity – somedays will be better than others. However, a client should be able to predict a reasonably consistent degree of handicap in certain situations. It is also no good trying to deal with behaviours that are no longer apparent nor occurring in the here and now. The client's problems should be causing him difficulties now and be a current handicap. These problems may have their origins in the past – morbid grief reactions for example – but the results should be expressed in the present if behavioural techniques are to be used.

3 Clear treatment goals can be specified

Behavioural psychotherapy is essentially a goal-directed approach. Therapy is aimed towards pre-defined targets. Therefore, clear treatment goals should be negotiated and agreed with the client. We have already discussed ways of establishing mutual trust and a good working relationship in the chapter on interview skills. Defining where the client wants to be at the end of therapy merely reinforces this process, firmly setting the agenda for the following sessions. Pre-defined targets are not the only goals, however. During the course of therapy it is often a good idea to discuss these targets again and there should always be room to re-negotiate further goals.

4 The client understands and agrees to the type of treatment on offer

This is a crucial criterion. We are unlikely to be as successful in therapy if the client does not know why we are asking him to carry out specific behavioural exercises. It is after all, just ordinary respect for the client to give him as much information as possible about both his problem and the most effective therapy for it. All too often, in our experience, clients with chronic disorders have never been given even basic information about their problems. A simple, straightforward rationale engages clients in the cooperative and collaborative style of therapy essential for therapeutic change. This will be discussed in detail in the chapter on the process of therapy.

5 There should be no contra-indications for behavioural treatment

As mentioned earlier, certain physical and psychological conditions inhibit behavioural methods or at least make them less likely to be successful. It has been demonstrated in several studies that up to 49% of psychiatric outpatients have some form of physical illness and in a significant proportion (12% — Gelder *et al.*, 1983) this had been previously undiscovered. As nurses we may not be used to determining physical or psychological differential diagnoses, but if we take on the role of main therapist it is crucial to be aware of some of the signs and symptoms of other serious disorders. Many of these, such as hyperthroidism, are often mistaken for anxiety disorders. In secondary impotence, for example, it is extremely important to check blood sugar for diabetes if this has not been done before. These and other physical and organic conditions are covered in Table 6.2. If physical illness is suspected, this should be discussed with the responsible medical officer and further investigations undertaken if appropriate.

The presence of serious biological depression is a contra-indication for behavioural psychotherapy. The slowing down of thought processes typical of severe depression seems to actively inhibit behavioural treatment mechanisms. If symptoms such as marked early morning wakening, diurnal variation in mood and suicidal ideas and plans are present the depression should be treated independently of, and before, the behavioural problem. Of course, many people with anxiety disorders may have depressive thoughts and ideas because of their problems. This does not inhibit behavioural methods at all, but these thoughts should be monitored routinely.

Substance abuse – alcohol, illicit and prescribed drugs – should be tackled before behavioural treatments like exposure are started in earnest. There is little point in helping someone to enter a feared situation if they are so sedated that they feel no anxiety at all. An effect called 'state-dependent learning' may be observed, where the effects of treatment are only apparent when the client is taking alcohol or drugs. In the case of sedative drugs, particularly benzodiazepines, a commitment to gradual withdrawal should at least be established before commencing behavioural treatment. Drawing up a withdrawal schedule is often the first stage in therapy and is covered in detail later in the book.

Consumption of caffeine is something that should be routinely assessed whenever a client presents with an anxiety problem. This substance is a powerful stimulant and occurs in coffee, tea, cola, some analgesics and many over-the-counter cold remedies. In regular coffee drinkers basal metabolic rate is increased by an average of 10%. Symptoms of excessive caffeine consumption closely resemble anxiety and include palpitations, tachycardia, nausea, irritability, agitation and insomnia. Since 50–200 mg of caffeine will produce measurable physiological effects and an average mug of coffee contains 100 mg of caffeine, it is easy to exceed doses where effects are noticeable. If a client is consuming more than 500–750 mg caffeine daily he should be advised to reduce his intake or replace coffee with a decaffeinated brand. This is especially true for clients with anxiety disorders since there is some evidence that these people have an increased caffeine

Table 6.2 Some Organic Causes of Anxiety and Sexual Dysfunction

Anxiety

Condition	Symptoms	Differentiating characteristics
Hyperthyroidism	Tachycardia, diarrhoea, sweating, weight loss, irritability	—Preference for cold weather —Weight loss despite increased appetite
Hyperventilation	Most anxiety symptoms, tingling and dizziness prominent	—Dizziness, ringing in the ears —See later chapter dealing with panic
Caffeinism	Irritability, headache, tachycardia, tremor, palpitations, insomnia	—Symptoms abate on reduction of caffeine intake
Hypoglycaemia	Disturbed behaviour, tremor, periods of unexplained fatigue	—Specific periodic anxiety, especially after having not eaten

Sexual disorders

Condition	Symptoms	Differentiating characteristics
Diabetes mellitus	Inability to achieve erection	—High blood sugar —Always check in secondary impotence
Endocrine disorders	Erectile impotence, low libido	—Eliminate in cases of sexual dysfunction —Look for any changes in secondary sexual characteristics
Other physical illness	Pain on intercourse	—Pain on deep intercourse indicates pelvic pathology in women —Menstrual disturbances also often present

sensitivity (Lee *et al.*, 1985). Over-the-counter analgesic consumption should also be checked since some brands contain up to 66 mg of caffeine per tablet.

When advising clients to reduce their caffeine consumption a gradual reduction should be implemented. One of the most common symptoms of caffeine withdrawal is severe headache (thus accounting for its inclusion in proprietary analgesics) which will be poorly tolerated and should be avoided if possible. Further information is included in a review by Greden (1974).

Acute and chronic psychoses are not conditions that respond to the collaborative, psychotherapeutic techniques covered in this book. That is not to say that behavioural *principles* are not appropriate, just that the specific therapeutic strategies used in behavioural psychotherapy have not been shown to be effective in psychotic illnesses. Behavioural principles, however, can be very useful. For example, behavioural methods have been used to eliminate auditory hallucinations with good success (see Morley, 1987 for an example).

Having gathered the information, reviewed it, decided that the client's problems are amenable to a behavioural psychotherapeutic approach and gained his active collaboration, we are now ready to translate his problems into a form that makes most clinical sense. This brings us to the important topic of clinical measurement.

MEASUREMENT

What is measurement?

Measurement is something we all do in our day-to-day lives. We make assessments of the dimensions of objects, situations, our feelings, etc., and compare them to other similar things or to a known standard we are familiar with. When driving, we may assess the space between a stationary vehicle and the oncoming stream of traffic and decide to drive around the obstruction only if there is enough room. To do this we must have compared the space available to the known width of our car. When buying new curtains we will have previously measured the window size and recorded it in some standard units so that the salesman can translate what we want into the real thing. We know if we are feeling ill, because we have a 'normal' state to compare ourselves with. We all make these daily judgements many times, but in a highly subjective way. What is the normal or acceptable state of affairs for ourselves may not be so for another person. It depends on the size of your car, your windows or what you consider to be good health.

Table 6.3

Measurement is:

— The objective assessment of a variable

This tells us...

— The *dimensions* of the variable
— The variable can then be compared against a

Known standard

Why measure?

At the start of treatment we need to have a measure of the severity of a client's problems. Once we have obtained an accurate measure, we have a *baseline* with which we can compare subsequent measurements. However, applying our own subjective values to his problems will not give us an accurate picture. We need to use other methods. If we can convert subjective words like 'awful' or 'panicky' to a numbered scale we can note changes more accurately and objectively. Such scales are more reliable than words. To put it another way, we can evaluate change, and then make judgements about the effectiveness of our therapy far more accurately if we use clinical measurement. Measurement in this context thus refers to a number on a scale.

One important reason for measuring problem severity is the feedback this gives to the client. A pre-therapy measure is a snapshot of a client's situation. Repeated measures, taken at various stages in therapy, can then be shown to the client and compared with the baseline. This gives welcome feedback of treatment gains, since it is all too easy to concentrate on what one *cannot* do rather than on one's achievements to date. This is far more reliable than repeatedly asking the client, 'How do you think you are getting on?' Measurement is thus a therapeutic exercise in itself.

The final reason for using measurement in routine clinical practice is that it aids the development of a body of nursing knowledge. Data collected in our day-to-day work can be analysed to provide information on the most effective strategies for change which can then lead to further research. In this way traditional, often institutional, practices can be replaced by nursing actions that have a sound research basis. This theme will be developed later in the section on quality assurance in Chapter 14.

What do we measure?

Whenever we set out to measure something we are only really measuring something else that indicates the length, depth, severity, etc., of a property that the first object possesses. The size of the window in our earlier example is indicated by the number of centimetres shown on our rule. The window possesses the properties of width and depth and it is these that we are measuring to indicate the window's *size*. In the other example, our upset stomach indicates we are not feeling 100% well. Here we are not measuring 'wellness' itself but a specific characteristic of a specific organ that we know will reflect the state of our general health. We can use similar 'indicators' to provide a tag to measure a client's problem severity. But, the assumption must be valid that:

Indicator improvement = Problem improvement

In other words, the indicator we have chosen to measure should be appropriate. It should be a way of accurately measuring improvement in problem severity. For example, avoidance behaviour is a measure of phobic anxiety, but is not an accurate measure of mood state. Conversely, raised mood will not necessarily indicate a reduction in phobic anxiety. If the choice of indicator is inappropriate then the measurement is invalid.

Case-specific measures versus validated questionnaires

A number of books (e.g. Ward, 1985) have described the importance of accurate assessment followed by appropriate interventions in psychiatric nursing. Part of this process has been the identification of relevant problems and the setting of targets for nurses and clients to aspire to. This problem-orientated approach lends itself readily to clinical measurement. Problem severity can be recorded on a scale, and the number thus obtained is at once relevant to the client's particular difficulties. We can refer to this measurement as 'case specific'.

Another way of measuring problem severity is to use questionnaires which have been developed and validated through research. These will have been shown to reliably indicate if a client is getting better or not by increases and decreases in the total questionnaire scores. Examples include the Fear Questionnaire (Marks and Mathews, 1979) and the Beck Depression Inventory (Beck *et al.*, 1961).

Both these types of measurement have their pro's and con's. The case-specific measures have great importance to the person, but do not tell us if improvements are generalizing to other areas of a person's life. More importantly, we cannot tell from case-specific measures how well one client is faring against the 'norm'. Case-specific measures also depend very much on the skill of the nurse in helping the client obtain a clear behavioural definition of his problems.

On the other hand, validated questionnaires can be daunting for the client to fill in and cannot cover all aspects of a person's problems. They can, however, be used to compare the effectiveness of different therapeutic approaches as they can be compared with data collected in various, even worldwide, centres. They also give us a range of scores that we know reflects the responses of a 'normal' population. Individuals' scores can be compared with this norm.

The best system is a combination of both case-specific measures and validated questionnaires. Behavioural problem definitions can be measured to give specific indicators of improvement for a particular client and then backed up with one or two validated measures to evaluate more generalized improvement.

Case-specific measures

(a) Problem statements

Problem identification is an essential step in any problem-orientated approach including the nursing process (Tiernay, 1984). Explicit definitions are much easier to measure than woolly ones. It is better to write a problem down in a simple but comprehensive way that is immediately understandable, than to miss bits out or to leave things open to misinterpretation. This is a lot easier said than done. One way to structure problem statements is to base them on the behavioural analysis that formed part of our assessment. An example is given below.

'Anxiety when leaving the house for fear of panicking, leading me to avoid pubs, clubs, shops and other crowded places and thus restricting my daily life.'

The components of this statement are:

1 The problem – anxiety
2 The feared consequence – fear of panicking
3 The antecedent – when leaving the house
4 The behaviour – avoiding pubs, clubs and shops
5 The consequence – restriction of daily life.

A problem statement is thus very exact and precise. Not only is the problem – anxiety – stated, but also made concrete are the exact nature of the client's fears, the context of his fears, the behavioural manifestation of his fears and the effects of fear on the person's life.

The important part of any problem statement is no doubt the first bit, e.g. 'compulsive urges to binge-eat' or 'inability to achieve erection', etc., but problem statements are most useful if we can put them into context as above. Two problem statements of this nature are usually enough to accurately describe a client's difficulties.

Problems are also best stated in the client's own words. We should always avoid putting words in the client's mouth, defining problems is no different. It can be quite a useful exercise to ask a client to say, in one short sentence, what their problem is. This can then be developed with the client until agreement is reached.

(b) Targets

Targets (or goals) are specific activities that clients currently find difficult and wish they were able to do were it not for their problems. Targets are:

- identified from problem statements
- precise
- stated positively
- client centred
- realistic
- measurable

Targets decided on at assessment are long-term aims and not the same as weekly treatment goals. The best targets are those derived from the problem statements and thus immediately relevant to the client's situation. They need to be precise in their description of what is to be achieved, i.e.

- *What* behaviour is to be demonstrated
- *The conditions* under which the behaviour is to be performed, e.g. alone or accompanied, where, etc.
- *Frequency, duration*, etc., to evaluate the behaviour.

An example of a target that is derived from our previous problem statement might be:

> Shopping alone, at a busy time, for one hour, twice a week in the local supermarket.

The components of this statement are:

1   The behaviour – shopping
2   The conditions – alone, at busy times
3   The frequency – twice a week
4   The duration – for one hour.

The target is not only precise but is directly related to the client's problem, i.e. fear of panicking in crowded places. Targets are normally stated in terms of what the client is to do and they should be realistic and practical. They should also be things that the client would actually *want* to do if he were not handicapped by his problems. Stating targets positively, i.e. what is to be achieved rather than what is not to happen is essential. Clients will feel much better about progress towards an achievable target than emphasis on reducing some other behaviour.

Measuring problems and targets

Problem severity can be measured by using a 9-point category scale. This is merely a straight line on a piece of paper which has 9 points along its length. Each point represents a category. In the scales used to measure problems and targets the line is categorised according to how much the problem upsets the client and interferes with his normal activities. So point 2 indicates that the problem slightly upsets the client and sometimes interferes with his normal activities, whereas point 8 indicates that the problem very severely upsets him and continuously interferes with his normal activities. In fact the 9-point scale has become an accepted standard in the clinical measurements outlined in this book. Different circumstances require different categories along the scale but the principles remain the same. The client chooses the category that best describes how he feels about the statement above the scale. This is then recorded on the form.

Thus, once problems have been defined, they can be measured by asking the client how much, 'This problem upsets me and/or interferes with my normal activities.' The scale used is reproduced below.

'This problem upsets me and/or interferes with my normal activities'								
0	1	2	3	4	5	6	7	8
does not		slightly/ sometimes		definitely/ often		markedly/ very often		very severely/ continuously

The client's self rating can then be recorded. It can sometimes be useful to include a 'therapist's rating' of the same problem, though this will rarely differ from the client's rating, especially at assessment. The client is usually the best judge of his problem severity.

Measurement of targets takes the same format. This allows targets to be partly achieved, rather than an all-or-nothing approach which can only emphasize failure. A similar scale is used but the emphasis here is on progress towards achievement of the targets. The client can be asked to rate his, 'progress towards achieving each target regularly and without difficulty'. The actual scale used is a percentage success rate, as follows:

'My progress towards achieving each target regularly without difficulty'					
	0	2	4	6	8
Discomfort	none	slight	definite	marked	very severe
Behaviour	complete success	75% success	50% success	25% success	no success

Again, a higher rating indicates greater difficulty with achieving the target and, if the targets are relevant, a greater problem severity.

Validated questionnaires

(a) Work and social adjustment – a measure of handicap
One thing that is very important to know is what effect the client's problems have on his day-to-day existence. We have already asked about this in the assessment, but we can quantify it by using a very useful measure, the Work and Social Adjustment scale (Marks

I. M., 1986). Again using our zero to 8 scale the client is asked to rate how his problems affect four key areas in his life. These are: work (earning money type of work), home management, social leisure (i.e. with other people) and private leisure. The full questionnaire is reproduced in Appendix A but one section is shown below.

				'Because of my problems my ability to work is impaired:'				
0	1	2	3	4	5	6	7	8
not at all		slightly		definitely		markedly		very severely I cannot work

Each area thus has a score of between 0 and 8 and we have a neat profile of the impact of the problem on the client's life. This measure, along with problems and targets is suitable for all clients regardless of their problems. In fact research has indicated that it is possible to extend this measure to many more psychiatric patients than those suitable for behavioural psychotherapy (Richards *et al.*, 1988). This is a reasonable assumption since the social adjustment scale asks for ratings of the effect of *any* problem on the person's life. Along with problem and target measurement this would give us an excellent outcome measure in quality assurance exercises.

(b)   The Fear Questionnaire

The Fear Questionnaire (Marks, I. M. and Mathews, A. M., 1979) was developed by analysing the responses of over 1000 people with phobias, and reliably picks out certain types of common fears. It has been used for over 10 years now and has facilitated comparisons of the results of treatments from many different centres and research studies. A full copy of the questionnaire is reproduced in Appendix A.

The Fear Questionnaire is divided into three parts. The client completes the questionnaire himself after explanation. In the first part, the top line is left blank for the client to write in a short definition of his main feared situation or object. Following this are 15 common phobic situations and then another space for any additional fears not covered in the previous 15 items. The client rates how much he avoids these situations on a zero to 8 scale, zero being 'would not avoid' and 8 being 'always avoid'. Within the 15 items are 5 typically agoraphobic situations, 5 blood and injury fears and 5 social phobic situations. These three subscales are added up independently and then totalled together. This therefore gives both a total score and a breakdown of the main areas of phobic avoidance. The 'main phobia' is also rated as is any additional situations if identified.

The second part of the questionnaire measures 'dysphoria'. This is the term used to describe the mixture of anxiety and related depression often found in phobias. Groups of symptoms are described, e.g. 'miserable and depressed', 'irritable and angry' and the client is asked to rate how troublesome these symptoms are in his daily life. The zero to 8 scale used here ranges from zero = 'hardly troublesome at all' to 8 = 'very severely troublesome'. This second section is then added together to give a total score.

The final section is a zero to 8 scale that asks the client to rate how disturbing and disabling his phobic symptoms are, and is referred to as the global phobia score. It ranges from 'no phobias present' to 'very severely disturbing and disabling'. This gives us an idea of the overall impact of the client's phobic anxiety.

The Fear Questionnaire, therefore, gives a lot of valuable information as well as being a reliable way of measuring treatment outcome. It should be used to complement the assessment and definition of a person's problems. It remains most useful, however, as an excellent outcome measure of overall phobic anxiety and can be given to all phobic clients taken into treatment.

(c) The Beck Depression Inventory (BDI)

This is a questionnaire developed by Aaron Beck (Beck *et al.*, 1961) famous for his work on the cognitive therapy of depression. In it, certain areas of depressive thoughts and feelings are identified. Each area then has a choice of statements about it, the client being asked to choose the statement for each area that best describes how they feel. The statements are ranked for each area, going from a fairly innocuous statement to a statement that is typical of very depressed thinking. Each statement has a score, the more depressive the statement, the higher the score. These individual scores are added together to get a total. An example is given below:

If depression is a prominent feature in a client's presenting problems or is hinted at in the dysphoria subscale of the fear questionnaire, the BDI can be given to assess mood. The BDI is

Table 6.4 Beck Depression Inventory –
example

---

3 I feel as though I am very bad or worthless
2 I feel quite guilty
1 I feel bad or unworthy a good part of the time
0 I don't feel particularly guilty

---

better than the dysphoria subscale at evaluating mood since it is
only concerned with depression. Certain scores ring alarm bells
and these are detailed in Beck et al. (1961). However, it is not
necessary to give the BDI to every client, only those for whom
there is a strong depressive element to their presenting problem.

Measurement – When and How

We have discussed the principles of measurement, why it is
clinically useful and what we are going to measure. But when is
the best time to do it?

Measurement is not only helpful in assessment, it is also used
to evaluate outcome. Therefore, a 'pre-post' system is used. After
the information has been collected and reviewed, and if the client's
problems have been identified and found suitable for behavioural
psychotherapy, then measures are taken to obtain a baseline. The
basic measures (problems and targets, Fear Questionnaire, work
and social adjustment) give us this standard against which we can
measure progress. Normally, a behavioural treatment programme
lasts more than five or six sessions, so 'mid-treatment' ratings are
taken during session 5. This involves repeating the measures taken
at assessment, which give us an objective indication of how
successfully therapy is going up to that point. This will help us
decide to change tack to another strategy if no improvement is
obvious. Conversely, however, it may be a source of extremely
positive feedback to the client. At the end of a period of treatment –
discharge – the measures can be re-rated to give the post-treatment
scores. This is our measure of outcome and from it we know how
successful our interventions have been.

The client's problems can also be re-rated after various periods
of time have elapsed following discharge. The conventional times
are one, three and six months follow-up. This monitors the
maintainance of treatment gains, since we need to know if our

therapy is durable. It also has the advantage of softening the discharge procedure so that there is not an all-or-nothing end to therapy. Should the follow-up appointments and measures indicate relapse, further 'booster' sessions of therapy can be arranged. Follow-up measures thus protect the time, or therapeutic investment, spent in the initial treatment programme.

The way we administer measures is also very important. There is little point in going to all the trouble of developing a system to get this objective evidence and then ruining it by sloppy administration. Several points are worth bearing in mind.

Measures should always be clearly explained. At the top of the form are usually some explanatory notes which should be read through carefully with the client point by point. Efforts should be made to ensure the client fully understands the scales, etc., before filling them in.

Measures should be taken at the same time each session, preferably at the beginning. This helps us to gain an accurate rating of how the client views his problems, before any extra sessional intervention from ourselves alters his perceptions.

When taking repeat measures, never show the client his previous ratings until the new ones have been taken. This avoids contaminating his ideas with previous scores. On the forms that are used repeatedly at each measurement session, e.g. Problems and Targets, the previous scores should be covered up before asking the client to re-rate. Only uncover the old ratings when the new ones have been decided on. The process of comparison and discussion of progress can then begin.

Table 6.5 gives a summary of all the measures that have been found useful in clinical practice. The table includes both case-specific measures and validated questionnaires. It also includes some very specific measures that should be used to assess particular problems. These are covered in the chapters dealing with these problems and copies of all the measures mentioned are included in Appendix A.

Summary

In this chapter we have taken assessment past the information gathering stage. We have discussed reviewing the information collected, identifying problems from this information and measuring the severity of the client's problems. We have also considered

Table 6.5

Which Clients	Measurement Which Measures
All clients	Problems and targets
	Fear questionnaire
	Work and social adjustment
Social phobia	Social situations measure
Obsessive-compulsive disorder	Obsessional checklist
	Time, discomfort, handicap
Depression	Beck Depression Inventory
Sexual dysfunction	Conventional sexual activity
Sexual deviation	Conventional sexual activity
	Unconventional sexual activity

All measures taken pre-, mid- and post-treatment and at 1, 3 and 6 months follow-up.

criteria that can be applied so that we can decide if the client's difficulties are likely to be amenable to behavioural psychotherapy. Although we have touched on the structure of therapy briefly, the next chapter will look in more detail at the implementation stage – the process of treatment.

REFERENCES

Aggleton P., Chalmers H. (1984). Models and theories. *Nursing Times*, 80(36), 24–28.

Beck A. T., Ward C. H., Mendelson M., Mock J., Erbaugh J. (1961). An inventory for measuring depression. *Archives of General Psychiatry*, 4, 561–571.

Dylak P. (1986). The state of the art? *Nursing Times*, 82, 42–72.

Gelder, M. *et al.* (1983). *The Oxford Textbook of Psychiatry*. Oxford: Oxford University Press.

Greden J. F. (1974). Anxiety or caffeinism: a diagnostic dilemma. *American Journal of Psychiatry*, 131(10), 1089–1092.

Lee W. A., Cameron O. G. and Greden J. F. (1985). Anxiety and caffeine consumption in people with anxiety disorders. *Psychiatry Research*, 15, 211–217.

Marks I. M: (1986). *Behavioural Psychotherapy: Maudsley Pocket Book of Clinical Management*, Bristol: Wright.

Marks I. M. and Mathews A. M. (1979). Brief standard self-rating for phobic patients. *Behaviour Research and Therapy*, **17**, 263–67.

Morley S. (1987). Modification of auditory hallucinations: experimental studies of headphones and earplugs. *Behavioural Psychotherapy*, **15**, 240–51.

Richards D. A., Butterworth J., Shrubb S. (1988). Outcome measures in community psychiatric nursing. *Community Psychiatric Nursing Journal*, **6**, 7–16.

Tiernay A. (1984). In *A Systematic Approach to Nursing Care: An Introduction*. Milton Keynes: The Open University Centre for Continuing Education.

Ward M. F. (1985). *The Nursing Process in Psychiatry*. London: Churchill Livingstone.

Chapter 7

Implementation – the process of therapy

Behavioural psychotherapy is a problem-orientated approach that has much in common with the nursing process. Table 7.1 shows the familiar four stages to the nursing process, first outlined in this country by McFarlane (1973) and subsequently adopted by nursing policy makers (GNC 1977; ENB 1982) as a 'helpful framework for nursing practice'. Professor Altschul (1984) has written that behaviour therapy nursing represents the nursing process 'par excellence'. In this chapter we offer guidelines on the implementation phase of this process. Firstly, however, we would like to emphasize the word *process*.

Although it may be conceptually helpful to split the problem orientated approach into sections dealing with assessment, planning, etc., in practice it is impossible to determine where one stage

Table 7.1 The 4 Stages of a Problem Orientated Approach

Assessment
↓
Planning
↓
Implementation
↓
Evaluation

Problems are identified from the assessment. A plan is agreed with clear goals based on the information gained at assessment. The plan is carried out and then evaluated to see if the goals have been achieved.

ends and another begins. A behavioural treatment programme is a complete process. It may start with an 'assessment' but this assessment is often a therapeutic exercise in itself as a client is given the time and space to outline his difficulties. Similarly, assessment does not end when treatment begins but is an ongoing process throughout the whole of therapy. We would argue very strongly against the belief that one can pick up behavioural treatment techniques and apply them in a 'cook book' fashion without regard to the assessment, planning and evaluation of therapy. Implementation must be seen as part of the whole process of therapy and occurs at all stages. Measurement, for example, plays just as large a part in the implementation phase of therapy as it does in the assessment and evaluation stages. Measurement, in the form of self-monitoring, is a powerful therapeutic strategy on its own and can result in significant behaviour change. Thus, the implementation stage of the therapeutic process cannot be seen as a separate entity.

Organizing treatment sessions

Most encounters with clients, including active treatment sessions, can be organized along roughly the same lines. The framework for consultation is similar to the principles used when organizing interviews, which we discussed in Chapter 4. We need a plan for the session which includes content and time. We should take care in the selection of the environment in which the session will take place and make sure that it is suitable for the needs of the client and the content of the treatment session. We need all our skills of attention, non-verbal communication, flexibility and direction if the session is to have a chance of being successful. Table 7.2 summarizes the stages in a typical treatment session.

Table 7.2 Organizing Treatment Sessions

1 Introduction and orientation
2 Review of previous week and homework tasks
3 Problem-solving of difficulties
4 Behavioural exercises
5 Summarizing the therapy session
6 Planning next week's activities and homework
7 Ending the session

1 Introduction and orientation

Just as described in the chapter on interview skills, we need to negotiate with the client just what we want to do during the session and come to an agreement on this. Introductions may be more informal at this stage but are still part of normal social behaviour and very necessary at the start of any session with a client. The orientation should allow for negotiation of session content and a time limit should be specified. This is sometimes known as 'setting the agenda'.

2 Review of previous week and homework tasks

Most behavioural treatments require a commitment from the client that they will carry out 'homework' exercises between treatment sessions. These should always be recorded in a diary or record sheet. Feedback from these diaries gives us detailed information about the client's activities since the last session. They are a crucial part of the treatment package and we need to spend as much time as possible with the client going over them. This will aid the client's recall of particular events or assignments and is much more useful than merely asking, 'How has the week gone?' They also give positive feedback on successfully completed exercises plus information to help us problem-solve any difficulties. Clients often spend a great deal of time filling in homework records or diary sheets and we should always acknowledge this by spending time in the session discussing them. We should never ignore them or pass quickly on to something else.

3 Problem-solving of difficulties

There is no point in reviewing homework records or diaries if no attention is paid to issues raised at this stage. We now believe that the work carried out by clients between treatment sessions is crucial to the success of therapy. Problems raised at this stage need to be looked at in detail to discover ways around any difficulties the client may be experiencing in achieving treatment targets. Support for clients as they tackle their problems can then be given. Additionally, all successes should be praised and positive feedback given to clients when they overcome difficulties. This stage may occupy the bulk of some treatment sessions. Issues raised, either positive or negative, can be discussed and solutions sought. This then leads on to negotiation of further homework goals.

4 Behavioural exercises

Some sessions may include specific behavioural treatment techniques. Such techniques can be grouped as follows:

A *Anxiety Reduction*
- graded prolonged exposure (*in-vivo* or in imagination)
- cue exposure and response prevention
- anxiety management: relaxation
  - controlled breathing
  - distraction
  - rational self-talk
  - other positive coping strategies

B *Drive Reduction*
- self-monitoring
- covert sensitization
- habit reversal
- aversive techniques

C *Encouragement of New Behaviours*
- education
- social skills training
- sexual skills training
- modelling
- role play
- shaping and prompting
- operant techniques

One or more of these treatment techniques may be used during any session. In keeping with our belief that we should use treatment techniques that have been shown to be effective and appropriate for certain problems, each technique will be described in much more detail later in the book when we deal with specific problems and their treatment, using examples from our clinical practice.

At this stage it is worth saying that the specific behavioural treatment exercises listed above have been shown to be *the* effective component in therapy. Some authors (Frank, 1984) have written that all psychotherapies share the same qualities – the 'professionalism' of the therapist, a secure treatment setting and a sympathetic listener – and that it is these factors that are effective, particularly in treating anxiety disorders. In other words a good therapist will achieve the same results whatever he does. Analyses like these have resulted in the development of many varied therapies.

It is impossible to deny that the factors cited by Frank and others are very important. They are, however, weak effects when compared to the specific behavioural interventions we will be describing in the rest of the book. Many studies of behavioural treatments have conclusively shown that the specific content of behavioural interventions is the most active component. The *non-specific* aspects of therapies can be controlled for in research studies by randomly allocating clients to either a therapy that includes all these elements or to a behavioural treatment programme that includes the same elements *plus* the behavioural strategy. For example, exposure has been shown in many studies to be significantly more effective than a non-specific therapy in dealing with phobic anxiety and obsessive-compulsive disorders. Examples include Gelder *et al.*, 1967, Mathews *et al.*, 1974, and Jannoun *et al.*, 1980. There are many more.

Whichever behavioural techniques are being used, the environment should be appropriate for the task. A quiet, undisturbed place is essential for imaginal exposure, whereas a crowded cafe may be the ideal place to take a client with a fear of eating in public. Group rooms need to be big enough to accommodate the group comfortably if clients are being seen in this way.

Most behavioural treatment techniques, particularly those involving the treatment of anxiety, require practical skills and effort from ourselves as well as the client. This may mean, for example, leaving our nice warm office and getting on the No. 9 bus, or it may mean enlisting the help of other people in practising conversation skills with a client. Although a lot of talking does obviously go on, behavioural psychotherapy is an active and practical form of therapy which often requires more than advice or 'counselling'. We should always be prepared for this.

There is no overall ideal time limit to a session other than how long it takes to complete the particular behavioural treatment being used. Therapist-aided *in-vivo* exposure, for example, can last several hours. Other sessions may involve only guidance and homework review and take a relatively short time. We should be flexible in our timetabling of sessions and be realistic as to how much time therapy takes. It is no use trying to cram in as many clients as possible at half-hourly intervals if this results in less than the optimum time being spent with each client for successful completion of particular behavioural exercises. However, we should always be aware of the limits of people's attention span.

Appointments that are of a non-stop, face-to-face nature should not really last more than an hour unless the content of the session is varied. After this time it is unlikely that clients will remember much of the information given or discussed.

5 Summarizing the therapy session

It is just as important to summarize the factual, emotional and practical content of a treatment session as it is to use summaries in an information-gathering interview. We should be clear and concise and use the client's own ideas about the session in this feedback. People remember best whatever is discussed last. This can then lead on to the final phase of the session.

6 Planning homework

As we have already noted, one of the main factors predicting the success of behavioural treatment is the determination of clients to practise specific exercises between treatment sessions. Success also depends on our skill in facilitating this. Planning homework is all about negotiation. Some clients will want to rush headlong into facing their difficulties, others will want to take a more hesitant course. Our role is sometimes to gently encourage and at other times counsel caution. At all times we are balancing what is the optimum clinical decision with what the client will find personally acceptable. Homework should aspire to be both lengthy and frequent to maximize its effect. It should also reflect what has gone on during the treatment session so that the setting of homework is a natural progression of the session towards a close. Homework is thus relevant and appropriate. If the client is not clear about recording the homework assignments on the diary sheets, this should be explained also.

7 Ending the session

Sessions should end on time with both ourselves and the client agreeing to the next stage. The principles outlined for ending interviews in the chapter on interview skills should be applied at this stage. A mutually convenient appointment is arranged and the session ended cleanly and tidily. It is good practice to give clients appointment dates written down with a contact telephone number in case they need to change the date in a hurry. If the session has been a home visit it may be harder to end the session on time and in control but it is wise to be firm and set limits.

ISSUES IN CASE-MANAGEMENT

The treatment rationale

When outlining the nature of a behavioural treatment programme to clients we must bear in mind two important points.

1 It is the duty of all health care professionals to provide information to the public on matters relating to personal health. We are very privileged in that we have access to information on health that most people do not have. This is especially true for experimentally derived information that has been shown to lead to significant improvements in health. Where this information relates to a mental health strategy that can be applied by anybody and needs only a small input from professionals to be effective, it is negligent to deny people this information.

2 We will not gain the agreement and cooperation of clients in carrying out what may occasionally be distressing treatment activities unless they fully understand the reasons they are being asked to comply. It is merely treating the client as an adult to present him with the true rationale for treatment. A half-baked explanation of therapy which leaves the client unsure and unclear about what is to happen will severely undermine our chances of success. It would be failing in our responsibility to the client if we offered him the best and most effective treatment available and he rejected it because of a poor explanation.

The rationale is thus probably one of the most important aspects of behavioural psychotherapy to get right. It requires much practice.

There is no magic formula that can be used to produce a perfect treatment rationale. We all develop our own styles. However, the principles of education and explanation should be employed to give a clear and understandable picture of what the client is experiencing and the course of treatment being offered. A very common fear that clients voice is that they are going 'mad'. Symptoms of anxiety can be extremely frightening so it is not surprising that people can react with terror and confusion. A straightforward explanation of the nature of anxiety, the origin of the physiological symptoms that occur and the knowledge that these symptoms are not abnormal can be an immense relief to many clients. As we stated before, it is our experience that many clients come to us with a long history of distressing anxiety symptoms which no one has ever taken the time to explain. Some clients feel that they might be about to have a heart attack when they start to feel panicky, so basic explanations help them reattribute their symptoms more realistically.

The explanation we give clients should be based on what we ourselves know about anxiety. The three-systems analysis, described earlier, is an excellent way to do this and can be expanded to include particular aspects that the client has described as being especially important to him. Some people use handouts when doing this, others draw diagrams. Either way it is probably a good idea to give clients something to take away with them so that they can reinforce what they have learnt when they go home.

This knowledge – that anxiety is a normal bodily reaction to stress and is not 'madness' or a serious physical illness – plus more in-depth information relating particularly to their own experience, is often the single most important factor leading to recovery for many clients. Time spent here is time very well spent indeed.

At this point *expectation effects* are again important. There are very few predictors of successful outcome for the types of problems that behavioural psychotherapy can help. However, expectations of treatment have been shown to be significant predictors with agoraphobic clients (Mathews *et al.*, 1976; Emmelkamp and Wessels, 1975). The greater the expectation clients have that treatment will be effective, the more likely it is that they will improve. The reverse is also true. There may be many reasons why a client believes a treatment will work, but a comprehensive and credible rationale will certainly be one of the most important.

When outlining the treatment approach being offered, the client can be encouraged to generate the next steps himself. Treatment explanations should follow on logically from the education phase. The main point we can make here, and this applies to any problem suitable for behavioural interventions, is that anybody can learn new ways to cope or deal with problems. The behaviour people use to cope with difficult situations may be useful at first but sometimes gets out of control and in the way. An example of this would be the cleaning rituals seen in some obsessive-compulsive problems, which start out as a response to anxiety about contamination and effectively reduce this anxiety. They end up, however, dominating the person's life. We can make the point that just as the cleaning rituals were learnt as a response to fear, so new, less handicapping, responses can be learnt to replace the compulsive handwashing.

When explaining the principles of exposure, time and effort is well repaid later if we are thorough now. A rough graph of habituation versus escape such as the one in Figure 7.1 can be understood by most people. If this is drawn in the session and the client taken through it bit by bit, understanding of the principles of exposure can be enhanced. The four key words need to be

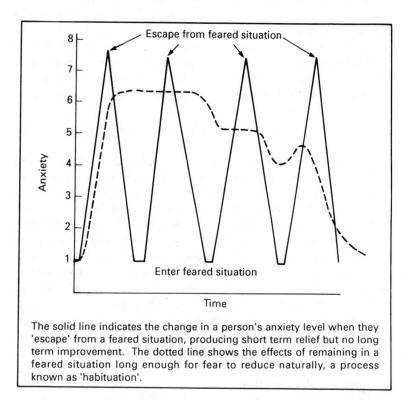

The solid line indicates the change in a person's anxiety level when they 'escape' from a feared situation, producing short term relief but no long term improvement. The dotted line shows the effects of remaining in a feared situation long enough for fear to reduce naturally, a process known as 'habituation'.

Figure 7.1   Anxiety – Escape v. Habituation

stressed; *graded, prolonged, repeated, homework*. It is at this stage that the commitment from the client to work at their problem between treatment sessions should be gained. We must make it clear that the problem belongs to the client and it is their own responsibility to tackle it. We can educate, advise, accompany, support and counsel but it is the client's responsibility to make efforts to change. At this point it is worth explaining to the client that treatment will take time and should be made a priority in their lives. If they cannot make space available in their daily routines for practice of therapeutic objectives they are less likely to be successful. Giving this message is not only part of our behaviour change strategy, it is also absolutely true.

The rationale should end with the client confirming that he understands the treatment being offered and agrees to commit himself to it. Time and space should be allowed for questions. If the client is unsure about accepting what we are offering it may be necessary to ask him to come back next time with further questions and then make a decision about commencing treatment.

Intervals between treatment sessions

There are two ways of organizing a course of treatment, 'short and fat' or 'long and thin'. In the former, sessions are given regularly and frequently, the total course of treatment being of a fairly short duration. In the latter, the opposite is true and there are long intervals between sessions, treatment lasting much longer. We believe that the intensive option is preferable, a stance for which there is some research evidence. Lengthy periods of exposure are better than repeated short exposure sessions (Stern and Marks, 1973). It is far better to offer weekly treatment appointments at first so that the client can be guided and supported through the first difficult steps in therapy. Any difficulties that arise can be dealt with immediately if this approach is taken and the commitment to therapy being asked of the client is mirrored in the approach of the therapist. Brief appointments, given at long intervals, hardly give the impression that we are committed to the client and are a much less effective organization of our time.

As treatment progresses the intervals between treatment sessions can be lengthened. This has the effect of giving the client more responsibility for carrying out his own therapy and solving his own difficulties. It helps to reduce any dependency on us that the

client may develop through a more lengthy period of frequent
contact. This then leads into the discharge (even if such a term is
not actually used with the client) and follow-up period when the
client can be seen at progressively lengthened intervals of one,
three and six months.

Settings for therapy

We have already touched on this subject briefly, but it is worth
emphasizing that we should consider the resources available for
a treatment session before we begin and that the environment in
which the session is to be conducted is one of the most important
factors to be organized. The best environment is a quiet, undisturbed office with two comfortable chairs, plenty of natural light
and all the resources necessary for the session. For most of
us, however, that will not always be possible. Whatever is
compromised it should neither be privacy nor quiet.

We have found it a far more economical use of our time if
clients come to us, unless there are exceptional clinical or practical
reasons why this cannot happen. Sharing the cumulative daily
burden of travelling among many clients is better than ourselves
travelling from house to house. Occasionally there may be good
clinical reasons why we need to go to clients' houses but it must
be remembered that even most people with agoraphobia can travel
accompanied to clinics or hospitals. If it is necessary to go to a
client's house it is quite in order to ask for the television to be
turned off or that the interview be conducted in a quiet room of
the house. If the visit has been organized in order to conduct a
specific treatment activity then we can ask the client to prepare
the ground for us. This may mean asking a client to have his
family at home when we visit, or organize baby-sitters if necessary.

Another option is to see clients in local health centres or GP's
surgeries. This has many advantages, especially if several clients
can be seen during one visit to a health centre. For people who
work from large psychiatric hospitals, often the subject of much
local folklore, it can be impossible to get clients to agree to come
and see them there. Arranging sessions at the place where the
client sees his family doctor can remove the stigma attached to
the psychiatric services. This type of therapy setting also aids
communications with the GP.

When conducting *in-vivo* exposure sessions that involve ourselves it is important to make sure the environment is as controlled and suitable as possible. For example, we cannot organize how full a particular bus is nor guarantee there will not be a fight on the bus, but choosing routes and times of the day that are suitable to the treatment session being planned rather than our own timetable is preferable.

The issue of whether to treat clients in groups or individually is a matter of debate. The obvious advantage is one of economy of effort on our behalf – we can avoid saying similar things to similar clients many times over if they are all in one place at the same time. On the other hand, does this somehow 'dilute' the relationship between ourselves and the client and make this approach less effective? It may be that clients gain support from each other over and above that lost by the reduction of individual attention from ourselves. There may be very positive interactions between group members that make group treatments *more* effective.

Several researchers have looked at this issue. On the whole, group treatments of phobics have been shown to be as effective as individual treatments, but no more so, on measures of main problem outcome. One study found a significantly greater benefit on measures of general social activities (Hafner and Marks, 1976) for group treatments, which is consistent with the opinion expressed by some writers that clients may be able to benefit from sharing problems and practising normal social skills in a group setting (Mathews *et al.*, 1981). There is also the suggestion that highly 'cohesive' groups can produce continued improvement after treatment has finished (Hand *et al.*, 1974), but this effect has not been replicated.

Group treatments are certainly worth considering when there are a number of clients with similar problems. Individual assessments should of course precede group treatment. This approach is bound to save us more time and enable us to treat more clients. However, groups can be very hard work and if clients are asked to wait until there are enough people suitable for a group, the advantage can be negated. Groups are probably most effective for clients with social skills deficits and social phobias. However, there are many examples of anxiety management groups for mixed groups of clients with anxiety problems (e.g. Powell, 1987). These have a much more educative content and are organized on a more self-help basis. Indeed, associations such as the Phobic Trust regularly operate in this way. Their effectiveness has not, unfortunately, been evaluated.

Behavioural methods have often been seen as best suited to a regulated ward-like atmosphere but this only really applies to operant approaches like 'token economy' regimes. Clients suitable for behavioural psychotherapy do not usually need to be treated as hospital inpatients. Whereas once it was thought the optimum conditions for the treatment of obsessive-compulsive disorders were in a hospital ward, we now know we can treat these clients just as effectively in the community. In fact it is probably more effective to treat such problems in this way, since the focus of many obsessional problems lies in the home. However, it may be necessary to treat very severe obsessional problems by admission to hospital but this is fraught with problems. The more staff that are involved in a treatment programme, the harder it is to ensure consistent messages are given to the client. Generalization of treatment gains to the home environment has to be worked at – with home-based treatment it is not an issue.

We may, however, receive referrals regarding clients who are already in hospital and, if appropriate, there is no reason why the same techniques cannot be applied. Being in hospital is not a contra-indication for behavioural psychotherapy, but we should be aware of the difficulties of organizing therapy effectively in such an environment.

If we are seeing a client who is or becomes severely depressed we should arrange a second opinion from the responsible medical officer or a consultant psychiatrist, especially if the client is expressing suicidal ideas and plans. This may mean a hospital admission, but we should still remain in contact with the client whilst he is in hospital to maintain continuity with previous treatment. Active behavioural treatment may then restart when the client's depression has lifted and continue as he is discharged from hospital.

Self-help vs. therapist-aided treatment

There has been a shift recently from an emphasis on assisting clients by active involvement in treatment exercises, particularly *in-vivo* exposure, to a minimal intervention strategy with reliance on self-help manuals. There is no doubt that self-exposure is crucial for successful completion of treatment but how much this can be directed without therapist contact remains the subject of some debate. Advice such as that given by Mathews *et al.* (1981) in their '*Programmed Practice*' manual and in books such as '*Living with Fear*' by Marks (1978) is extremely useful. We should consider recommending these texts to clients to reinforce the information we give them. Ghosh *et al.* (1984) reported a study of phobics who were given either computer-assisted, therapist-assisted or self-help manual-directed exposure and found similar results for each condition. However, of the 123 patients found suitable in this study, only 88 accepted treatment and only 71 completed the course.

Despite this move towards minimal intervention strategies based on the obvious cost-effectiveness arguments, it is our belief that too many severely disabled clients may not accept, or drop out from, treatment if offered this self-help package alone. We prefer to take a middle course. For example, it is not necessary to trudge around the streets with an agoraphobic client week after week. Most sessions take the form of homework planning and problem solving but it may be necessary to carry out a few therapist-aided *in-vivo* sessions as well, especially in the early stages of treatment. In the absence of clearly definable criteria for self-help or therapist-aided treatments it is better to err on the side of a little over-involvement.

Co–therapists and family involvement

The involvement of family members and significant others with a client's problems may vary from minimal to overwhelming. We do not accept the contention put foward by other models of human behaviour that anxiety symptoms fulfil a symbolic role. One of these models, put forward by systems theorists, is that an individual expresses the hurt of a system, e.g. a family, through his own symptoms and that it is the family which needs therapy. There is absolutely no data to support this idea. In fact, treating phobics who have concurrent marital problems using behavioural methods usually results in improvement in both the phobic problem and the marital problem with no further problems emerging, contrary to the predictions of such theories.

When assisting one member of a family to change his behaviour, however, obviously there will be significant effects on the family system as a whole as other members come to terms with the change. Involving family members in the process of change makes this effect a positive force and not a negative one. Not only will a 'cotherapist' assist and support the client in the sometimes difficult process of therapy, but being directly involved in treatment helps the family adjust to the change in the client more smoothly. As a principle of case management we should always try to talk to and engage significant others in therapy. They should have access to the same information about the client's problems and projected treatment plan as the client (if this is OK by the client, of course), so that messages given at home will be consistent with those given by ourselves.

Ethical considerations

Ethics, or the science of morals, gives us the principles and rules with which we operate as professionals. Some of these principles have been incorporated into law and others form part of professional codes of practice (e.g. UKCC 1984). Sometimes these different ethical systems may conflict. An example might be the client who informs us of something he has done that is against the law of the land. Do we respond to our legal responsibilities or do we respect the client's right to confidentiality? An extreme example of this dilemma, although obviously hypothetical, may help to illustrate the point.

Suppose we are asked to treat a client with a problem of sexual deviancy – exhibitionism. During treatment the client tells us of a recent occasion when he exhibited his genitals in the local park. Nobody but himself knows that this happened and we are the only other person he has told. He has told us this information because, while treating him for his exhibitionism, we have gained

Table 7.3 UKCC Code of Professional Conduct

Each registered nurse, midwife and health visitor shall act, at all times, in such a manner as to justify public trust and confidence, to uphold and enhance the good standing and reputation of the profession, to serve the interests of society, and above all to safeguard the interests of individual patients and clients.

---

his trust. We need this trust and his honesty since frequency of deviant urges and acts must be a critical outcome measure for our therapy. The fact that he feels he can tell us of this act makes these outcome measures all the more valid. Do we respect his confidence or respond to point 9 in the UKCC code of professional conduct (1984), i.e. 'Respect confidential information obtained in the course of professional practice ... except where disclosure is required by law or by the order of a court or is necessary in the public interest.'? We will leave you to come to your own conclusions.

There are no easy answers to such ethical dilemmas and we would not attempt to give them here. There are, however, certain principles that we should always adhere to, the two most important being confidentiality and consent.

Confidentiality

Adherence to the principle of confidentiality is both a professional and legal requirement of all health workers. If we break this principle we may lose our job, our professional qualification and be sued by clients. All clinical information is confidential and should only be discussed by those people directly involved in the client's care. There is enormous potential for social distress and damage, especially in the field of mental health, if we release information that clients have given us in private. We should ask the client's explicit permission if we wish to divulge any information he has given us to anyone else. This includes both other professionals and the client's own relatives. We should not even admit to anybody else that we are seeing a client unless we are sure to whom we are speaking and that explicit, preferably written, permission has been given by the client.

The appearance of computers in nursing for administration and research puts new dimensions on the issue of confidentiality. The Data Protection Act (1984) makes our responsibility with regard to personal data explicit. Clients can request and subsequently view any information we may have about them held in electronic data management facilities. We have a legal requirement for confidentiality that includes maintaining adequate data security, keeping only appropriate records and using data only for the purposes declared to the data protection registrar.

There are, even in the field of confidentiality, grey areas. Some clients may not wish us to communicate with their general practitioners, although we almost always do this routinely. It is probably worth getting into the habit of checking with clients that they are happy for us to do this before sending out letters to GPs and other involved agencies. There may be exceptional, though perfectly reasonable reasons, why clients would want some information kept between ourselves and they alone. Their best friend may work at the local health centre, for example.

Another issue of confidentiality is that of access to notes. Notes should always be stored in a locked cabinet in a locked office. If travelling to health centres or clients' homes we may carry their notes about with us – necessary if we are carrying out repeat measures for example. In this case a locked briefcase carried with us and not left in the car is the best plan.

Some mental health units are adopting a policy of 'open records' where clients have a right to examine their own notes. Hopefully this will become a universal practice as we should have written nothing in the notes that we could be ashamed of. We prefer to see the notes written in behavioural psychotherapy as a shared record of a collaboration between ourselves and a client. There is no reason to deny clients access to such records.

Occasionally we may have recorded clients on audio or video tape, perhaps for teaching purposes. The same rules of confidentiality apply, but more so. We must make sure that such tapes are only seen or heard by people for whom permission has been specifically given by the client. This brings us on to consent.

Consent

Inherent in our treatment suitability criteria is the principle of consent. Clients must understand and *agree to* any behavioural treatment technique we wish to use. On most occasions it is not necessary for this consent to be given in writing, but there are exceptions. The viewing of explicit sexual material or consenting to be interviewed on close circuit television are examples. If we wish to video clients in an interview or treatment session it is prudent to obtain written consent first, and then begin the filming with a statement of consent from the client. Just as we stated in the section on rationale, clear explanations are essential. If there is any doubt about the client fully understanding any treatment technique or therapeutic strategy we should not continue. Consent is not valid if it is given by a client who does not fully understand what is being asked of him.

The above are examples of our moral responsibilities to individual clients. What about our wider responsibilities to society as a whole? How ethical is it to spend a great deal of time with one client, achieving little progress, when our time could be spent more profitably with other people for whom treatment could be more effective? Our obligations to these other people means we should generally only treat suitable clients and we must discharge clients if we are unsuccessful *after an adequate trial of treatment.* 'Adequate' is at least five sessions and also refers to the use of as many different strategies as possible before admitting defeat. It may be very difficult, especially for nurses – with our tradition of caring and giving – to say, 'I'm sorry, I can't help you.' However, is it right to deny others access to treatment which might be the key to a new life, simply because we feel obliged to persevere?

Ethical issues are usually very difficult to resolve, and rarely is this achieved to the satisfaction of everyone. We have raised some in this chapter in order to put across the idea that there is often no right and wrong when making decisions affecting the care of others. As the nature of psychiatric nursing has changed, especially with the development of community psychiatric nursing services over the last 20 years (outlined by Simmons and Brooker, 1986), nurses have taken on the role of 'main therapist' more and more. The nursing process, key workers, primary nursing and accountability are all concepts that feature regularly in the thinking of many nurse educators and policy makers. In another development, the idea of 'community mental health workers' outlined by MIND (1983) proposes the idea that training for this generic worker would include aspects of nursing, social work and occupational therapy. As nurses move out of traditional roles and into a more autonomous position, some of the ethical issues raised here will be encountered and need to be prepared for.

Summary

This chapter has examined how we structure treatment sessions to get the most out of them for ourselves and our clients. However, implementation of behavioural treatments cannot be seen in isolation from the complete process of therapy but is an integral part of the whole. This whole resembles the four stages of the nursing process and is essentially a problem-orientated approach to people's difficulties. The way in which this therapy is implemented can greatly affect the outcome of treatment and we have spent time discussing issues of case-management that we see as crucial to the success of behavioural treatments. Taking on the role of 'main therapist' and thus making crucial treatment decisions makes it necessary to consider certain ethical issues. We have done this in such a way as to promote discussion of the alternative solutions available, since most of these issues have no right or wrong answer.

The specific content of treatment sessions is best described in relation to individual problems. We can now move on to Part 3 of the book and outline in detail the treatment of clients for whom behavioural psychotherapy has been found to be a highly effective treatment strategy.

REFERENCES

Altschul A. T. A. (1984). A Challenge to Psychiatry. *Nursing Times*, 80(29), 49–51.

Emmelkamp P. M. G., Wessels, H. (1975). Flooding in imagination vs. flooding *in-vivo*: a comparison with agoraphobics. *Behaviour Research and Therapy*, 13, 7–15.

English and Welsh National Boards for Nursing, Midwifery and Health Visiting (1982). Syllabus of Training. Professional Register Part 3. Registered Mental Nurse. Bedford: Burts.

Frank J. D. (1984). The psychotherapy of anxiety. In *Psychiatric Update Vol 3* (Grinspoon L., ed.). Washington DC: American Psychiatric Press.

Gelder M. G., Marks I. M., Wolff H. H. (1967). Desensitization and psychotherapy in the treatment of phobic states: a controlled clinical inquiry. *British Journal of Psychiatry*, 113, 53–73.

Ghosh A., Marks I. M., Carr A. C. (1984). Controlled study of self-exposure treatment for phobics: preliminary communication. *Journal of the Royal Society of Medicine*, 77, 483–487.

General Nursing Council for England and Wales (1977). *Statement of Educational Policy*. Circular 77/19/A. London: GNC.

Hafner J. and Marks I. M. (1976). Exposure *in-vivo* of agoraphobics: contributions of diazepam, group exposure and anxiety evocation. *Psychological Medicine*, 6, 71–88.

Hand I., Lamontagne Y., Marks I. M. (1974). Group exposure (flooding) *in-vivo* for agoraphobics. *British Journal of Psychiatry*, 124, 588–602.

Jannoun L., Munby M., Catalan J., Gelder M. (1980). A home-based treatment program for agoraphobia: replication and controlled evaluation. *Behaviour Therapy*, 11, 294–305.

Marks I. M. (1978). *Living with Fear*, New York: McGraw Hill.

Mathews A. M., Gelder M. G., Johnstone D. W. (1981). *Agoraphobia nature and treatment*. London: Tavistock Publications Ltd.

Mathews A. M., Johnston D. W., Lancashire M., Munby M., Shaw P. M., Gelder M. G. (1976). Imaginal flooding and exposure to real phobic situations: treatment outcome with agoraphobic patients. *British Journal of Psychiatry*, 125, 362–371.

Mathews A. M., Johnston D. W., Shaw P. M., Gelder M. G. (1974). Process variables and the prediction of outcome in behaviour therapy. British *Journal of Psychiatry*, 125, 256–264.

McFarlane J. K. (1973). *The Nursing Process*. Unpublished seminar paper. University of Manchester, Dept. of Nursing, Manchester.

MIND (1983). Common Concern. London: MIND Publications.

Powell T. J. (1987). Anxiety management groups in clinical practice: a preliminary report. *Behavioural Psychotherapy*, 15, 181–187.

Simmons, S., Brooker C. (1986). Community Psychiatric Nursing. A Social Perspective. Oxford: Heinemann Medical Books.

Stern R., Marks I. M. (1973). Brief and prolonged flooding. A comparison in agoraphobic patients. *Archives of General Psychiatry*, 28, 270–276.

The General Nursing Council for England and Wales (1977). A Statement of Educational Policy. Circular 77/19/A.

United Kingdom Central Council for Nursing, Midwifery and Health Visiting (1984). Code of Professional Conduct for the Nurse, Midwife and Health Visitor 2nd Edition. London: UKCC.

Part 3

Chapter 8

Fearfulness and panic

THE NATURE OF ANXIETY

Feeling anxious is one of the commonest and most pervasive of all human experiences. It is a fundamental part of our being. It has helped us to survive and adapt to all manner of situations and is part of the reason we are such a successful species. We have already outlined current research and thinking with regard to anxiety but it is worth summarizing some of the main points here.

1 Human beings experience irrational fear in only a few common categories:
   (a) The presence or absence of other people
   (b) Certain small animals
   (c) Open or enclosed places
   (d) Injury and illness.
   (e) Heights
   As we are more likely to be anxious in the presence of certain stimuli this selectivity can be seen as part of the innate nature of fears.
2 People with certain personality characteristics are more likely to have problems with persistent anxiety.
3 People's responses when anxious will be highly individual and consist of:
   (a) Autonomic responses
   (b) Behavioural responses
   (c) Cognitions
   These three responses may occur in unison to the same degree (synchrony) or in varying degrees (desynchrony).
4 The effect of life events is probably highly significant. This

may account for why people have problems with particular types of anxiety at certain times in their lives. Life events refer not just to obvious stressors like bereavement, etc., but also to generally raised levels of background stress in people's lives.

5 The responses an individual adopts when anxious contribute greatly to the ensuing course of the problem. New responses can be learnt by the person which deal more effectively with the anxiety being experienced.

In this and subsequent chapters we are going to outline treatment techniques for particular anxiety problems. Because anxiety is such a wide term which covers many different types of experience, we shall organize our chapters using generally accepted categories of anxiety found in a system called DSM III(R) (1987). This is a descriptive system which makes no attempt at determining causes. It merely describes the problem as presented by the client and includes room for autonomic, behavioural and cognitive descriptions of anxiety. Once we have determined which broad area of anxiety the client is having problems with, we shall put into practice the client-centred assessment skills outlined previously in Part 2 and use examples of clients treated by nurses to illustrate the principles of behaviour therapy.

General anxiety and panic

There is some discussion and disagreement among researchers in the field of anxiety disorders about the relationship of panic to anxiety. One view is that panic is a separate entity probably with a biochemical basis; the opposing view is that panic is just a severe form of anxiety. Whatever the truth, it is still useful to see the two separately from a clinical standpoint. Therapeutic strategies are different for anxiety and panic. Panics may also occur in clients with phobic anxiety and the same general principles can be used.

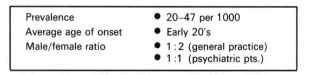

Prevalence	● 20–47 per 1000
Average age of onset	● Early 20's
Male/female ratio	● 1 : 2 (general practice)
	● 1 : 1 (psychiatric pts.)

Figure 8.1   Clinical Anxiety States: Basic Information

1 General anxiety

The essential feature of this problem is a persistent, generalized feeling of anxiety that has no apparent cause and is not related to a specific situation or object. These anxious feelings usually manifest themselves in the following way.

(a) Motor tension, e.g. muscle tension, shakiness, restlessness, tiredness, inability to relax.

(b) Autonomic hyperactivity, e.g. sweating, tachycardia, dizziness, dry mouth, nausea.

(c) Apprehension, e.g. worry about untoward things happening to client or family, over-preoccupation with health.

(d) Vigilance and scanning, i.e. people feel 'on edge' and are constantly checking for danger; they may have difficulty getting off to sleep.

It is crucial, when seeing a client with such a problem, to eliminate other possible causes of their symptoms. When no situational cues exist it may be that a physical illness is to blame. It is part of our nursing role to make the responsible medical practitioner aware of our suspicions and ask that physical investigations be undertaken to check for things like hyperthyroidism (see Chapter 6, Table 6.2). Other possible causes such as the excessive use of caffeine can be checked out by ourselves in the assessment. It is well worth asking anybody with such symptoms to cut out caffeine from their diet to rule out this cause. Another possibility is that the client may be suffering from withdrawal symptoms, perhaps from benzodiazepines or alcohol. Past and present drug and alcohol use can be assessed during our interview with the client. If this is a likely interpretation then the client can be counselled as to what he is likely to expect as a result of withdrawal. We may have to negotiate with the appropriate doctor a graded withdrawal regime for the client, especially from benzodiazepines. A full explanation of the clinical difficulties produced by combining behavioural psychotherapy and benzodiazepines is given at the end of this chapter along with a sample benzodiazepine withdrawal schedule.

Behavioural treatments of general anxiety

The three-system model of emotion we discussed earlier can be used to organize treatment. We need to direct therapy at all the components of the anxiety response, and alter them all by action directed at either the autonomic, behavioural or cognitive component. The first and most commonly used strategy has been relaxation.

Relaxation is used widely in psychiatric care. There are many variants of this technique, the commonest being Jacobson's progressive muscular relaxation (Jacobson, 1938) where the client is taught to relax the voluntary muscles, leading to a state of psychological as well as physical calm. This usually occurs in a safe place away from the stresses that provoke the person's anxiety. Unfortunately, outcome studies of relaxation used alone have been very disappointing. Generalization of ability to relax and improvement in performance does not appear to occur to any great degree. In his comprehensive review of the topic, Mathews (1984) states that only 'modest effects are usually achieved, regardless of exact relaxation technique'. Even 'cue-controlled relaxation', where clients are taught to relax *when* they are feeling anxious rather than in a cosy controlled environment, shows little significant effect. Despite this lack of evidence, relaxation continues to be one of the most widely used psychological approaches to anxiety.

Behavioural techniques, particularly those based on the exposure principle (see Chapter 9), are difficult to apply to clients with a generalized anxiety problem since there may be no consistent behavioural avoidances. However, some therapists have adapted behavioural interventions such as systematic desensitization to this problem. In this procedure clients are first taught to relax and then instructed to imagine scenes which evoke anxiety. At the point when they are feeling anxious they then revert back to a relaxed state. Thus, the scenes which initially provoked anxiety are said to cue in antagonistic relaxation responses. This is known as Anxiety Management Training (AMT) and was first outlined by Suinn and Richardson (1971). Again, there is little outcome data on this approach, although two studies (Jannoun *et al.*, 1982; Hutchings *et al.*, 1980) have shown significant clinical improvements. The study by Hutchings *et al.* (1980), although only with anxious volunteers, showed that AMT was more effective than just relaxation. This approach may, therefore, be promising but much more research is needed.

Cognitive techniques have flourished recently and take many forms. Examples include: simply teaching the client to use positive statements to counteract negative thoughts when they occur;

'stress inoculation training' (Meichenbaum and Turk 1976); and 'cognitive therapy' (Beck *et al.*, 1985). Cognitive therapies take as their basic premise the idea that cognitions are the *cause* of autonomic and behavioural events and, therefore, cognitive therapists aim their treatments directly at the cognitions. Various techniques are used ranging from simple 'self instructional training' (Meichenbaum, 1977) where the client is taught to rehearse positive statements about the feared situation prior to facing it, to highly complex procedures designed to unearth and alter 'negative automatic thoughts' said by Beck (1979) to underlie emotional responses.

Despite the recent explosion of interest in cognitive therapies, the evidence for the specific effectiveness of many cognitive procedures is scanty and it is not known whether they are more effective than simpler procedures. Some of the cognitive therapies are very complicated to apply and it has to be questioned whether the extra effort is worthwhile. They also have a theoretical basis that owes much to the American analytical tradition rather than to a rigorous experimental rationale. These traditions include beliefs in the mind/body dualism, that the mind is the most important component of what makes us human, and a tradition of highly paid experts that one consults for answers to life's problems. These ideas do not match with our model of holistic care delivered by nurses with specific skills.

However, in Chapter 3 we talked of the importance of paying less attention to the labels that people give themselves and the things they do than to the actual content of therapy. We saw how behavioural nurse therapists were misperceived as being rigid, simplistic and mechanistic when they were actually found to be more humanistic in outlook and in the delivery of their care than virtually all other groups of nurses (Gournay, 1986).

Many 'cognitive' therapies include basic behavioural strategies. For example, Beck encourages clients with phobias to undertake 'behavioural experiments' to assist in challenging negative beliefs. These experiments are, of course, about facing difficult situations and so it may be that they are actually no different from the exposure instructions given to clients in behaviour therapy. Similarly, many behaviour therapists encourage the client to use 'coping statements' such as 'it's only panic, it will not harm me' when facing up to feared situations, calling these 'induction aids', etc. Such coping statements are directed at the cognitive component of anxiety in just the same way as cognitive therapies are designed to do.

The key difference between behaviour therapists and cognitive therapists is the equal weighting the behaviour therapist gives to all three components of anxiety in contrast to the cognitive therapists' emphasis on the importance of a single component. In view of the similarity of actual practice, it would seem to be better to drop all the different terms and use elements of cognitive and behavioural therapies to the best advantage of our clients. There are, therefore, two basic rules which we should adopt when designing a treatment programme for a generally anxious person.

1   Make a thorough assessment of what the client's experience of anxiety means to *him* in terms of its autonomic, behavioural and cognitive components.

2   Choose strategies aimed at the specific manifestation of the client's anxiety, i.e. we should use more cognitive techniques where the principle response is a cognitive one, predominantly behavioural interventions for behavioural symptoms and techniques aimed at reducing autonomic activity for physical anxiety responses. In fact, what is more likely is that we will use a combination of all three types of techniques.

A treatment strategy for general anxiety

Gordon was a 32-year-old self-employed businessman who owned a number of shops. For over a year he had found it impossible to relax and enjoy himself. He complained of muscular tension, lack of concentration, a feeling of not being on top of his work and irritability with his colleagues and family. He worked long hours at the office, including the weekends, and usually took work home with him. He felt other people were becoming critical of his performance and so he was working harder to prove he was capable of the work. He drank six or seven cups of coffee daily, smoked 30 cigarettes a day but drank alcohol only occasionally. He was taking no medication and took no regular exercise.

He came from a working class background and had started his business up from scratch ten years ago. He had married six years ago and had two sons aged five and three. The relationship with his family had become strained and he was concerned that he had little time to see his children. This last effect was one of the reasons he had sought treatment along with concern and worry as to why his performance was suffering.

After the assessment, when the physical, behavioural and cognitive aspects of his problem were identified, some basic education was given as to the causes and effects of anxiety. Feeling anxious was explained as a normal response to stress and danger and the three systems were outlined. Gordon found this information immensely reassuring as he had actually harboured a secret fear that he was 'going mad'. Once his feelings had been put into context the next phase was to tackle his problems on two fronts. We considered what Gordon could do to alter his daily routine so that he experienced less stress. Gordon identified an imbalance between the time he devoted to his business and the time he allowed for personal and family recreation. Changes he made to his personal lifestyle included taking up a weekly game of squash, which he had stopped playing three years ago, and promoting somebody in the office to handle the mundane paper-work and office management which he had previously felt unable to delegate.

The other area considered was his own coping strategies. He was advised to cut down on his caffeine intake and was given a relaxation tape to listen to three times a week at first and then use the techniques learned when he was feeling particularly tense. Gordon did not find this particularly useful, preferring to jog around the block if he felt very tense. Behavioural strategies involved making time to be with his family and engaging in other activities which he found pleasurable. He quickly realized that he had been neglecting this side of his life and arranged a baby-sitter once a fortnight so that he and his wife could go out for a meal. They began to enjoy each other's company again.

Gordon still felt that his work performance was not up to scratch and that others were negatively evaluating him. These thoughts were examined with Gordon and alternative explanations were explored. Any setback that Gordon experienced at work he tended to blame on himself and then generalize this to his performance as a whole, regarding himself as a failure. Cognitive strategies were used to help Gordon identify when these thoughts occurred and then to challenge them with more realistic explanations.

An example of this was when Gordon received an unexpected telephone call from his accountant informing him that he was coming to visit and wanted to stay overnight. Gordon interpreted this as being bad news and identified thoughts such as 'He must have bad news, he wouldn't want to stay so long if things were ok', etc. Gordon was helped to examine these thoughts in the light of what he knew about his business and he came up with some alternative, more logical explanations, e.g. 'He must have a lot of work on', 'perhaps he's behind with the accounts', 'I know my business is doing well', etc. He challenged his catastrophic misinterpretation of events with a more realistic appraisal of things, although some doubts remained. When the accountant arrived it was with better-than-expected news, the reason for his extended stay being that he had another client in the area to see the following day! This graphically pointed out to Gordon the errors of his thinking and he quickly became skilled at identifying logical alternatives to anxious cognitions.

After three months of this multi-faceted approach – physical, behavioural and cognitive strategies with lifestyle changes emphasizing more leisure time — Gordon reported a 75% reduction in his anxious feelings. He felt much more on top of his work and his family life had improved. Most importantly, he felt he could deal on his own with future episodes of anxiety if they should occur as he now had a battery of techniques to apply if needed. This gave him considerable comfort and optimism.

The above example shows how a treatment programme was tailored to Gordon's specific problems and encompassed a variety of strategies to deal with his difficulties. These can be summarized as:

- Education about anxiety.
- Enhanced personal coping skills.
- Lifestyle changes.

Coping skills included techniques to control the autonomic aspects of anxiety (relaxation and exercise), behavioural change (time with family) and cognitive strategies (reappraising negative thoughts).

2 Panic

Panics are characterized by a 'sudden onset of intense apprehension, fear or terror, often associated with feelings of impending doom' (DSM III(R) 1987). They differ from more general anxious feelings both in this sudden onset, and in that many more physiological symptoms are experienced, particularly breathlessness, tachycardia, dizziness, tingling of the extremities, sweating, shaking and a feeling of derealization or depersonalization. For many people the experience of a panic is absolutely terrifying and the symptoms are often misinterpreted in a highly catastrophic manner. Many people fear that they are about to have a heart attack or some other grave physical illness is upon them. Other people feel that they are going mad. Often people become so afraid of panicking that they go to extraordinary lengths to avoid the possibility of a panic.

Many agoraphobias are maintained by this 'fear of fear' as people, not unreasonably, remain at home in safety. In fact, there is some debate at the moment among clinicians and researchers as to whether agoraphobia is a distinct clinical entity at all. It may be a cluster of similar types of problems that are nonetheless separate and are maintained by different mechanisms, one of these mechanisms being panic. It may be that different agoraphobias need to be treated differently according to which mechanism is in operation. On balance, since this debate is still unresolved, we have opted to discuss agoraphobia in the chapter on phobic problems, but the reader should be aware that the way in which we understand things is in a constant state of debate and change.

Chemotherapy has been the traditional treatment for panic. Until recently the use of the benzodiazepines was almost universal. However, problems with drugs such as diazepam, lorazepam, etc., include waning effectiveness with time, dependence, severe withdrawal symptoms when coming off these drugs and public disquiet about the vast quantities prescribed. Tricyclic antidepressants have been shown to effectively reduce panic but suffer the same problem of relapse when the drug is discontinued. These disadvantages have led to other ways of dealing with panic being investigated.

Behavioural strategies have consisted of helping the client face up to the situations that provoke panic in a graded, repeated and prolonged way, letting the panic subside naturally. Clients can be taught coping statements such as, 'it's only panic, it cannot harm me' and 'if I stay here my panic will subside in time'. These have been successful but do require the client to show considerable courage at times and also rely on there being situations that reliably provoke panic.

Hyperventilation and panic

For some years there has been a lot of interest in the role of hyperventilation in panic. The symptoms of panic can be produced artificially in a laboratory situation by a number of means, one of which is by asking the subject to voluntarily hyperventilate. Breathing very fast and deep for a few minutes is a very effective way of making someone feel many of the same feelings typical of a panic attack. The reason is that hyperventilation reduces the level of carbon-dioxide in the bloodstream, raising the blood pH. A small rise in pH is enough to produce the same symptoms as seen in typical panic attacks. Since one of the commonest symptoms of panic is a rapid gasping for breath the possible link between hyperventilation and panic has been recently explored.

The work of Clark and his co-workers (Clark, 1986; Clark, Salkovskis and Chalkley, 1985; Salkovskis *et al.*, 1986) has been particularly influential. They have developed a treatment programme which involves the client voluntarily overbreathing to see if they can reproduce the symptoms they experience when panicking. If this is shown to be the case, they then instruct the client in controlled breathing techniques, using a recorded audio-tape to pace their breathing, eventually hoping the client will be skilled enough to use this technique in situations where they are likely to panic. They maintain that the crucial element to this treatment is that the client reappraises his experience in the light of the knowledge that he can make himself panic. If one can make oneself panic voluntarily, then one should also be able to prevent and control the process of panic directly.

This 'cognitive model of panic' (Clark, 1986) is backed up by laboratory evidence that some people can experience panic and enjoy it! This is not as unlikely as it seems, many of us enjoy being deliberately frightened, on wild fairground rides or by watching horror films for example. The catastrophic misinterpretation of panic symptoms as much more frightening than they really are is said to be the reason panic develops and snowballs into a vicious circle of panic symptoms ⇒ hyperventilation ⇒ increased symptoms ⇒ catastrophic misinterpretation of these symptoms ⇒ more anxiety and more symptoms of panic. Characteristic misinterpretations include fears of death, serious illness and loss of control (Hibbert, 1984). The cognitive model of panic is reproduced in Figure 8.2.

As this work is recent there is not too much in the way of reliable outcome data to support the claims of the authors. However, work is being done to remedy this and our own clinical experience is that this method of helping clients reattribute their

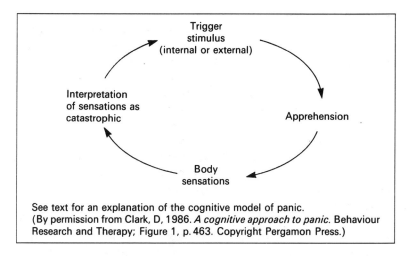

See text for an explanation of the cognitive model of panic.
(By permission from Clark, D, 1986. *A cognitive approach to panic.* Behaviour
Research and Therapy; Figure 1, p. 463. Copyright Pergamon Press.)

Figure 8.2   The Cognitive Model of Panic

panic symptoms to a cause which they can then learn to control is highly effective. The next case example will illustrate this technique more fully.

Julia

Julia, aged 32, was referred to a nurse therapist with a history of panicking three to four times a day. These panics were unpredictable and of sudden onset. They were extremely frightening, giving rise to fears that there was something physically wrong with her. Cardiac investigations had revealed no physical cause for her panics, but she still experienced tachycardia, shaking, sweating, shortness of breath and dizziness regularly. The panics usually subsided after an hour or so but had been known to last up to five hours. They occurred just as frequently in the home as outside and Julia was being careful not to let the panics prevent her from doing the things she enjoyed. However, she was finding this harder to manage and the fear that things were getting worse had prompted her to visit her GP. He had suggested lorazepam but she had declined to take this as her mother had a history of similar problems and had been taking tranquillisers for 20 years with little relief. She did not want to become dependent on drugs in the way her mother had.

*There were no family, financial or personal worries and Julia
could think of no reason for her panics continuing since their first
onset five years ago. Although fed up, she was not depressed and
was determined to do whatever was necessary to prevent her life
being ruled by her panics.*

The first stage in therapy after the assessment was a detailed
explanation of the nature of anxiety including information on the
mechanisms of anxiety maintenance – the three vicious circles of
anxiety shown in Figure 8.3.

Next, Julia was asked to fill in a questionnaire which lists some
of the common symptoms of panic and hyperventilation. She was
asked to rate how much she experienced each of the symptoms
during a naturally occurring panic from 'not at all' to 'very severe'.
This questionnaire (Clark and Helmsley, 1982) is detailed in
Appendix 1. The next step was to ask Julia to voluntarily
hyperventilate. It is important to present the rationale for this so
as not to prejudice the outcome. Therefore, the procedure was
presented as a 'test' to determine factors which may be important
in panic and no mention was made of specifically trying to
reproduce the symptoms of panic, since this could influence Julia's
experience. Just in case she did feel very uncomfortable Julia was
instructed in using a paper bag to control these feelings during
the test. Breathing into a paper bag causes the levels of CO_2 in

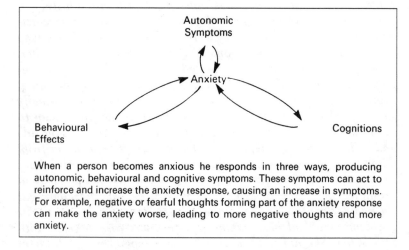

When a person becomes anxious he responds in three ways, producing
autonomic, behavioural and cognitive symptoms. These symptoms can act to
reinforce and increase the anxiety response, causing an increase in symptoms.
For example, negative or fearful thoughts forming part of the anxiety response
can make the anxiety worse, leading to more negative thoughts and more
anxiety.

Figure 8.3   The Three 'Vicious Circles' of Anxiety

the lungs and blood to increase rapidly and thus is an effective emergency measure to control panic. It was stressed that she should try to continue without resorting to the paper bag if possible. She was then asked to breathe deeply and rapidly for two minutes, pacing herself with the nurse. Julia managed to do this for only 45 seconds before she felt she had to stop and use the paper bag.

Julia had felt very dizzy during the latter part of the test and this was shown up when she was asked to fill in another copy of the same questionnaire she had filled in earlier, this time relating to her experiences whilst overbreathing. The nurse and Julia examined the two questionnaires and found dramatic similarities between them. There was 80% agreement between physical feelings experienced during a typical panic and the voluntary hyperventilation, differences being mainly one of degree to which particular symptoms were experienced. The nurse helped Julia to reappraise the significance of this fact by careful questioning, striving to facilitate Julia's acknowledgement of two things:

1　If voluntary overbreathing can produce typical panic symptoms then she may be hyperventilating during naturally occurring panic attacks.
2　Controlling her breathing when she is panicking may help control her panics.

Following this Julia was shown the model diagram (Figure 8.2) and a system of controlled breathing was explained to her. The salient features of a controlled breathing technique are:

- Shallow
- Smooth
- Diaphragmatic
- 8–12 breaths per minute
- No sighing or gasps for air

To help Julia practise this type of breathing first, before using it to control panics, an audio-tape had been prepared to help her pace her breathing. This consisted of the nurse saying 'in two three, out two three' at the correct pace. Julia was asked to listen to this tape for half an hour daily for the next week. At first she found herself tempted to draw extra breaths at frequent intervals. She realised that she had been habitually breathing rather faster than normal for some time, but she persevered and eventually became skilled at breathing in a smooth, shallow and controlled fashion. Gradually she was asked to wean herself off the tape and start to use this technique during actual panics. She found it highly effective in reducing her symptoms to 50% of what they were and eventually her panics ceased altogether as she learnt to breathe calmly all the time. She learnt to identify the first signs of an impending panic. Rather than respond in an anxious way, she dismissed these signs as of no consequence since she could easily control them. No further intervention was required as soon as Julia became competent in using her new-found skill to control her feelings.

The above example illustrates the main points of this technique.

1   Demonstration that hyperventilation produces panic.
2   Voluntary reproduction of these symptoms.
3   Training in controlled breathing.
4   Reattribution of symptoms to a more appropriate cause.

We do not know how many people who experience panic regularly can be helped by such an approach. Salkovskis and Clark (1986) note that 60% of these people recognize a strong similarity between panic and the symptoms of voluntary hyperventilation, so it may be a significant number. The best advice is that should there be any indication that breathing quickens during panics it is probably worthwhile carrying out the test described in the case example. In addition the same multi-modal approach used for clients who are generally anxious should be employed, emphasis again being on the client-centred, individually tailored approach.

Behavioural psychotherapy and benzodiazepines

A chapter on general anxiety and panic would not be complete unless it considered the problem of anxiolytic drugs, in particular the benzodiazepines. Many clients with the type of difficulties described in this and the following two chapters will be taking such medication. This section will concentrate on the most important aspect of benzodiazepines for nurses considering a behavioural treatment programme – the potentially destructive interaction of benzodiazepines with behavioural psychotherapy. This can cause extreme clinical difficulty when assessing and treating clients.

The emergence 30 years ago of drugs like chlordiazepoxide and diazepam – the benzodiazepines – was greeted with much excitement, as they seemed to offer a safe alternative to previously existing anxiolytics such as barbiturates. However, since the early enthusiastic reports and almost reflex prescribing of these drugs for anybody reporting symptoms of anxiety there has been mounting disquiet. The chief problems are dependence, side effects with chronic use and withdrawal symptoms on cessation of the drugs (Petursson and Lader, 1981; Tyrer *et al.*, 1983). We often find that clients who ask for help with their anxiety problems are on dosages of benzodiazepines that are both large and chronic. At the moment some $1\frac{1}{4}$ million people are entering their second year of benzodiazepine use, i.e. they are chronic users. This is despite the evidence that after 4 months of acute use the anxiolytic effect of benzodiazepines wanes and 50% of people will develop dependency effects.

The interplay between these drugs and behavioural treatments of anxiety has been comprehensively reviewed by Sartory (1983). She found no evidence that they have a beneficial effect on the outcome of therapy, particularly for phobias and obsessive-compulsive disorders, and may in fact be detrimental.

The main objections are:

1 Anxiolytic effects of benzodiazepines could not be reproduced when people were faced with their phobic stimulus.
2 Attention and memory need to be unimpaired during exposure. Both are affected by benzodiazepines.
3 Follow-up of gains made whilst taking benzodiazepines were less stable than improvement achieved when not taking drugs.

Thus, benzodiazepines, especially used chronically, should not be mixed with behavioural psychotherapy. We may only be helping a client cope temporarily and, should he come off his drugs, he may relapse to his original condition or even become worse. The ideal approach would be to have a client come off all his drugs before starting therapy but this may not always be possible. Withdrawal from benzodiazepines can take many months and symptoms can persist for up to one year after complete cessation of the drug. However, because of the difficulties associated with behaviour therapy and benzodiazepines it is important to at least get a commitment from the client that he will begin to withdraw from them.

There may be difficulties with other professionals, perhaps doctors, in getting agreement to a withdrawal regime. Communication and diplomacy are the key skills. If we are going to function as independent practitioners, even within a team, we need to make others aware of our competence. We are only doing the client a disservice if we try behavioural treatments under unfavourable conditions so we should quote the evidence for the incompatibility of behavioural treatments and benzodiazepines. Most other professionals uninterested in behavioural psychotherapy will probably not be aware of Sartory's 1983 review so we should introduce this diplomatically. Other good articles include the work by Tyrer *et al.* (1983, 1987), Ashton (1984) and Petursson and Lader (1981). Most people will listen to us if we can put across good reasons for our objections to benzodiazepines.

Not all benzodiazepines are as easy to withdraw from as others. The most difficult ones are the short-acting drugs such as lorazepam. Because the active metabolite breaks down quickly in this drug, blood concentrations rapidly decline, leaving the client craving for another dose. Longer-acting drugs like diazepam are much less harsh as the decline in active metabolite is slower. This drug is also broken down into desmethyldiazepam, an active tranquillizing substance, by the body which prolongs the effect of the drug. Therefore, as suggested by Ashton (1984), it is a good idea to replace lorazepam by an equivalent dose of diazepam. Ashton suggests 1 mg lorazepam to 10 mg diazepam but local pharmacists may differ in their practice. It is better to seek advice locally, but the usual equivalent dosages are between 5–10 mg diazepam to 1 mg lorazepam. Diazepam can be substituted for lorazepam dose by dose on a daily basis until all the doses have been changed.

An example of a withdrawal schedule follows, but the important points are:

- Clients usually find the last few mg the hardest to stop.
- Clients tolerate loss of sleep badly so the night-time dose should be the last one cut out.
- Adjust the withdrawal schedule to meet the client's needs. Some will want to come off very slowly, others will regard this as prolonging the agony and want to come off in a few weeks.

- Education about the possibilities of serious side-effects, which may mimic the very anxious feelings the drugs were prescribed for in the first place, is important or the client may think he is experiencing a relapse in his main problem.
- Self-help groups for clients undergoing withdrawal from benzo-diazepines may provide a useful source of support. There are many such groups around, and usually one in the locality. Some of the major symptoms seen in benzodiazepine withdrawal are listed in Table 8.1.

A withdrawal schedule

Current dose: lorazepam 3 mg daily.

Stage 1 Substitute diazepam for lorazepam.
One dose substituted at a time, starting with the midday doses, then the morning dose and the evening dose last. This can be done at weekly intervals or more frequently if the client prefers.

Stage 2 Gradual withdrawal of diazepam.
Diazepam withdrawn over 4–16 weeks usually in steps of 0.5–2.5 mg per dose. Night-time dose reduced last. Final stages should be more drawn out and reductions graded more finely.

Table 8.1 Principle side-effects of benzodiazepine withdrawal

Sadness	Reduced sexual interest
Reduced sleep, nightmares	Unsteadiness, abnormal sensations of movement
Depersonalization	
Concentration difficulties	Dizziness
Pessimistic thoughts	Hallucinations
Indecision	Paranoid thoughts and feelings
Muscle tension	Change in appetite
Tremors and shaking	Convulsions
Nausea, diarrhoea, constipation	Clinically significant depression
Tiredness, fatigue, lethargy	Increased sensory perception – noise, light, etc.
Agitation	

Table 8.2 An example of a benzodiazepine withdrawal schedule

Stage 1.				Substitute 3 daily doses of 1 mg lorazepam for 3 daily doses of 8 mg diazepam over 2 weeks.											
Stage 2.				Gradual withdrawal from diazepam.											
Weeks	2	3	4	5	6	7	8	9	10	11	12	13	14	15	16
Daily mg diazepam	24	20	16	12	10	8	6	5	4	3	2	1.5	1	0.5	0

During any withdrawal regime we should be sensitive to some of the more serious side-effects such as hallucinations, hypersensitivity to sensory inputs and depression. Clinically significant depression may occur in 10% of people but often occurs only after six months have elapsed since withdrawal. If this becomes serious we may have to ask for help from the responsible medical practitioner and antidepressants may be needed.

The principles of a benzodiazepine withdrawal schedule are therefore no different from the principles we have adopted throughout this book. The schedule is client-centred, education as to the expected symptoms likely as a consequence of withdrawal is given and a graded programme is organized after agreement with the client. As the withdrawal gets under way we can then start appropriate behavioural treatment for the client's main problem.

Summary

This chapter has discussed the treatment of two major areas of anxiety – general anxiety and panic. Particularly for general anxiety we can offer no hard and fast 'treatment of choice'. Instead we must pay attention to two of the major themes running through this book – accurate assessment and the tailoring of therapy to meet a client's individual needs. It has also been important to present in detail a withdrawal schedule from minor tranquillizers, since so many anxious people are addicted to such drugs.

There are some techniques which are of proven use and others which show great promise for the years to come. The emergence of better validated cognitive techniques in the future may be an example of the latter. Hyperventilation control and the cognitive theory of panic, whilst still in its infancy, show that researchers

are investigating more thoroughly ways of helping people overcome this most distressing problem. However, in the next chapter
we are on firmer ground where we will describe the treatment of
the many and varied types of phobias, so common in our society.

REFERENCES

Ashton A. (1984). Benzodiazepine withdrawal: an unfinished story. *British Medical Journal*, 288, 1135–1140.
Beck A. T. (1979). *Cognitive Therapy and the Emotional Disorders*. New York: International Universities Press.
Beck A. T., Emery G., Greenberg, R. L. (1985). *Anxiety Disorders and Phobias: A Cognitive Perspective*. New York. Basic Books.
Clark D. (1986). A cognitive approach to panic. Behaviour Research and Therapy, 24, 461–470
Clark D. M., Helmsley D. R. (1982). Effects of hyperventilation and its relationship to personality. *Journal of Behaviour Therapy and Experimental Psychiatry*, 13, 41–47.
Clark D. M., Salkovskis P. M., Chalkley A. J. (1985). Respiratory control as a treatment for panic attacks. *Journal of Behaviour Therapy and Experimental Psychiatry*, 16, 23–30.
Diagnostic and Statistical Manual of Mental Disorders 3rd Edition – Revised. (1987). Washington DC: American Psychiatric Association.
Gournay, K. (1986). A pilot study of nurses' attitudes with relation to post-basic training. In *Psychiatric Nursing Research – Developments in Nursing Research Vol. 3.* (Brooking, J. J. ed.) Chichester: Wiley and Sons.
Hibbert G. A. (1984). Ideational components of anxiety: their origin and content. *British Journal of Psychiatry*, 144, 618–624.
Huthchings D. F., Denny D. R., Basgall J., Houston B. K. (1980). Anxiety management and applied relaxation in reducing general anxiety. *Behaviour Research and Therapy*, 18, 181–190.
Jacobson E. (1938). *Progressive Relaxation*. Chicago: University of Chicago Press.
Jannoun L., Oppenheimer C., Gelder M. (1982). A self-help treatment program for anxiety state patients. *Behaviour Therapy*, 13, 103–111.
Mathews A. (1984). Anxiety and Its Management. Chapter 13. In *Current Themes in Psychiatry*, Vol. 3. (Gaind R. L. *et al.* ed.) New York: Spectrum.
Meichenbaum, D. (1977). *Cognitive Behaviour Modification: An Integrative Approach*. New York: Plenum Press.
Meichenbaum D., Turk D. (1976). The cognitive-behavioural management of anxiety, anger and pain. In *The Behavioural Management of Anxiety, Depression and Pain*. (Davidson, ed.) New York: Brunner/Mazel.
Petursson H., Lader M. H. (1981). Withdrawal from long-term benzodiazepine treatment. *British Medical Journal*, 283, 643–645.
Salkovskis P. M., Clark D. M. (1986). Cognitive and physiological processes in the maintainance and treatment of panic attacks. In *Panic and Phobias*. (Hand and Wittgen eds.) Heidleberg: Springer Verlag.

Salkovskis P. M., Warwick H. M. C., Clark D. M., Wessels D. J. (1986). A demonstration of acute hyperventilation during naturally occurring panic attacks. *Behaviour Research and Therapy*, 24, 91–94.

Sartory G. (1983). Benzodiazepines and behavioural treatment of phobic anxiety. *Behavioural Psychotherapy*, 11, 204–217.

Suinn R. M., Richardson F. (1971). Anxiety management training: a non-specific behaviour therapy program for anxiety control. *Behaviour Therapy*, 2, 498–510.

Tyrer, P., Murphy S. (1987). The place of benzodiazepines in psychiatric practice. *British Journal of Psychiatry*, 151, 719–723.

Tyrer P., Owen R., Dawling S. (1983). Gradual withdrawal of diazepam after long-term therapy. *The Lancet*, i, 1402–1406.

Chapter 9

Overcoming phobias

Phobias are characterized by a persistent and irrational fear of a specific object, activity or situation resulting in a compelling desire to avoid the phobic stimulus. This type of fear which, unlike generalized anxiety has a specific focus, is the most common manifestation of the anxiety response. Most people have some object or situation which causes us unease when we are in its presence. Normally we do not find this interferes with our day to day activities but sometimes fears can get out of control and dominate a person's life, causing severe handicap. People who experience fear to this level usually recognize the unreasonable and excessive nature of their fear but still need to respond by getting as far away from the feared object or situation as possible in order to reduce their anxious feelings. There are three general categories of phobias:

- Specific (or simple) phobias
- Agoraphobia
- Social phobia

Specific phobias

A specific phobia is a persistent irrational fear of an object or situation excluding those situations avoided as a consequence of agoraphobia or social phobia. They are very common, most people having some fear or other. However, specific fears only become a problem if the avoidances interfere with the person's life or the lives of people around him. In these cases people may request help. The commonest fears are those of small animals like spiders, snakes, dogs, etc., followed by other specific fears like claustrophobia, height phobia and blood-injury phobia. Fear of flying is also very common.

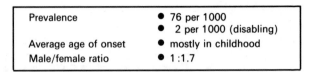

Prevalence	• 76 per 1000
	• 2 per 1000 (disabling)
Average age of onset	• mostly in childhood
Male/female ratio	• 1 :1.7

Figure 9.1   Specific Phobias: Basic Information

People with specific fears often experience very high levels of anxiety when confronted with the feared object or situation. Autonomic arousal is high and there is almost total avoidance of anything that resembles the phobic stimulus. For example, a person with a snake phobia may be unable to look at pictures of snakes and may even find squiggly lines on a piece of paper difficult.

With all specific phobias, apart from fears of blood and injury, autonomic arousal follows the typical pattern of high anxiety, i.e. tachycardia, sweating, shaking, etc. However, people with severe blood-injury fears have a *diphasic* response to blood, etc. Initially their autonomic response is the same, but quite quickly their blood pressure drops to such low levels that they often faint. We are all very familiar with the concept of feeling faint at the sight of blood and these fears are very common indeed. For example, one study reported that 15% of people attending a blood-donor clinic fainted (Graham, 1961) and this of course excluded people who were too afraid of blood to attend the clinic in the first place.

The high levels of autonomic arousal and the ease with which people with specific phobias can become fearful in the presence of their phobic stimulus means that we must structure treatment carefully. A hierarchy of fears is important and we should take the client gradually through each step. The starting point for treatment depends on the person and how much anxiety he can tolerate. It is probably best to start low and enable the client to experience successful habituation to his anxiety at an early stage, in other words demonstrate that anxious feelings will actually reduce during prolonged exposure.

Exposure to feared situations and objects can be done in imagination or in real life, although many writers maintain that real-life exposure is better (Marks, 1981). This assertion has been challenged recently, particularly in regard to specific phobias (James, 1986; Richards, 1988). Where real-life exposure can be readily arranged it is probably the best option, but exposure to less readily available feared objects like snakes or aircraft may be done in imagination.

As discussed in earlier chapters, the crucial determinant of successful treatment is the amount of practice undertaken by the client between treatment sessions. Any exposure undertaken in the treatment session must be repeated by the client at home.

The guidelines for effective exposure are that:

Exposure must be: Graded
                    Prolonged
                    Repeated
                    Practised as homework

Treatment sessions should only end when the client has experienced a reduction (i.e. habituation) of his anxiety during the exposure session. The following is an example of a client with a specific phobia, treated using graded, prolonged exposure.

Helen was a 13-year-old girl who asked for help because of her fear of dogs. She could not stroke or pet dogs and ran away from them if she saw one on the street. This was beginning to restrict her activities as she could not go to her friends' houses if they had a pet dog and other school children were beginning to make fun of her. She had had this fear as long as she could remember but recently her fears had generalized to other furry animals such as cats, rabbits, etc. and she even found it difficult to touch fur coats and gloves. She had no other anxiety problems and had a happy and stable family life.

The first stage of therapy was to construct a hierarchy of feared objects with Helen. From this hierarchy it was decided to start the first session by touching furry objects. She arrived for this session with her mother, having been crying on the way to the session at the thought of touching the furry scarf her mother had brought with her. She was determined to continue, however, and the scarf was placed on the table. Using the same anxiety rating scales we described in the earlier chapter on measurement, where o represents no anxiety and 8 is panic. Helen rated how anxious she felt at regular intervals throughout the session. At the beginning Helen rated her anxiety at 8. During the next five minutes, she was persuaded to hold her hand gently on the scarf and after 10 minutes of this her anxiety had reduced to 3. Twenty minutes later she only rated herself at 1.

Homework practice was to touch furry objects for at least half an hour daily but Helen did much more, even sleeping with the scarf in her bed. Following a review appointment, it was arranged that the next session should involve exposure to a cat. During this session Helen was encouraged to touch and stroke the cat who roamed around the room. Within 20 minutes her anxiety ratings had reduced from 8 to 2. Between sessions Helen petted and stroked two cats belonging to friends. The next session was a repeat of the last but Helen was able to pick the cat up and was hardly anxious at all. Finally, a dog was bought into the last session and interestingly Helen only rated her anxiety at 6, quickly decreasing to 2 as she petted the dog and then took it for a walk. She needed no further assistance in overcoming her fears and was no longer handicapped or embarrassed by her dog phobia. The total time taken to overcome her fears, excluding homework, was less than six hours.

The above example illustrates in a very clear way the principles of exposure. Helen worked through a hierarchy towards her worst fear, individual sessions lasted until her fears had reduced *during the session* and she engaged in repeated homework practice. Working up her hierarchy enabled her to face her greatest fear – a dog – much more easily than expected.

A more complex specific phobia

Jennifer was a 32-year-old woman who avoided any situation associated with blood or injury. She could not attend the doctor's surgery for a routine blood test and would not watch television programmes where there was the slightest chance of scenes involving blood or injury. She would always check with her boyfriend or family to see if there was any chance of gory scenes on television or in films if she went to the cinema. She would then avoid the situation. She was particularly concerned because she was planning to get married and wanted to have children. She could not envisage this because she knew it would mean having blood tests. She also felt that she would not be able to cope with any accidents her children had.

When confronted with anything that reminded her of blood and injury, she felt extremely panicky, her heart raced and her temperature increased. After about 30 seconds she became very nauseous and felt faint. If she did not leave the situation or lie down she would actually faint. Things had become so bad that she spent a great deal of time worrying about the possibility of coming across her feared situations. This actually made her continually anxious and attentive to anything remotely connected with blood and injury. This was interfering with her ability to concentrate on other aspects of her life such as her job, and she considered herself to be severely handicapped by her fears. Her mood was also becoming a little depressed as she was despondent about the future.

Despite being a little more inventive, treatment followed the same lines as that for Helen in the previous example. First, a hierarchy of feared situations was drawn up and used as the basis for therapy. The first treatment session involved showing Jennifer, who was accompanied by her boyfriend, a video of blood being taken from the nurse organizing the treatment. This video had been prepared earlier using equipment from the local school of nursing. It showed in detail the equipment needed for taking a blood sample, progressed to the blood being taken from the nurse's arm, finally ending with a scene where a sample of blood was swirled around in a glass. This sequence was repeated four times on the video, the whole video lasting about 40 minutes.

Jennifer was shown the video whilst lying down on a couch. She initially rated her anxiety at maximum intensity, feeling extremely nauseous and faint but her feelings reduced to 50% after about 15 minutes. At this point she sat up and watched the rest of the video, her anxiety dropping to around 30% of the initial level. The nurse then left the room and Jennifer watched another 30 minutes of the video with only her boyfriend present. At the end of this time her anxiety was only 2 on the 0 to 8 scale mentioned previously.

Homework was to take the video home and watch it at least four times weekly for two weeks. This she accomplished so the next session was an *in-vivo* exposure session where she watched one of the psychiatric registrars take blood three times from the nurse. Again she started by lying down but was quickly able to sit up. Instant photographs were taken of this session and she was instructed to take them home and look at them daily for half an hour. The final stage of the session was to take a sample of blood from Jennifer's arm. Although this was done, she was highly anxious. The sample of blood taken was put in a blood bottle containing anti-coagulant and Jennifer took this home to examine with the photographs daily.

Only two more sessions were required. The local haemophilia

centre were kind enough to allow Jennifer and the nurse to sit in the clinic and watch blood being taken from many different people. Again Jennifer was initially very anxious but her anxiety dropped to minimal levels at the end of twenty minutes. Homework was to continue the previous exercises plus to watch as many 'gory' videos as possible.

The final session involved the registrar taking two samples of blood from Jennifer's arm. The first sample caused her anxiety level to rise to maximum (8) but this reduced to 2 after five minutes. The second sample was taken without Jennifer feeling anxious at all. Homework from this session was to donate blood at the blood transfusion centre near her home. She did this successfully and was overjoyed at her accomplishment. She was no longer preoccupied with thoughts of blood and injury and was able to visit her GP for a blood sample. Her mood also improved significantly.

A final piece of advice was given to Jennifer. This was that she should continue to look at the photographs, gory films and the blood bottle regularly and to donate blood as often as the transfusion service recommend. Since blood and injury situations may be quite rare it is important that clients continue a rather artificial exposure programme for some time after therapy has finished to maintain their progress.

Imaginal exposure
The same rules for exposure, i.e. graded, prolonged and repeated as homework, can be applied when using imaginal exposure. Here, the client is asked to imagine scenes from his hierarchy and verbalize them in the form of a narrative. It is important that we ask the client to speak in the first person and talk about what he is *doing and feeling* not just what he is seeing. In this way the client imagines the situation in as vivid a way as possible. We should not interject unless it is strictly necessary to guide the client onto relevant material. A hierarchy can be used to choose imaginal scenes and exposure should be prolonged and repeated. Sessions can be audio-taped to enable the client to continue at home by listening to the tape and using it to guide his imagination. Alternatively, the client can take something home with him from the session, such as a photograph of his feared object, to enable him to undertake successful imaginal exposure homework.

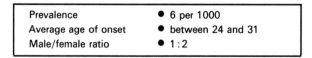

Prevalence	● 6 per 1000
Average age of onset	● between 24 and 31
Male/female ratio	● 1 : 2

Figure 9.2   Agoraphobia: Basic Information

Agoraphobia

Agoraphobia, with or without panic, is one of the major phobic problems that people seek help for from health professionals. Other phobias may be more common, but agoraphobia can be crippling. Most people assume it is a fear of wide open spaces but in fact it is defined as a fear of being alone or in public places from which escape might be difficult or help not available in case of sudden incapacitation. This leads people to avoid crowded shops, buses, trains, cinemas, etc. and can severely restrict a person's life.

Typically, a person with agoraphobia will describe a 'fear of fear', especially if they experience panics. They often avoid feared situations because they are afraid of bringing on a panic, not because the situation is inherently fearful. During such episodes they may fear collapsing, losing control, going mad or being unable to escape to safety. They also experience great anticipatory anxiety before entering a potentially frightening situation and often suffer from generalized anxiety (see Chapter 8) as a background to their agoraphobia. The presence of this background anxiety or panic should not be confused with general anxiety or panic. A person needing help with agoraphobia will always have very specific avoidances and can identify cues which consistently provoke anxiety.

The treatment of agoraphobia

Agoraphobia has been the subject of a great deal of research over the last 20 years or so. Behavioural treatments have been developed which have been extensively evaluated and improved through controlled studies. Other treatments have also been investigated. Anxiolytic and anti-depressant drugs have been shown to give temporary relief of autonomic symptoms, but little behavioural improvement, and relapse is likely when the drugs are stopped. Passive psychotherapies are not helpful (i.e. psychoanalysis, analytical psychotherapy, hypnosis, relaxation, etc.) and most therapists, whatever their method, stress the need for practice in entering the feared situation. Even Freud wrote, 'One can hardly ever master a phobia if one waits until the patient lets the analysis influence him to give it up ... one succeeds only when one can induce them by the influence of the analysis to ... go about alone and to struggle with their anxiety while they make the attempt.' (Freud, 1919). There is no evidence that psychological exploration is necessary for the successful resolution of an agoraphobic problem, neither is it true that agoraphobia is a result of family or system disharmony. Such assertions are not supported by research evidence.

The development of behavioural therapies for agoraphobia reflects the development of behavioural psychotherapy as a whole. From systematic desensitisation, through graded retraining, flooding and implosive therapy we now know that *in-vivo* exposure is the treatment of choice for agoraphobia.

To be effective, *in-vivo* exposure should fulfil the following conditions:

- Anxiety is not avoided
- Exposure is long enough for habituation to occur
- Exposure is regular
- Situations faced are appropriate to the fear
- Homework is used to encourage self-reliance

The manner in which graded, prolonged *in-vivo* exposure is undertaken is very important. Mathews *et al.* (1981) identify certain important factors and potential problems.

1 Therapist-assisted exposure alone requires much therapist time.
2 Clients may attribute progress they make to the help that they receive from the therapist and thus feel dependent on continued contact with him.
3 Progress may not continue after active treatment stops.
4 Clients who later experience a recurrence of acute anxiety may be unable to cope successfully without the therapist's help and so relapse.

It is therefore clear that factors which help clients practise self-exposure to phobic situations may be crucial to long term success (Mathews *et al.*, 1981). These factors are further illustrated in the following case history.

Irene was a 54-year-old woman who went to her GP requesting help for her fears when outside her house. She experienced palpitations, nausea, sweating and extreme tension whenever she travelled a long way from her home. She therefore avoided long journeys altogether and would not travel on buses at all. She also found crowds extremely difficult and would do all her shopping very early in the day to avoid the busiest time. In crowded situations she felt hemmed-in and feared she would not be able to escape back home. She rarely socialized and wanted help so that she could visit her grandchildren who lived away from the immediate area. She also wanted to be able to go out socially with her husband.

Until one year ago Irene had been taking diazepam in varying dosages for 20 years, ending up on 15 mg daily. She had recently listened to a radio programme about tranquillizers and followed the advice given, eventually stopping all her diazepam six months ago. Unfortunately she then found it increasingly difficult to get out and about as her anxious feelings when away from home became worse. It was at this point that she sought help. There were no other psychiatric or psychological difficulties and she was not depressed. Irene was determined to overcome her fears but was a little disheartened that they had worsened when she had stopped her medication.

She attended for her first appointment with her niece who had accompanied her on the bus. This was a great achievement for Irene, who was rather anxious when she came for the appointment. However, she became calmer as the session went on and the nature of anxiety was explained to her. She accepted the treatment rationale and returned the next week, again with her niece, with a hierarchy of feared situations. Irene decided that she would like to tackle a few short bus journeys with her niece to start with, and so for the next two weeks she practised travelling to and from a local shopping street. She managed quite well, eventually using the bus alone on two occasions.

Irene had trouble with the next stage, which was to travel on a bus further afield, and so the nurse offered to accompany her on a long bus journey. This was accomplished the next week and Irene's anxiety habituated over one hour, reducing from 7 to 3. The return journey was much easier, her anxiety never going above 4. The nurse then got off the bus with Irene's agreement and she completed the last half hour of the journey alone.

Telephone contact established that she had found this harder but her anxiety had reduced during the journey as she neared home. Over the next month Irene practised longer bus journeys, at first with her niece and then alone as she gradually became more confident until she triumphantly announced that she had managed to visit her grandchildren who lived over an hour's journey away.

During the time that she was trying bus journeys out, Irene was also entering crowded situations. She did this gradually and started to do her shopping at more usual times and in supermarkets. She began to find shopping a pleasure again and enjoyed discovering bargains at the various new shops she was exploring.

One particularly difficult situation was a family wedding which she attended. She felt very anxious during the reception and never really felt comfortable. Having discussed this with the nurse it was felt that this situation had probably come along a little too soon. She arranged with her husband to go out locally once a week and found that social situations started to feel gradually easier although they still remained her most uncomfortable situations.

After seven sessions, of which only one involved the nurse going into a situation with her, Irene felt she could manage to face her remaining difficulties alone with time and so the active phase of treatment was stopped. At one and three month follow-up appointments Irene continued to maintain her progress and had achieved all her main aims. Social situations were still difficult but she was avoiding few of her originally feared situations and she remained much less handicapped by her problem. She was delighted to be both off her tranquillizers and able to travel to visit her family.

The resolution of Irene's problems illustrates how we can work together with the client to tackle the areas of concern that the client feels are important. Therapy was client-centered and directed largely by Irene herself. Sessions consisted of explanation and problem solving together with planning of the next step. When Irene got stuck at a certain point the nurse became actively involved, but only to facilitate further self-exposure by Irene herself. This input clearly repaid itself and did not result in Irene becoming dependent on the nurse for continued support.

Social phobia

Social fears are common in the general population. Most of us can remember feeling embarrassed, awkward and insecure at various times in our lives, particularly during adolescence. These feelings generally reduce with time as our confidence and experience grows. If they persist into adult life or become worse, so that we begin to avoid contact with other people, the problem can be severely handicapping. Many of us still remain anxious in some situations, however, without it having a severe effect on our lives. Situations that spring to mind include speech making and dealing with people in authority. Only when these normal anxieties become so severe that they begin to handicap a person's life can we talk in terms of a social phobia.

Because people with social phobia find crowded situations difficult it is often confused with agoraphobia. There are, however, striking differences between the two and this illustrates the importance of an accurate three-systems analysis of anxiety forming part of the initial assessment.

(a) Autonomic symptoms
People with social phobia report more blushing, shaking and sweating, unlike agoraphobia where the predominant physical symptoms are dizziness, tachycardia and hyperventilation.

(b) Behavioural effects
Although very fearful, people with social fears often do not avoid the situations they are afraid of. They may continue to enter feared situations but careful assessment can reveal surreptitious avoidances such as sitting with their backs to others or drinking alcohol prior to going out, as 'dutch courage'.

(c) Cognitions
There are dramatic differences in the thoughts of people with social phobia compared to those suffering from agoraphobia. With social phobia there is discomfort in situations where the person is exposed to possible scrutiny by others for fear of *negative evaluation*. People with social phobia often fear that they will act

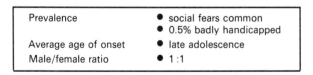

Prevalence	● social fears common
	● 0.5% badly handicapped
Average age of onset	● late adolescence
Male/female ratio	● 1 :1

Figure 9.3   Social Phobia: Basic Information

in an embarrassing or humiliating manner and that other people will judge them badly because of this.

Because the autonomic symptoms seen in social phobia are often very visible a vicious circle of anxiety can develop. For example, if a person shakes when anxious he may feel this is very obvious to others and that they will think him inadequate because of it. This can lead him to become more anxious with a consequent increase in his shakiness and further feelings of inadequacy. A similar pattern of negative thoughts often occurs with people who blush severely. This cognitive aspect of anxiety contrasts strongly with the thought pattern of people who have an agoraphobic problem, where the thoughts are about some physical catastrophe occurring to the person themselves. These differences are important as they have implications for treatment.

The treatment of social phobia

As with other phobias the treatment of choice for social phobia is exposure *in-vivo*. There are, however, a number of difficulties associated with the use of exposure alone when helping people with social anxiety. These are discussed in detail by Butler (1985) and are summarized below.

(a) Many people with social phobia do not avoid their feared situations, but repeated, naturally occurring exposure seems to have no effect on their fear.

(b) Social situations are constantly variable and complex. It may be impossible to grade, prolong or repeat situations consistently. It is also impossible to predict the outcome of social interactions since they often rely on the participation of others.

(c) Exposure may actually have a negative effect since obvious anxiety or poor social performance may produce an adverse reaction from other people, confirming the person's negative evaluation of their performance. An example could be the person who blushes and is teased by others as a consequence.

(d) The cognitions associated with social phobia may actually play a key role in maintaining people's fears. If a person with agoraphobia consistently enters his feared situations successfully, his fear that he will have a heart attack or faint, for example, may be disconfirmed by his experience. This is not the case with social fears since the person will receive no information from others around him to disconfirm his fears of negative evaluation. The crucial link to break may be the connection between the visible symptoms of anxiety and the fears that these will be negatively evaluated. Exposure alone is unlikely to do this.

Thus, there are practical as well as theoretical difficulties with an exposure approach alone. Exposure remains, however, a highly effective approach when dealing with social anxiety as shown in a study by Butler *et al.* (1984). In this study exposure alone was compared with exposure combined with anxiety management. Anxiety management refers to the type of procedure we described in Chapter 8, basically a combination of relaxation, distraction and positive self-talk. Both treatments were found to be effective but the combined treatment showed better results on measures of the cognitive component of anxiety and no clients in this group requested further treatment, as opposed to 40% of the people treated with exposure alone. Most clients found the positive self-talk the most useful. This consisted of identifying negative thoughts that occurred in the feared situations and rehearsing logical and constructive thoughts to counter the negative ones. These were then used to help the client control his anxious thoughts when undergoing exposure practice.

Organizing exposure for social phobias
The pitfalls associated with treating social phobia can be overcome by attention to the following questions:

1 Grading exposure – because it is often not possible to grade situations, we should stress that frequency and variety of exposure is important. Many different practice situations can be repeated frequently (up to an ideal total of one hour daily). Close scrutiny of the situations that provoke anxiety can reveal common elements and practice can be organized to tackle these specific elements.

2 Prolonging exposure – because social interactions can be very short (a conversation may only last a couple of minutes) the emphasis should be on repeated practice. Feared situations can be repeated frequently on a daily basis to facilitate effective exposure.

3 Counteracting surreptitious avoidances – people who are socially anxious often avoid exposure to their fears by not

engaging fully in the situation. This cognitive avoidance or disengagement enables people to enter situations they fear without facing their anxiety, but of course leads to greater problems in the long term. For exposure to work effectively we must help people fully face up to their fears. We therefore need to encourage people to become active participants in the social situations they have difficulty with. This may mean practising eye-contact, active listening or introducing new topics of conversation, all skills that require an active participation in events.

4   Dealing with fears of negative evaluation – we can use the cognitively orientated techniques described in the section on general anxiety, including Butler's positive self-talk, to help people reappraise the significance of their fears and help them substitute a more realistic assessment of the situation they are in.

The following person's experience may help to put together some of the points discussed above.

June was a 35-year-old woman who presented at her initial appointment with a 15-year history of fear and avoidance of all social situations. In these situations she became very shaky, her concentration was severely affected and she invariably left to return home. She lived with her common-law husband and their two children aged 15 and 13. Her husband had long ago developed a social life that did not include June and as her children became more independent she felt left out and alone for much of the time. She found all social events difficult, especially those where she was expected to contribute to the conversation. Even buying groceries from shops could be difficult if the assistant tried to engage her in conversation. Travelling was also a problem for June in case anybody talked to her whilst she was on a bus. She feared that people would expect her to perform well in conversation with them and regarded her own performance as inadequate, something she felt others thought too.

During the appointment June was highly and visibly anxious. She shook, became tearful at times and found it difficult to concentrate on the interview. There was no evidence, however, of underlying depression. Towards the end of the interview June relaxed significantly and found it easier to discuss her difficulties. She understood the principles of the three systems of anxiety and agreed that this represented how her social anxieties had become out of control. Group treatment was offered to her and after some hesitation she agreed to try it.

The groups consisted of weekly sessions lasting 90 minutes, run over an eight-week period. There were five other people in the group, all having problems with social phobia, with two nurses as facilitators. The group sessions consisted of education on anxiety, exposure instructions, monitoring of exposure homework, anxiety management instructions and practice and, of course, the opportunity to discuss fears with people who had similar difficulties.

The two nurses gave information to the group members and facilitated discussion and problem solving within the group. The group was asked to help each member in turn come up with exposure practice tasks and the whole group problem-solved difficulties any members were having between sessions. The very fact that treatment was carried out in a group setting was a form of exposure in itself.

June had great difficulty in the first session. She contributed very little to the group and at one point was disengaging so completely that she appeared to be going to sleep despite being obviously severely anxious. During the first session the three-systems model of anxiety was described in detail. June paid little attention but took a handout, summarizing the information given during the session, away with her. The last half-hour was given over to a relaxation session, but June again found it almost impossible to engage in the session. She took a tape away from the session to practise relaxation at home.

Gradually June was able to feel less anxious as the sessions progressed. She began to contribute to the groups and became more relaxed. She teamed up with another group member and they met a few times outside the group for further practice. She concentrated her homework practice on bus journeys and shopping trips and would go into half a dozen small shops daily to practice speaking to strangers. She was able to use the rational self-talk aspect of the anxiety-management package quite well and she found her concentration improving as the weeks went by. At the end of the 8 groups she was much less handicapped although she had not yet tackled her main fears of going out socially. This she intended to do, and informed the group at the last session that she would be negotiating with her husband to go out to a club once a week.

Unfortunately, at a follow-up appointment three weeks later June presented in a highly distressed state. Her husband had refused to go out with her and had admitted to a long-term affair he had been having with another woman. She had barred him from the house and their relationship was effectively over. The next few sessions were spent allowing June to explore her feelings and consider her next move. Paradoxically, she became more determined than ever to forge a new independent life for herself. She went to the local library and found the address of a social club for older single people, plucked up her courage and went along one night. This she found initially very difficult especially when approached by men who asked her to dance. However, after a few weeks she began to feel more comfortable and found the positive self-talk skills she had learned at the group especially useful in dealing with each new situation. Six months after the groups finished, June was going out socially twice a week and had started a new relationship with another man. She was much more confident and outgoing and rated herself as 75% improved.

June's problems illustrate some of the difficulties encountered when treating social phobias. Cognitive avoidance leading to an almost total disengagement from the situation is unlikely to lead to successful confrontation of fear, but had the nurses pointed this out initially June may never have returned for the second group. Even with such high anxiety levels people can both learn to control their feelings and experience habituation. The groups were deliberately made one-and-a-half hours long to make sure that there was time for habituation to at least start to occur. Group treatments for social fears seem like the most appropriate setting as they are themselves feared situations.

Summary

This chapter and the previous one have described the detailed treatment of several of the most common types of anxiety problems that are known to respond to a behavioural approach. We have tried to emphasize the importance of a thorough assessment of the client's problems, using the three-system analysis of anxiety. This analysis has a critical bearing on treatment and allows us to tailor our interventions to the particular aspects of the client's anxiety that cause him distress.

Multi-faceted anxiety management strategies, controlled breathing and graded prolonged exposure are all techniques that are known to be clinically effective. Other techniques such as relaxation have been shown to be less effective and we should not use them alone or in situations where there are known to be more effective strategies. Difficulties in adapting the principles of exposure to certain phobias, particularly social phobia, have been outlined and solutions offered.

Although behavioural treatments have been shown to be the treatments of choice for phobias, we can now move on to outline one of the most dramatic success stories in modern psychiatry – the development of behavioural treatments for obsessions and compulsions.

REFERENCES

Butler G. (1985). Exposure as a treatment for social phobia: some instructive difficulties. *Behaviour Research and Therapy*, 23, 651–657.

Butler G., Cullington A., Munby M., Amies P., Gelder M. (1984). Exposure and anxiety management in the treatment of social phobia. *Journal of Consulting and Clinical Psychology*, 52, 642–650.

Freud S. (1919). Collected Papers 2. 399–400. London: The Hogarth Press.

Graham D. T. (1961). Prediction of fainting in blood donors. *Circulation*, 23, 901–906.

James J. E. (1986). Review of the relative efficacy of imaginal and *in-vivo* flooding in the treatment of clinical fear. *Behavioural Psychotherapy*, 14, 183–191.

Marks I. M. (1981). Cure and Care of Neurosis. New York: Wiley.

Mathews A. (1984). Anxiety and its management. Chapter 13 In *Current Themes in Psychiatry*, Vol. 3. (Gaind R. L. *et al.* ed.) New York: Spectrum.

Mathews A. M., Gelder M. G., Johnston D. W. (1981). *Agoraphobia, Nature and Treatment*. London: Tavistock.

Richards D. A. (1988). The treatment of a snake phobic by imaginal exposure. *Behavioural Psychotherapy*, 16, 207–216.

Chapter 10

Obsessions and compulsions

Consulting a psychiatric textbook dating from only 25 or so years ago (Slater and Roth, 1969), one finds a depressing description of the outcome for people suffering from obsessions and compulsions. Such problems were considered intractable with the sufferer consigned to a life of severe handicap. For example, Slater and Roth state that 'the outlook in the true obsessional state ... is at best maintainance *in status quo*, more usually imperceptible decline downhill' (p. 135). The options for treatment were either long-term care in an institution or psychosurgery (despite the lack of evidence for the success of such surgery). Over the last 20 years, however, psychological treatments have been devised and tested which means that we can effectively treat at least 75% of these problems. This is a quite remarkable turn round in the prognosis for such a major source of psychological distress.

Obsessions are usually characterized by fearful or doubting thoughts which the person finds extremely distressing. In order to rid themselves of the anxiety caused by these thoughts they feel compelled to undertake some activity, usually in a set manner. A few examples of the diverse ways in which obsessions and compulsions present will help to illustrate the complexity of the problem.

1   *Lillian, a mother of six children, found herself becoming increasingly concerned with cleanliness. She spent long periods of time disinfecting her house from top to bottom and washed her hands up to 40 times a day. Certain parts of the house were safe (e.g. her babies' bedrooms) whilst others, such as the back porch, were dangerously unclean. She felt very unhappy about people coming into the house*

in case they were contaminated by germs and would make her husband and family remove their outer clothing in the porch before going upstairs to shower. She would not allow other people to touch her baby and had to change her own clothes four or five times a day in case she contaminated the baby. Not surprisingly, she found little time to get on with ordinary social activities and became very tired and depressed.

2 *Mike had a problem with checking. If he saw an article in a newspaper he felt compelled to read it thoroughly, several times over, until he was satisfied he understood the story. Local news programmes on the radio caused him to feel very uncomfortable and he avoided going into shops and houses where a local radio station might be playing. He could not buy local newspapers or read stories about events close to home. He could not clearly identify what caused him distress when he read such a story, but if he asked his girlfriend if she had seen the article and she replied, 'yes' then he was immediately reassured that everything was 'alright'. Unfortunately, the frequency of this reassurance-seeking increased with time. He also could not tolerate being alone in the house with very sharp knives and would always look back at people when they had passed him in the street to ensure nothing had happened to them. Although he could not define his fearful thoughts exactly, he worried about being responsible for unpleasant events and needed to check and seek reassurance from trusted others to calm his fears.*

3 *Mary was a very religious woman in her late forties who was extremely distressed when she started having thoughts about the devil. She felt that bad things would happen to people if she thought about the devil. When these thoughts occurred, she had to cancel them out by touching wooden objects a certain number of times or by praying and trying to think about God until the initial thoughts went away. This process could take up to five minutes, during which time she was unable to continue with her everyday activities. Although the thoughts were not very frequent, she was very distressed by them because of her religious beliefs. Counselling by the local priest did not reassure her for any length of time and the frequency of her thoughts had started to increase.*

4 *John spent many hours a day examining himself for signs of cancer. He would stand in front of the mirror in the early morning checking to see if there were any skin imperfections that could be signs of impending cancer. Any physical symptom that emerged in himself or his family provoked strong fears of cancer and he would immediately make an appointment with his GP for reassurance that the symptoms were not cancerous. He had an extensive home medical library and would spend hours in medical libraries checking his symptoms. He attended the GP's surgery at least once a fortnight and gained initial reassurance that he was well. As soon as new symptoms emerged, however, his anxieties returned. He became depressed and found it hard to continue with his job. His family became intolerant of his constant checking and reassurance seeking, especially when he involved them in trips to the GP's surgery.*

5 *Pauline could not stand the thought of things being out of order. Each ornament in her house had to be in a special place and she became highly anxious if things were moved. One of her main problems was getting the bed clothes straight. This took her up to an hour each morning as she had to straighten all the creases and pleats, making sure each was in the correct position before going on to the next one. She had been known to iron the bedcover to remove creases whilst it was on the bed. If she was unable to do this, she became very anxious and quite aggressive towards her family. They, therefore, did not interfere with her rituals. A further problem was going to bed. She could not check the house without taking hours to lock up so her husband assumed responsibility for this. Unfortunately, she had another ritual in the bathroom that involved sitting for half an hour on the toilet making sure she had expelled every last drop of urine. This took so long that she often had to wake her husband up to get him to make the house secure. Their relationship was very strained as a result of Pauline's behaviour.*

The treatment of obsessions and compulsions

Many different approaches to treatment have been tried for obsessions and compulsions. We will briefly summarize these before outlining behavioural treatments in depth.

(a) Drugs

Drugs used to treat anxiety, such as benzodiazepines, β-blockers and major tranquillizers have little effect on behaviour in obsessive-compulsive problems. This is similar to the situation in phobic anxiety problems which we discussed in the last chapter. Drugs may, in fact, retard the action of behavioural treatments.

Antidepressants, particularly clomipramine, have been the subject of much speculation and investigation. Several studies have asked the question – do these drugs have a specific anti-compulsive effect? (Marks *et al.*, 1980; Mawson *et al.*, 1982; Rachman *et al.*, 1979; Thoren *et al.*, 1980). All these studies show that clomipramine has no specific anti-compulsive action but that it acts on the depressed mood seen in about a third of people with obsessional problems. Unfortunately, on stopping the drug there is a tendency for the depression to reoccur. It must be stressed that in these studies clomipramine did not reduce compulsive rituals *per se*, any improvement was as a consequence of general improvements in mood and well being. Clomipramine had no effect in people who had obsessional problems uncomplicated by depression.

(b) Relaxation

Studies by Hodgson *et al.* (1972); Roper *et al.* (1976) and Marks *et al.* (1980) showed that relaxation has minimal effect on compulsive rituals.

(c) Psychosurgery

A few workers maintain that psychosurgery, usually a stereotaxic leucotomy, is a useful treatment for chronic and intractable obsessional problems. Although there have been a number of reports extolling the virtues of such operations, there have been no random controlled trials of this approach. Jack Rachman, who has spent many years researching obsessional problems, makes the point that, 'the use of such radical procedures can only be justified on the grounds of demonstrable success, in the absence of satisfactory alternatives ... neither of these conditions is met and therefore the psychosurgical treatment of obsessional patients cannot be justified at present.' (Rachman, S., 1979). Psychosurgery is still used, however, but the Mental Health Act Commissioners in the UK insist that the person has an adequate trial of behaviour therapy, conducted by an appropriately trained person, before allowing consent to be given.

(d) Psychodynamic approaches

Psychoanalysts postulate that people with obsessional problems
have a tyrannical super-ego and use concepts of mental defence
mechanisms, particularly regression to an anal-sadistic level of
development, to explain the confusing picture presented by
obsessions. Psychoanalysts themselves admit that treatments tried
out from such ideas have been unsuccessful. A well known and
experienced psychoanalyst, Malan, has written that he has never
seen an obsessive-compulsive problem treated successfully by
analytical methods (Malan, 1979). Furthermore, analytical predictions of symptom substitution following removal of rituals by
behavioural treatments have not been borne out in practice. Other
'talking' therapies have been comprehensively reviewed by Kazdin
and Wilson (1978), who show that all psychodynamic methods
have no effect on obsessive-compulsive problems.

Other approaches have been tried (e.g. Janet, 1925) and often
include elements of behaviour therapy under different names. Only
in the last few years has a consistent behavioural treatment with
reliable results been evolved. In order to understand this treatment
we need to understand the behavioural model of obsessions and
compulsions.

Obsessions and compulsions: a behavioural model

Although the problem a client presents with may be very individual,
obsessive-compulsive problems share many basic characteristics.
Obsessions and compulsions are usually seen together but we can
define them independently to make the picture clear. Rachman
and Hodgson (1980) have the best definitions which are:

> 'An obsession is an intrusive, repetitive thought, image or
> impulse that is unacceptable and/or unwanted and gives rise to
> subjective resistance. It generally produces distress. Obsessions
> are difficult to remove or control. During calm periods the
> person acknowledges the senselessness of the thought or impulse.
> The content of the obsession is repugnant, worrying, blasphem-
> ous, obscene, nonsensical – or all of these – and frequently
> takes the form of doubting.'
>
> 'Compulsions are repetitive, stereotyped acts. They may be
> wholly unacceptable or, more often, partly acceptable, but are
> regarded by the person as being excessive and/or exaggerated.

They are preceded or accompanied by a subjective sense of compulsion, and provoke subjective resistance. They generally produce distress. In his or her calmer moments, the person usually acknowledges the senselessness of these activities.'

The content of obsessions
Obsessional thoughts usually provoke distress and commonly refer to:

- dirt and contamination
- sex
- religion
- illness
- aggression
- orderliness
- socially unacceptable actions

Interestingly, thoughts with all the characteristic intrusive qualities of obsessional thoughts occur in 88% of a 'normal' population (Rachman and de Silva, 1978; Salkovskis and Harrison, 1984). It seems, therefore, not the thought which is the problem but the person's response to it. Most of us can dismiss such intrusive thoughts. However, when a person with an obsessional problem experiences an intrusive thought he is unable to do this and the thought provokes extreme distress and anxiety. The person then tries to deal with the anxiety by cancelling it out, usually with a compulsive ritual.

Compulsive rituals are therefore no different in intent from the avoidance or escape behaviour seen in people who have phobias. Thus, Lillian's fear of contamination results in excessive washing rituals which reduce the possibility of contamination, whilst doubts about physical health lead John to check his body constantly and seek reassurance from various sources. Both activities are designed to reduce the anxious feelings the person is experiencing as a consequence of his or her intrusive thoughts.

Ritualizing, therefore, is just the method the person has evolved

Prevalence	• 1 per 2000
Average age of onset	• late teens and early 20s
Male/female ratio	• 1 :1

Figure 10.1   Basic Facts. Obsessions and Compulsions

in order to cope with the anxiety produced by the intrusive thoughts. Whereas people with phobias reduce their anxiety by avoiding the situation that provokes their distress, people with obsessional problems reduce their anxiety in a more active way, by engaging in rituals.

In the same way that avoidance of feared situations in phobias, whilst giving short-term relief of anxiety, leads to an increase in phobic anxiety in the long term, the more a person engages in obsessional rituals the greater the long-term problem. If a person increasingly avoids the feared situation or object by engaging in rituals the less effective and more complicated the rituals become and the more frequently they have to be employed. They can eventually become so overpowering that they come to dominate a person's life.

This model of anxiety is one arm of the three-systems analysis we have often referred to in this book and is known as the 'Fear and Avoidance' model. See Figure 10.2 for a diagram of the Fear and Avoidance model as applied to obsessions.

We would not suggest that the behavioural model provides all the answers to the phenomenology of obsessions and compulsions. Many rituals, for example, require the person to expend a great deal of effort, whilst for some people anxiety does not decrease during ritualizing. Salkovskis (1985) has suggested a revision of the model that tries to explain why obsessive thoughts, common in the general population, should provoke such distress for some people. Gray (1987) relates some of the new knowledge about psychophysiology to propose a 'behavioural inhibition system' in the brain that produces, amongst many things, the typical behaviours seen in obsessive-compulsive problems. Many researchers are beginning to see that whilst anxiety creates obsessive-compulsive behaviour, dysphoria and depression maintain the problem and make it resistant to treatment. Rather than a criticism of the behavioural model, this continuing debate illustrates the extent to which the behavioural model is a 'live' theory. It is being constantly updated and changed to take into account the data produced by clinical trials and research. In this book we cannot do more than alert the reader to some of the current debates and suggest references to those who wish to study the subject further.

Usually the content of intrusive thoughts is less important than the mechanisms with which they are maintained. People's past and present lifestyles may influence the thought content, however.

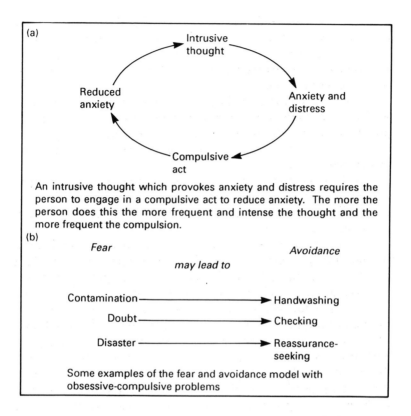

(a)

Intrusive thought

Reduced anxiety

Anxiety and distress

Compulsive act

An intrusive thought which provokes anxiety and distress requires the person to engage in a compulsive act to reduce anxiety. The more the person does this the more frequent and intense the thought and the more frequent the compulsion.

(b)

Fear   Avoidance

may lead to

Contamination ⟶ Handwashing

Doubt ⟶ Checking

Disaster ⟶ Reassurance-seeking

Some examples of the fear and avoidance model with obsessive-compulsive problems

Figure 10.2   The Fear and Avoidance Model of Obsessive-Compulsive Problems

For example, a devoutly religious person will find normal intrusive thoughts more disturbing if they are blasphemous, the example of Mary given earlier illustrates this. However, it is generally counter-productive to discuss at great length the content of thoughts with people suffering from obsessions. This can be used by clients as a source of reassurance, reducing their anxiety (but only in the short-term) and prolonging their obsessions. Examples later will make this clear. The *strength* of intrusive thoughts may be relevant, however, for some of the 20–25% of people with obsessive-compulsive problems who do not respond to behavioural psychotherapy.

Unlike most people, including those with severe obsessions, some clients do not regard their thoughts and fears as completely senseless. These people are identified by Foa (1979) as people with 'overvalued ideas' and they make up a small but significant population who usually do poorly in behavioural psychotherapy. There has been some investigation into using cognitive techniques to help these people reduce the strength of their overvalued ideas (e.g. Salkovskis and Warwick, 1985). However, it must be stressed that in most cases this is not necessary and may be counter-productive.

Rachman and Hodgson's definition of obsessions also includes obsessional images and impulses. Images are mental pictures which may intrude into a person's mind in the same way, and with the same characteristics, as an intrusive thought. This is *not* the same as an hallucination. The person will have no loss of contact with reality and the image will be regarded as intrusive and unwanted, provoking behaviour which neutralizes the image. Intrusive images are rare whereas impulses are quite common. Many people untroubled with obsessional problems have felt momentary impulses to jump off railway platforms at the approach of a train. Obsessional impulses may be of this nature, but are often concerned with danger to others, for example an impulse to pick up a kitchen knife and stab a child would be very distressing to many mothers. If these impulses are repetitive, intrusive and provoke distress and resistance they can be seen as obsessional. It should be stressed that if they are of this nature they are rarely, if ever, carried out. Instead, just as obsessional thoughts are resisted or neutralized by other behaviours, the person may engage in many avoidances to limit his contact with sharp knives and possibly use neutralizing thoughts or compulsive behaviours to reduce the anxiety evoked by these thoughts.

The themes of compulsions

The two most common compulsive rituals are washing and checking. Handwashing is the most usual response to fears of contamination, often accompanied by avoidance of contaminated objects and excessive washing or disinfecting of these objects. Handwashing can be so frequent that it causes severe skin problems, whilst disinfecting household objects can be an expensive exercise.

Checking is also very frequently seen in clients with obsessional problems. This may be simple, overt checking such as making sure the doors are locked at night, or can be done cognitively. In the latter case, people may be counting to a certain number whilst doing a certain activity in order to feel it has been done correctly. For people with checking rituals, whether overt or covert, the connection between obsessions and doubt is most vividly displayed. For example, after switching the light off, a person may doubt that it has been done and return to repeat the action. They may actually switch the light on and off again several times before believing that it is off, despite the evidence of their eyes every time the room goes dark.

Reassurance seeking is another obsessional behaviour that people often engage in. A client may wish to use another person's assertions that everything is 'alright' to calm the anxious feelings produced by intrusive and doubting thoughts. This is most clearly seen in people who display obsessional illness fears, where in response to fears for their health they may make extremely frequent visits to doctors, hospitals, etc. This often leads to labels such as 'hypochondriac' being applied with all the attendant negative connotations associated with such concepts. Seen in the context of a behaviour designed to reduce obsessional anxiety, such attendance at hospitals is more understandable and should lead to more constructive attitudes being adopted by health workers.

Ruminations have been the most puzzling of all obsessional problems and the most difficult to treat. Ruminating refers to the cognitive, or internal, side of the obsessional problem. A person may spend long hours just thinking, being unable to carry on normal activities until he has finished. At first, researchers considered this to be just a preoccupation with intrusive thoughts but treatment approaches based on this idea did not really work well. It now seems clear that when people ruminate they are engaging in the same battle with anxiety that produces overt rituals. In this case the rituals are internalized. Therefore, ruminating consists of intrusive, anxiety-*provoking* thoughts which are neutralized by anxiety-*reducing* thoughts. This explanation of ruminations has very important implications for treatment, and has led to some promising new techniques being developed for helping people with obsessional ruminations.

A final point about compulsions is that they are often endowed with a magical property, particularly where doubting is a strong feature. It is easy to see the connection between fears of contamination and compulsive handwashing but less obvious is why, for example, reciting the 7 times table backwards seven times should protect a mother's children from harm. People's compulsive acts often bear no relation to the feared consequence other than that they somehow ward off the possibility of future danger. Although the vast majority of people with such rituals know this, they still feel compelled to carry out the ritual. Confronting a person about the senselessness of his obsessive thoughts and compulsive acts is probably the single most destructive thing one can do, serving only to remind him of his own crippling irrationality.

The treatment of obsessive-compulsive problems

Dealing with what appear to be confusing and baffling problems with reference to a fear and avoidance model gives us clear indications for treatment. If someone is avoiding a feared object then exposure to this object should reduce anxiety. However, this is not likely to be successful if rituals remain that are acting as an escape from the anxiety. A second component of treatment must be to help the client prevent this neutralization of anxiety. In this way exposure can be prolonged. The two components of behavioural treatment for obsessions and compulsions are therefore:

1 Cue Exposure
2 Response Prevention

Cue exposure means exposure to any stimulus that provokes intrusive thoughts and therefore makes one anxious. Response prevention refers to stopping the rituals that the client usually employs to cancel out his anxiety.

There has been much research into developing this type of treatment since the first successful report of behavioural therapy with obsessions was published (Meyer, 1966). Foa *et al.* (1984) deliberately compared the effects of exposure alone, response prevention alone and a combination of the two procedures. All three treatments were effective but the combined approach was the most effective and the most durable. It seems that exposure is the essential component in reducing anxiety whilst response prevention has more impact on compulsive rituals. How then do we go about putting all this into practice?

1 Cue exposure

Cue exposure is no different from the exposure we use to help people overcome phobias. We should stick to the same principles that apply when using exposure generally, i.e.: Exposure is

- Graded
- Prolonged
- Repeated
- As self-exposure homework

The crucial factor when organizing practice with clients is that we should devise ways of making exposure positive and *active*. For example, it is easy to say to a client that he should reduce his handwashing after he touches outdoor clothes, but it is quite another thing to actually do this regularly. Instructions about what a client should *not* do are rarely effective. Additionally, for exposure to be prolonged and repeated, agreeing on exercises that rely on clients coming across exposure situations by accident will not be effective. Exposure sessions should be organized to happen at a particular time in the day when the client decides to concentrate all his efforts on confronting his fears. This point cannot be stressed enough. Exposure should last at least an hour, during which time the client's attention must be exclusively centred on the relevant cues. To continue with our earlier example, contamination exercises during which time a client concentrates solely on deliberately touching and handling outdoor clothes for an hour each morning will be far more effective than sporadic accidental exposure.

After the assessment, rationale and baseline measurement have been undertaken, the client can be helped to formulate a hierarchy of his fears, obsessions and compulsions which can then be used to commence exposure practice. We should help the client choose a situation or object that is fairly close to the bottom of his list and facilitate him practising exposure to it in a regular, prolonged and repeated fashion.

Let us now look at how we used this approach in the treatment of Lillian's fears of contamination.

1 Lillian

After identifying the many areas of concern she felt, Lillian elected to spend an hour a day touching kitchen utensils which she found difficult to touch because they had been used by other members of her family. During this time she handled various items thoroughly, transferring the 'contamination' she feared was on them to other 'clean' utensils. She did this by touching clean utensils immediately after she had touched 'dirty' ones, repeating this until she had handled all the kitchen utensils whether she considered them to be contaminated or not. She thus started to break down the rigid boundaries that divided her home and its contents into 'safe' and 'contaminated' areas.

Gradually, week by week, she progressed to touching more and more feared objects, transferring the contamination from these objects to other things she felt were clean. When she was able to touch her family's outside clothes it was no longer necessary for them to change and wash on entering the house. She began to practise holding her baby whilst wearing clothes that she had worn outside the house and did not change into special indoor clothes after coming back from shopping. She was eventually able to accept visitors coming into the house which meant that her social life improved dramatically.

As Lillian's fears of contamination reduced with regular, active exposure to previously feared objects she became far less handicapped and troubled by her problems. Importantly, not only were there dramatic improvements in her behavioural symptoms, but treatment effects generalized (as they usually do). Her mood elevated and her buoyant and active personality reasserted itself.

Lillian's treatment programme demonstrates the principles by which exposure should be employed. She adopted a graded series of exercises which steadily confronted her fears. These exercises were undertaken most days and lasted about an hour. As well as confronting feared objects, she actively broke down the barriers between 'contaminated' and 'clean' areas of her house. This division between areas and objects is a very common strategy that people with obsessional problems use in order to make their lives bearable. After a while, however, so much time can be spent organizing routines around this division that it becomes disablingly complicated. Thus, exposure involves not only touching contaminated objects but also transferring the 'contamination' to previously clean objects to break down this artificial barrier.

However, this active exposure would have been of little use if Lillian had continued to wash her hands during the exercises, since this would have been ritualizing to reduce anxiety, allowing no time for habituation to occur. This brings us to the second aspect of treatment – response prevention.

2 Response prevention

As previously described, response prevention describes the reduction or blocking of rituals which a person would feel compelled to engage in following exposure to a feared situation or object. Rituals exist to reduce the anxiety a person may feel after they have come across a feared situation or have experienced an intrusive, distressing thought. Exposure-based therapies rely on prolonged contact with a feared object or situation allowing the anxiety this causes to abate naturally – habituation. Exposure cannot work effectively if a person continues to reduce his anxiety by engaging in rituals.

To ask a person with an obsessional problem to stop engaging in their rituals is, therefore, an essential part of therapy, but we must not forget that we are asking people to resist the very actions that have previously enabled them to cope with their fears. This illustrates the importance of establishing a sound therapeutic relationship with our clients and maintaining the policy of honesty with them that we have stressed throughout this book. We are asking people to take what is for them an enormous risk, and so we should have presented both an honest and convincing rationale for this approach and have made it very clear that we have understood the difficulty the task presents.

Lillian was asked initially to record the number of times she washed her hands daily and then, during the first stage of treatment, to refrain from washing her hands during the exposure practice times. Quite quickly, however, Lillian found it was possible to 'save-up' her fears until after the hour was finished, heading straight for the sink the moment her time was up. She realized this was unlikely to make her problem better and so a different strategy was used. She kept a contaminated object – a cup – by the sink and touched it immediately she had washed her hands after feeling contaminated. She was therefore 'recontaminating' herself after each handwash, thus making handwashing redundant. She was helped to identify those times in the day when it is acceptable to wash one's hands – before preparing food, after going to the toilet, etc. – and tried to keep her handwashing to these times only. She also altered the way in which she washed her hands and began to mostly rinse, rather than vigorously soap, her hands. Although this was difficult she was able to reduce the frequency with which she handwashed to a quarter of what it was.

Housework was also tackled and she was helped to reduce the frequency with which she cleaned the house. This was much easier than she expected because as she confronted more objects in the exposure sessions she felt less compulsion to clean everything anyway.

By a combination of cue-exposure and response prevention Lillian was able to confront her fears and reduce her handicapping rituals. Her mood lifted and she began to find more time to do the things she had previously enjoyed. The relationships within the family also improved as her rituals impinged less on the other family members. She remained more scrupulous than most, but was careful not to let this get out of control in the way it had before.

A number of clinical issues arise from the treatment of Lillian's problems:

(a) Self-exposure versus assisted practice

Although Lillian undoubtedly spent many hours confronting her fears, we merely advised and guided her in her treatment. It was not necessary to spend large amounts of time practising exposure exercises with her. This *self-exposure* approach, just as for phobic problems, is the one we should try first, only becoming more actively involved if the person has difficulty getting started with treatment exercises. Experimental evidence for this comes from a recent study by Ghosh *et al.* (1988).

The opposite approach is sometimes necessary, especially for those people who have difficulty formulating a hierarchy of feared objects and situations, and who do not feel able to undertake guided self-exposure at first. We may go to the client's home for several hours, perhaps half a day, during which time we would undertake a massive exposure session helping the client to continuously touch contaminated objects in his house and refrain from handwashing. During this time, we ourselves could act as sources of contamination, touching objects in the house to contaminate them and then asking the client to contaminate himself with things we have touched. Although half a day may seem a long time to spend with one client all at once, in the long term this can be an extremely effective use of our time. Exposure homework remains essential when we have gone, of course, and if lengthy assisted exposure sessions have to be repeated many times we must look for other reasons why we are not being successful.

(b) Prolonged exposure

For fears such as Lillian's, exposure to feared situations and objects will be almost continuous anyway, which is why response prevention is so important. Although we know that habituation of anxiety often takes more than an hour, Lillian was asked to practise for one hour for mainly practical reasons. Exposure to contaminated objects during that hour, plus response prevention of rituals both then and at other times, gradually increased Lillian's confidence in facing up to other feared objects without handwashing. As she conquered her fears of more and more objects and simultaneously reduced her handwashing she spent more time in daily effective exposure.

Now we have established the principles of cue-exposure and response prevention, how can they be applied to the other problems we outlined at the beginning of this chapter?

2 Mike

Mike was able to put his rituals in some sort of order. He felt that he could face his fears about newspapers first, starting off with national papers. He elected to read a national newspaper once a day, making sure he did not re-read any of the stories after he had read them through once. His girlfriend came with him for one appointment and they discussed ways to reduce his seeking reassurance from her. She practised a neutral response to his reassurance seeking. Whenever he asked for reassurance that everything was 'alright' she replied, 'The nurses at the clinic have asked me not to answer those questions.' Such a reply helped reduce potential friction and arguments between Mike and his girlfriend.

At first highly anxious, Mike persevered and his anxiety soon dropped to manageable levels. Pleased with his success, he progressed to buying and reading a local paper daily, throwing it away as soon as it was read. He found this harder but overcame his fears. He also began to listen to the national news and then the local news on radio and television.

He had a setback after a few weeks of success when he went with his girlfriend to the local large city. He became anxious about people he passed in the street and a feeling of responsibility and dread came over him. He began constantly asking his girlfriend if people they had passed in the street were OK, and also looked behind very frequently. His girlfriend was unable to maintain the neutral response practised in the clinic and, as his requests became more desperate, she started to reassure him that everything was alright. Unfortunately, this merely increased his reassurance seeking. The day was a disaster.

Following this, exposure exercises were directed at graded confrontation to crowds in shops and markets and Mike soon regained his former optimism. Finally, a series of exercises was devised where Mike spent time with sharp knives, at first in different rooms to him and eventually in his pockets. At the end of treatment he was no longer troubled by urges to check and did not avoid any situations because of exposure to newspapers, etc. His anxiety was greatly reduced.

3 Mary

Mary's main difficulty was a nagging belief that if she thought about the devil she could bring evil down upon others and would be responsible for bad things happening to other people. This had not been resolved by religious counselling. She started out by trying to clarify her fears during the assessment interview, asking if it was in fact possible to cause evil by thinking evil. The nurse had to be very careful not to give her reassurance by discussing such concerns (since this had been done before by a priest but to no avail) and clearly explained to Mary why this approach was necessary. Mary readily agreed that discussing her concerns was only making them worse and understood why a ban on reassurance-seeking was necessary. The nurse used a bland and neutral statement, similar to that used by Mike's girlfriend, to help Mary when she felt the need to seek reassurance.

Active treatment took the form of deliberately bringing on the blasphemous thoughts and then refraining from both overt and covert neutralization. Mary found it relatively easy to eliminate her overt rituals but much harder to stop herself ruminating to rid herself of the blasphemous thoughts. She was able to bring on the thoughts by writing them down when they appeared spontaneously and then used this written record as a cue to provoke the thoughts at other times. She was asked to practise this regularly, for about an hour and not to engage in neutralizing her unpleasant thoughts with prayers or other anxiety-reducing thoughts. The purpose was to help her habituate to the anxiety provoked by her fearful thoughts so that she felt less need to neutralize them.

Mary found this very difficult. At first she only managed to hold her blasphemous thoughts for five minutes before cancelling them out. After a while she could go for fifteen minutes or more but still experienced some anxiety. At the end of treatment she rated herself as 60% improved overall with all overt rituals eliminated but some anxiety remaining about blasphemous thoughts. Her belief that she may be affecting others by her thoughts was reduced but not entirely removed.

4 John

Branded as a hypochrondriac, John had a very low self-esteem. When the rationale for both his fears and the treatment was explained to him he became both relieved and uneasy. He was glad that people were taking his problems seriously, but apprehensive about the treatment programme. A gradual approach was taken, the emphasis in the first stage being to reduce his rituals. He agreed with the nurse, his GP and his family to refrain from reassurance seeking and it was decided by everybody, including John, that if he felt the need to seek medical advice he should approach the nurse carrying out the behavioural programme. This decision was taken only after John had had one final thorough physical examination to exclude physical illness.

Initially, John was asked to reduce the amount of time he spent examining himself in front of the mirror, reading textbooks, etc. Self-examination was gradually reduced until he limited it to one minute each morning. He locked his textbooks away in a cupboard and did not consult them at all after the first treatment session. He stopped attending medical libraries and his GP's surgery. He also reduced the amount of time he spent asking his family to check for cancer on his body to 10% of what it was. All this was achieved in just a few weeks.

His fears of cancer, however, remained strong. To help him face these fears he was asked to bring on thoughts of cancer and sit quietly thinking them through. At first he did this with the nurse in an imaginal exposure session, imagining the progress of a cancer on his body from small mark to disfigurement and death. He repeated this at home, once a day. In addition, whenever he had thoughts about having cancer, he was asked to respond to them by paradoxically 'making them worse'. This was practically more difficult as he often had the thoughts during work when it was impossible to break off and concentrate on his fears. He therefore concentrated on the daily imaginal practice. This achieved its aim of reducing the frequency of his thoughts and intensity of his fears to less than 10% of what they were. He not only checked less, but felt less anxious about cancer generally. His mood improved and he was able to continue with his job. His relationship with both his family and his GP greatly improved.

5 Pauline

After writing down her hierarchy of fears, Pauline attempted to do some self-exposure exercises. This initially involved deliberately moving certain ornaments away from their usual places and then leaving them there for the rest of the day. Pauline could not manage this at all and so she asked that the nurse come to her house and do some practice with her. An exposure session of two hours was undertaken where Pauline went around the house disturbing the rigid set pattern of ornaments, etc. She was also helped to remake the bed, taking two minutes to put the clothes straight and then leave the room. Finally, Pauline walked around the house checking each electric socket and window once only before she and the nurse left the house to go to the local shops. Pauline was asked to stay out for a further two hours. This session was highly stressful to Pauline but the presence of the nurse helped her contemplate and complete actions that she had previously found impossible.

Since Pauline found these exercises almost impossible to do alone, an appointment was made for both herself and her husband to attend together. Pauline's husband was very hostile to this suggestion but eventually agreed. During the session her husband remained hostile towards treatment until they were shown a video explaining the nature of her problem and containing scenes of somebody being treated. After this he became more accepting of her problems and agreed to help her in exposure exercises at home. He stopped taking responsibility for household security and helped Pauline reduce her checking.

Specific exercises included checking the house last thing at night, initially together, each appliance, window, etc., only being checked once. Once she had been through a room her husband helped her resist the temptation to return and check again. She managed so well that she started to do this alone and the frequency of her checking reduced markedly. She still found excessive neatness a problem and so a series of exercises was devised where she actually rumpled the bed clothes up after making the bed. After a few days of this she was able to spend much less time in her rituals and started to feel her life was less dominated by her fears. By working together on her problems she and her husband became much closer. At the end of treatment she rated herself as 80% improved and, despite being somewhat more concerned about neatness and order than most people, hardly handicapped at all by her problems. Most importantly she knew how to tackle her fears and obsessions should they reoccur.

Ruminations

Ruminating, or the cognitive component of obsessions and compulsions, is generally harder for people to overcome. Ruminations take the form of intrusive thoughts or 'noxious stimuli to which patients have difficulty habituating' (Rachman, 1971). They are then neutralized by the person actively thinking other thoughts. These neutralizing thoughts may be directly antagonistic to the intrusive thoughts or they may be of a more ritualistic 'magical' nature – e.g. reciting a sequence of numbers a certain number of times. Some people repeat a thought identical to the original intrusive one in order to neutralize it, and it can be difficult to tease out just which thoughts are anxiety-increasing and which are anxiety-reducing in these cases. A very small number of clients do not admit to any neutralizing phenomena.

Many ruminations are provoked by distinct cues, so it is often possible to use cue-exposure to provoke the thoughts and then ask the person to refrain from neutralizing them. This is especially true where the person has to neutralize his thoughts before carrying out a certain activity. Exposure instructions have to emphasize carrying out the activity in the presence of the intrusive thoughts, i.e. *without* neutralizing them first.

Some people who ruminate do not seem able to carry out such exercises and cue-exposure may not be appropriate in all circumstances. 'Thought stopping' has been suggested as a treatment for ruminations since the mid-1970s. In this procedure clients are instructed by a variety of training methods to stop their thoughts as soon as they occur. How this is any different from neutralization is not clear and Rachman makes the point that thought stopping is an *ad hoc* technique that rests on its empirical strength (Rachman, 1971). Moreover, a controlled study (Stern *et al.*, 1973) found only slight improvements, with thought stopping appearing no better than the control treatment. It has largely been abandoned in favour of better approaches.

More recently other more promising techniques have been investigated. Salkovskis (1983) reported treating a person with ruminations by asking him to voice his unpleasant thoughts, audio-taping them and then playing them back to him for initially 20 minutes daily and then 90 minutes daily. This eventually reduced his ruminations to zero. The recording was of standardized and high intensity thoughts presented so rapidly that the client was unable to neutralize them.

Another example was reported by Headland and McDonald (1987) who also audio-taped their client's cognitive rituals but asked him to listen to the tape whenever he experienced a spontaneous rumination and to continue until the ruminations stopped. This too was highly successful in eliminating the client's ruminations, and in an extremely short time.

Much more investigation needs to be done on the treatment of obsessional ruminations, but there are indications that we may be able to treat such problems consistently well in the near future.

Obsessions and depression

The relationship between obsessions and depression is complex and varied but includes the following aspects:

1 Depression is a complication in one-third of people with obsessive-compulsive problems.
2 Obsessional behaviour is common in people with depressed mood.
3 13% of depressed people had obsessional problems prior to their depression (Gittleson, 1966).
4 A small percentage of people with obsessive problems lose their obsessions when they become depressed (Gittleson, 1966).
5 Many obsessional problems start from a period of depression but remain when the depression has lifted.
6 There is a higher incidence of depression in the families of people with obsessional problems.
7 Severe depression has been identified by Foa (1979) as one of the two conditions that makes clients less responsive to cue exposure and response prevention.

The link between depression and obsessions is the reason so much attention has been paid to anti-depressant treatments of obsessive-compulsive problems. We have already said that anti-depressants only work in the presence of depression and are not anti-compulsive drugs. However, should we be asked to treat a client with both obsessions and a severe depression we should always contact the responsible medical officer and discuss the prescription of an anti-depressant. Not to do so may mean that we persist with behavioural treatments under unfavourable conditions. If behavioural treatments fail under these conditions, such strategies may be subsequently rejected on the erroneous belief that they will be of no use.

Cue-exposure and response prevention has been shown to have durable effects on people's compulsive rituals beyond the end of treatment. Unfortunately, the same cannot be said of anti-depressants and depression. People's mood often relapses when anti-depressants are stopped but if cue-exposure and response prevention have been successful it is less likely that recurring depression will result in a relapse of the person's obsessional problem.

Thus, it is vitally important that we assess someone's mood correctly and if we suspect them to be depressed we should ask the responsible medical officer to see them and give his opinion. The prescription of an anti-depressant under these conditions is an appropriate use for such medication.

Overvalued ideas

Some people have intrusive thoughts which, while although in no sense delusional, they do not consider to be senseless in the way most people with obsessions do. For example, a person may actually *believe* he will catch leukaemia from others and that his rituals do actually protect him from this eventuality. People with these 'overvalued ideas' make up the second group identified by Foa (1979) who are less likely to respond to behavioural techniques.

As treatment methods have become established to help the majority of people with obsessions and compulsions, so attention has focused on this group. Research into this problem is in its infancy but some workers have used cognitive techniques to help the person re-examine his beliefs more realistically. Salkovskis and Warwick (1985) presented a single case where an irrational belief (that the client would get a disfiguring cancer by exposure to contaminated cosmetics) was altered by helping the client to re-examine her beliefs in the light of opposing evidence she generated herself. The strength with which the client believed this notion was reduced enough to allow successful exposure sessions to be undertaken where previously exposure had been unsuccessful.

Although overvalued ideas are relatively rare, the use of cognitive techniques may improve the outlook where they do exist. Such techniques are not a replacement for exposure, as Salkovskis and Warwick point out, but may facilitate habituation during exposure exercises when it had previously not occurred. Unless the client experiences difficulty habituating to obsessional cues, exposure should, however, remain the first treatment option.

Summary

In this chapter we have outlined effective strategies for helping people severely troubled by obsessions and compulsions. These problems are usually complex and convoluted but, by the use of a behavioural 'fear and avoidance' model, we have tried to make the nature of these problems clear. We have also cited experimental evidence to illustrate that for the majority of people with such problems the outlook is very positive. However, because each person with an obsessional problem will be unique we can only really scratch the surface of the subject. Our examples of clients we have treated is only a sample of the types of difficulties people with obsessional problems present with. We would strongly urge anybody considering treating people with such problems to read around the subject in more depth using some of the references at the end of this chapter. Doing that, and obtaining behavioural supervision at least initially, will ensure that these severely troubled and handicapped people get the help that was for so long denied them.

REFERENCES

Foa E. B. (1979). Failures in treating obsessive-compulsives. *Behaviour Research and Therapy*, 17, 169–176.

Foa E. B., Steketee G., Grayson J. B., Turner R. B., Latimer P. R. (1984). Deliberate exposure and blocking of obsessive-compulsive rituals: immediate and long term effects. *Behaviour Therapy*, 15, 450–472.

Ghosh A., Marks I. M., Carr A. C. (1988). Therapist contact and outcome of self-exposure treatment for phobias: a controlled study. *British Journal of Psychiatry*, **152**, 234–8.

Gittleson N. L. (1966). The effect of obsessions on depressive psychosis. *British Journal of Psychiatry*, **112**, 253–259, 261, 705, 883, 889.

Gray J. A. (1987). *The Psychology of Fear and Stress*. Second Edition. Cambridge: Cambridge University Press.

Headland K., McDonald B. (1987). Rapid audio-tape treatment of obsessional ruminations. *Behavioural Psychotherapy*, **15**, 188–192.

Hodgson R., Rachman S.J., Marks I.M. (1972). Treatment of obsessive compulsive neurosis; following up and further findings. *Behavioural Research Therapy*, **10**, 181–84.

Janet P. (1925). Psychological healing, vol. 2. New York: Macmillan.

Kazdin A. E., Wilson G. E. (1978). *Evaluation of Beheaviour Therapy: Issues, Evidence and Research Strategies*. Cambridge, Mass: Ballinger.

Malan D. (1979). *Individual Psychotherapy and the Science of Psychodynamics*. Surrey: Butterworths.

Marks I. M., Stern R., Mawson D., Cobb J., McDonald R. (1980). Clomipramine and exposure for obsessive compulsive rituals I and II. *British Journal of Psychiatry*, **135**, 1–25.

Mawson D., Marks I. M., Ramm L. (1982). Clomipramine and exposure for chronic obsessive-compulsive rituals: III. Two year follow-up and further findings. *British Journal of Psychiatry*, **140**, 11–18.

Meyer V. (1966). Modification of expectations in cases with obsessional rituals. *Behaviour Research and Therapy*, **4**, 273–280.

Rachman, S. (1971). Obsessional ruminations. *Behaviour Research and Therapy*, **9**, 229–235.

Rachman S. (1979). Obsessional-compulsive disorders, In '*The Psychosurgery Debate?*' (Valenstein, E. Ed.) San Fransisco: Freeman.

Rachman S. J., de Silva P. (1978). Abnormal and normal obsessions. *Behaviour Research and Therapy*, **16**, 233–248.

Rachman S., Cobb J., Grey S., McDonald B., Mawson D., Sartory G., Stern R. (1979). The behavioural treatment of obsessional-compulsive disorders, with and without clomipramine. *Behaviour Research and Therapy*, **17**, 467–478.

Rachman S. J., Hodgson R. J. (1980). *Obsessions and Compulsions*. Englewood Cliffs, New Jersey: Prentice Hall.

Roper G., Rachman S.J., Marks I.M. (1975). Passive and participative modeling in exposure treatment of obsessive compulsive neurotics. *Behavioural Research Therapy*, **13**, 271–79.

Salkovskis P. M. (1983). Treatment of an obsessional patient using habituation to audiotaped ruminations. *British Journal of Clinical Psychology*, **22**, 311–313.

Salkovskis P. M. (1985). Obsessional-compulsive problems: a cognitive-behavioural analysis. *Behaviour Research and Therapy*, **23**, 571–583.

Salkovskis P. M., Harrison J. (1984). Abnormal and normal obsessions – a replication. *Behaviour Research and Therapy*, **22**, 549–552.

Salkovskis P. M., Warwick H. M. C. (1985). Cognitive therapy of obsessive-compulsive disorders: treating treatment failures. *Behavioural Psychotherapy*, **13**, 243–255.

Slater E., Roth M. (1969). *Clinical Psychiatry*. 3rd Edition. London: Bailliére, Tindall and Cassell.

Stern R., Lipsedge M., Marks I. (1973). Obsessive ruminations: a controlled trial of a thought-stopping technique. *Behaviour Research and Therapy*, 11, 659–662.

Thoren P., Asberg M., Cronholm B., Jornestedt L., Traskman, L. (1980). Clomipramine treatment of obsessive-compulsive disorder. I. A. controlled clinical trial. *Archives of General Psychiatry*, 37, 1281–1285.

Chapter 11

Sexual diversity

There are two main ways in which our sexuality can become problematic. We might become dysfunctional in the sense that we have difficulty in carrying out the sexual behaviour that we are used to or expect to be able to do.

Alternatively, we may find that situations, people or objects which generate arousal are unacceptable to ourselves or society and we might then be termed as deviant. The word 'deviant' now has unacceptable connotations and 'diversity' has largely supplanted it.

This chapter will discuss sexual diversity, considering how this might be acquired and what therapeutic options exist. Sexual dysfunction will be discussed in the following chapter.

Sexual diversity – heterosexuality and homosexuality

We make no apology for including homosexuality in this discussion. Although most people now agree that homosexuality is an acceptable preference which should not be treated as an 'illness' and that individuals should not be disadvantaged as a result of their preference, it remains the case that some people do seek orientation change. When the option of counselling aimed at improving homosexual adjustment is rejected, we need to know what, if anything, we can offer. It is also the case that homosexuality has been much more extensively studied than any other diversity and it is invaluable to be able to include this data in any discussion of the area.

Biological issues

The norm for sexual orientation throughout the animal kingdom is attraction towards an adult member of the opposite sex and same species. Clearly, this makes a lot of adaptive sense in terms of procreation and, in most species, sexual behaviour is completely stereotyped and clearly innate.

To a large extent, this is also true of humans and it is very likely that a large part of our sexual orientation is determined by genetic and prenatal influences. It has been demonstrated (Reinisch, 1974) that sexual attraction and social role behaviour of chimpanzees can be influenced by levels of prenatal circulating steroids. What happens when testosterone levels are decreased, in the case of a male foetus, or increased in the case of a female, is that the chimp later shows both sexual and social behaviour characteristic of the opposite sex.

In chimps, as in humans, one of the behavioural patterns by which males and females can be distinguished is the frequency of 'rough-and-tumble-play'. When biological females show male levels of this activity and males show a decreased level more characteristic of females, their behaviour is described as being 'sex-dimorphic'.

If this is true of our nearest primate relatives, then we must be prepared to accept that such influences may play an important role in determining whether humans are heterosexual or homosexual. There is, in fact, evidence (Erdhardt and Baker, 1974) that 'tomboyish' behaviour in young girls is at least partly controlled by foetal steroid levels.

We also have to consider the possible influence of genetic factors. The concordance rate (how often both of a pair of twins show the same characteristic) for homosexuality is around 50% for monozygotic twins and about 15% for dizygotic twins. This argues strongly for an important role being played by genetic influences and further strengthens the importance of taking biological factors into account.

Of course, one of the costs that higher mammals pay for their increased plasticity of functioning is that they become liable to acquire through learning, a diversity of behaviour, not all of which will necessarily be useful long-term additions to their behavioural repertoire, and it also has to be accepted that life experiences can also be instrumental in determining sexual preference. However, models of orientation which ignore biological factors are seriously flawed as a brief discussion of the two major ones should make clear.

The psychoanalytic model of homosexuality

The currently preferred psychodynamic model, and there have been quite a few, says that the mothers of homosexual men establish close, often sexually explicit relationships with their sons. The sons, as a result, become hypersexual and fearful of heterosexual activity. This leads to compulsive homosexual behaviour. The fathers tend to be detached and hostile and fail to act as role models which would protect their sons from demasculation.

The evidence proposed in favour of this is that adult male homosexuals frequently report behaviour patterns in childhood more typical of female children.

While one could argue that this could be attributed to maternal overprotectiveness, it is much more parsimonious to assume that the 'sex-role dimorphism' (the adopting of behaviour more typical of the opposite gender) seen in chimpanzees following the deliberate manipulation of prenatal circulating steroids can also occur in humans due to accidental variations in these levels. If we accept this, then it may well be the case that fathers appear distant because of sex-dimorphic interests and behaviours in their sons.

The behavioural model of homosexuality

There have been a few of these as well and they can be dismissed even more succinctly than the psychoanalytic model.

Some models have depended heavily on the reinforcement of homosexual behaviour in adolescence and sometimes incorporate a 'critical period' for the development of orientation. The main problem for such a model is a complete lack of supporting data. There is no evidence that homosexual experiences in early adolescence is strongly predictive of later homosexual preference.

Other behavioural models have emphasized conditioned heterophobia but these find it very hard to explain the lack of exclusivity discussed below.

Criminality and sexuality

It is worth reminding ourselves at the outset of this discussion on treatment that many sex offences and acts of sexual diversity are carried out by individuals who commit these deeds in the context of generalized social deviancy. When there is evidence of a range of asocial behaviours and where there is no subjective resistance to carrying out the deviant act, we certainly would not consider behavioural treatment.

Treatment of unwanted sexuality

You will find that our description of treatment techniques in this section is considerably less detailed than that in others. This is because we firmly believe that, in particular, a therapist carrying out the treatment of sexual diversity requires extensive supervised experience in order to practise safely.

Covert sensitization is a technique which has a central role in the treatment of sexual diversity. It consists of the repeated pairing in fantasy of the activity which the individual wishes to discontinue with a fantasy of the social or personal consequences of that activity. Thus, an individual who wished to suppress homosexual urges in favour of a heterosexual adjustment might imagine a homosexual encounter which would be interrupted by a rehearsed fantasy of his wife, friends and family finding out about his previously secret activities.

These fantasies would be paired a large number of times (on average, over a hundred) and practised outside the clinic until the thoughts of the aversive consequences were an automatic accompaniment to thoughts of homosexual activity.

Usually, this approach would be paired with a technique called *Orgasmic reconditioning* in which the individual is encouraged to exchange fantasy of the unwanted behaviour for their target activity during masturbation or coitus.

Exclusivity and limits to change

It is worth bearing in mind that neither homosexuality nor heterosexuality are usually exclusive in terms of sexual attraction and are, by and large, not exclusive in behavioural terms either. For example, Kinsey *et al.* (1948) found that 37% of caucasian

American males reported at least one incident of homosexual arousal leading to orgasm although only 8% of his large sample reported being exclusively homosexual. More recently, McConaghy *et al.* (1979) found that 50% of 196 male and female medical students reported some homosexual attraction and 15% of the females and 8% of the males said that this attraction was as strong or stronger than their heterosexual attraction.

When we consider people who declare themselves to be homosexual, we find that 60% of males report arousal in heterosexual situations, 48% report heterosexual coitus at some time and 10% have a current heterosexual partner. The equivalent figures for women are 70%, 79% and 9%.

Behavioural psychotherapists are no longer faced with large numbers of homosexual people presenting for treatment because of the marked change in social attitude leading to greater acceptance of this preference. Recently, however, some males have been coming along because of concern about sexually transmitted immune deficiency syndromes.

It should be said very clearly that, as we will discuss in more detail later, behavioural treatment is a reasonably effective means of inhibiting unwanted sexual behaviour but there is simply

Table 11.1 Incidence of homosexuality.

Kinsey (1948)	Caucasian males
	• 37% had at least one experience of homosexual activity leading to orgasm
	• 25% had regular, but episodic, experiences
	• 18% had consistent, but not exclusive, homosexual experiences
	• 18% were exclusively, homosexual
Kinsey (1953)	Caucasian females
	• 20% reported arousal in a homosexual setting
	• 15% reported orgasm in a homosexual setting.
McConaghy (1979)	Medical students
	• 50% reported some homosexual attraction
	• 15% of females considered their homosexual attraction as greater than their heterosexual attraction
	• 8% of males considered their homosexual attraction as greater than their heterosexual attraction

no evidence that heterosexual arousal will occur following the suppression of homosexual behaviour in individuals where heterosexual arousal did not pre-exist. In other words, when homosexuality is primary in the sense that it does not co-exist with heterosexuality to some extent, there is no firm evidence that orientation change is possible, or desirable. Where both homosexuality and heterosexuality co-exist then behavioural psychotherapy can be useful in emphasizing the preferred orientation and suppressing the other in the same way that we would with other unwanted sexuality.

Fetishes, bondage and sadomasochism

The usual definition of a fetish is arousal to a part of the body which is not a secondary sexual characteristic, a deformity or an inanimate object (often an item of clothing).

Masochism refers to sexual arousal produced by the experience of pain or humiliation and Sadism to sexual arousal produced by inflicting pain or humiliation on another.

In bondage, an individual obtains gratification from being physically restrained or by restraining a partner.

Very little is known about the prevalence of these, often trivial, diversities but they are likely to be very common with the vast majority occurring in consensual circumstances – an ongoing sexual relationship or a commercial one.

This group of problems rarely makes demands on the clinician and we, therefore, know little about onset. Although treatment successes have been frequently reported these take the form of single cases from which it is difficult to come to firm conclusions about how successful treatment is in general. Covert sensitization and orgasmic reconditioning are the current specific approaches of choice. Although onset is unclear, it has been demonstrated (Rachman, 1966) that fairly durable fetishes can be acquired by simply pairing common fetish objects with sexually arousing material in a classical learning paradigm.

Exhibitionism

In men, this is the exposure of the penis to women, usually strangers, in a public place. It is the most common sex crime and appears to split into two groups. About half of those arrested and convicted are never convicted again. The other half, however re-offend very frequently indeed. Stricter judicial responses to further offences seems to have little effect and untreated individuals often have extensive forensic records.

They have been regarded traditionally as 'passive, shy, dependent and inhibited' as a group but it is unclear whether this is connected with the origins of the problem or the result of the social disruption caused by frequent offending.

While it would appear that the behaviour is usually acquired in adolescence and is strongly associated with sexual arousal at that stage, for many it becomes non-sexual and has an obsessive quality. A recent concept which is an attempt to explain this type of phenomenon is that of the 'Behaviour Completion Mechanism' which suggests that a well-practised sequence of behaviour may become extremely difficult to resist once it has been initiated.

Exhibitionism usually responds well to covert sensitization. There is an alternative technique called 'Shame Aversion' which would appear to be powerful although ethically problematic and unpleasant for the individual. It consists of the individual exposing himself to an appropriate audience who have been instructed to produce the response, usually mockery, which the individual most dreads encountering in the real situation.

While the outcome data are impressive, we regard the degree of aversiveness and the ethical dubiety of the shame aversion approach as mitigating against its use.

Non-aversion variants have been tried and the simplest involves the individual 'exposing' himself frequently while imagining unpleasant consequences and that does seem to have some success. A difficulty in establishing what is successful in treatment is that while the disorder is common, few are referred or refer themselves for psychological help and fewer still are seen until a decade or more after they begin offending.

Peter

Peter was first arrested for indecent exposure when he was 22. He had exhibited his erect penis to a 17-year-old girl in a pedestrian subway. Over the next five years, he was convicted a further eight times for similar offences and his most severe sentence was a three-month imprisonment. He was referred to us by a new probation officer on his release from his latest custodial sentence.

There was little of significance in his early history. He came from a stable family background and was the fifth of seven siblings. There was no psychological disorder in the family that he knew of. He had always been 'shy' and had been bullied at school although he had managed to make a few close friends. He left school at fifteen and worked first as a delivery boy and then as a counter hand in a butcher's shop.

He had two girlfriends during his teens but neither relationship had continued beyond a couple of weeks and he had never had sexual intercourse.

He was very interested in archaeology and read numerous books on the subject and was a keen chess player, although he mostly studied theory and played by post.

He seemed to have led a very isolated life over the decade before we saw him and was living in a probation hostel where he had been placed after his release from prison. He had no real friends and little contact with his family. His mother had died when he was 23 and his father had virtually 'cut him off' as a result of his offending.

He told us he wanted to stop exposing himself to avoid further imprisonment, which he found very unpleasant, but felt unable to control himself and feared re-offending if left to his own devices. He said he would like to have a girlfriend and, eventually, get married.

He had seven sessions of covert sensitization which consisted of him pairing the fantasy of exposing himself to an attractive female with a fantasy of being in prison and being humiliated by the other prisoners because of the nature of his offence. He practised this many times in our sessions with him and during assigned 'homework' periods and became able to refrain from exposing himself and was reporting no urge to do so at this stage. We then passed him to some colleagues who were able to include him in a social skills training group.

He persevered with the group and managed to enlarge his social opportunities. When we last saw him, he was not experiencing urges to exhibit himself, was socialising regularly but felt disappointed that he had not yet found a girlfriend.

Voyeurism

This can be defined as the attempt to view others in a state of undress without their consent in an attempt to obtain sexual gratification from this. Very little is known about its origins although it has been suggested that voyeuristic fantasy, and possibly activity, is a fairly normal developmental phenomenon. It has also been suggested that onset might be related to an accidental first experience but substantiating data for this is elusive.

It does seem to occur most commonly in shy adolescent males and to then acquire a compulsive quality and often co-exist with interpersonal sexual behaviour. There is very little treatment data, but there are a number of single case studies which report success and covert sensitization is probably the best choice.

Transvestism and transexualism

These were always considered to be the same thing until Benjamin (1954) made the distinction between those who dress in opposite-sex clothes for sexual gratification and those who do so because they have a sense of identity with the opposite sex.

By and large, they can be considered to be separate entities which happen to share the wearing of clothes of the opposite sex although, as we shall see, there may be a degree of transition in some transvestites and a level of ambiguity in some transexuals.

Transvestism

Transvestism is best considered a fetish and appears to be most usually acquired in adolescence when it is used as a means of generating arousal and does not appear to interfere with normal sexual development.

In later life, if the individual continues to cross-dress then sexual gratification appears to become less important (in one study, only 12% considered it a significant motivation) and relaxation or a feeling of attractiveness become the most common reasons given. Some of this group have been reported to make the transition to transexualism.

Very few come for treatment and, while covert sensitization might be successful initially, it is our impression that relapses are common. It seems likely that most transvestites find a socially acceptable outlet for their preference, with some even being paid highly for cross-dressing on peak-time television.

Transexualism

Transexualism refers to a strong wish to be, or a belief that one is psychically, a member of the opposite sex. The incidence has been estimated at 1:34,000 males and 1:108,000 females.

A distinctive sign is an insistent demand for sex-change surgery and, if this is denied, mutilation (e.g. self-castration or mastectomy) has been reported. They frequently report that their desire or belief began very early in life and continued powerfully throughout although a proportion may acquire such feelings gradually following a period of apparent transvestism.

Social and learning influences seem unlikely to be able to account for the phenomenon. As an example, male children suffering from pseudohermaphroditism due to 5-α-reductase deficiency are almost all raised as females because of the appearance of their genitalia. At puberty, their maleness becomes obvious and the vast majority (17 out of 18 in one study) are able to adopt male identity.

There is no recorded case of an undoubted transexual being helped by any form of psychotherapy and behavioural methods have been exhaustively tried.

The outcome of reconstructive surgery is unclear. Many report subjective improvement although observers may continue to note psychological and social adjustment problems.

Paedophilia

It is difficult to summarize the literature on this topic because of a lack of an agreed definition. Some authors use definitions like 'sexual activity of a post-pubertal person with a pre-pubertal person' while others emphasize age differences. Operationally, it is probably best to combine the two to produce something like 'adult sexual interest in pre-pubertal individuals or individuals less than 16 years of age when the adult is over 25'.

Another difficulty in the way of understanding of this phenomenon is that it is a highly emotive subject which most people, particularly parents, find difficult to consider dispassionately and logically. This is also fuelled by the lurid and prurient way in which legal proceedings are reported in popular newspapers.

Perhaps because of the inherent emotionality in the topic, there is little public consideration of the complexity of the topic. One step that is helpful in attempting an understanding is to classify paedophilic activities as in Figure 11.1.

As soon as we begin to consider the different subgroups, we begin to discover important ways in which they differ from one another which will influence our management of the problem and we also uncover gaps in our knowledge which we clearly need to make good.

Incestuous heterosexual paedophilia is almost certainly the most common. The real incidence is almost impossible to assess although Lukianowicz (1972) reported 26 cases of father-daughter incest in 650 unselected females. Only two of these fathers had been charged with the offence and this may provide an indication of what is almost certainly a low reporting (and, therefore, detection) rate.

Recent UK interest in the topic, highlighted by the Butler–Schloss inquiry into events in Cleveland have hinted at a high prevalence but have obscured the issue by focussing on anal intercourse which is one of the least probable activities to take place in this context. The majority of offenders in this category do not have generalized sexual attraction to young people and usually have a conventional heterosexual orientation. They are better considered to have a failure in their ability to create effective boundaries in their relationships to their children (and, strikingly commonly, stepchildren) rather than to be sexually deviant. This does have management implications. When an incestuous relationship is suspected or discovered, the inevitable consequence is the removal of the father from the household. In most cases, that is an effective end to the problem since the perpetrator is not usually a danger to young people in general. In any case, custodial remands and sentences are almost invariable and it is not our view

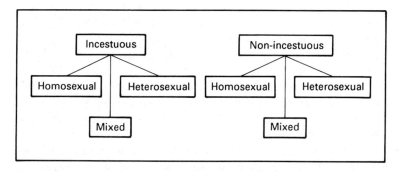

Figure 11.1 A Taxonomy of paedophilia

that successful treatment is possible under these circumstances.

Most people would say that incarceration was an appropriate response to such offences. That may be so, but it is worth pausing to consider the plight of the potential offender who might spend months and years wrestling with increasing temptation. There are horrifyingly few mental health professionals who are aware of the treatment facilities available and are conversant with the outcome data.

Given this, it is hardly surprising that the relatively unsophisticated individuals who are the majority of offenders are unable to find their way to help until, almost invariably, it is too late. Because they are so rarely seen before forensic involvement, it cannot be demonstrated that behavioural approaches would work. On the other hand, we have no reason to suggest that they would not be effective.

Incestuous Homosexual Paedophilia has been reported, both in association with heterosexual incest and as a separate entity. Prevalence is unknown and treatment reports are sparse.

Non-Incestuous Heterosexual Paedophilia refers to a generalized interest in young females who are, most commonly, in the immediate pre- or post-pubertal years.

It is usually, but not invariably, an accompaniment to adult heterosexuality although, even then, interest in young girls usually exceeds that to adults.

Offenders generally seek consensual contact with children with force occurring on about 2% of incidents. As far as is known, reporting rates are high and detection latency (the time between first offence and arrest) low in comparison with other sexual crimes.

There is considerable experience of behavioural treatment of this group although no controlled studies. The reason for the lack of controlled outcome research in this area, in sharp contrast to other areas of behavioural psychotherapy, stems from a reluctance to conduct research in such a sensitive area which involves withholding, even temporarily, what our experience informs us is the most effective. From a scientific point of view this is, admittedly, sloppy thinking which in this instance is overridden by a moral imperative.

However, based on the uncontrolled data which has amassed over the years, a combination of covert sensitization, orgasmic reconditioning and adult sexual skills training appears a potent approach. It is our impression that virtually all who comply with treatment and had some pre-existing adult sexual interest cease to have paedophile interest and activity after treatment. It is unclear how successful, in the long term, our treatment approaches are for that small group who lack adult sexual interest before treatment. The key to maintainance of treatment gains would appear to be the establishment of stable adult sexuality. Follow-up needs to be protracted and regular and it is our approach to encourage 'open-access' should the individual experience any difficulty.

John

John was 45 when we first saw him. He was a labourer on building sites and was married with two boys, aged 14 and 17.

We were treating his wife because of agoraphobic problems and, although we had already met him during our assessment of her, were surprised when he requested a consultation for himself. He told us that he was attracted to young girls of 12–14 years of age, particularly if they wore school uniforms.

He told us that he had been particularly attracted to girls of that age group since his late teens. He told us a number of stories about how he had enticed schoolgirls onto the building sites where he worked and about the sexual fondling which had taken place. He had been arrested once by the police but released for lack of evidence. There had been no coercive incidents that we could determine.

He had been brought up in South London and was very much a product of the working-class tradition of the area. His father had run a market stall until his death from liver cancer and his mother had continued with this until she retired at 68. He was the third of five children. They all lived locally and were in regular contact with each other. There was nothing untoward about his upbringing although his father drank a lot and there were some rows between his parents.

He had an uneventful childhood and was very much an average scholar. Although he had been in a large number of jobs since leaving school, he had never been unemployed. He was a moderate drinker and had never smoked.

He had always been sexually active. He was unable to recall all of his sexual liaisons but it seemed clear that he had always had at least one relationship ongoing at any time. Besides this, he

*reported masturbating at least once per day, even in the context
of a continuing sexual relationship. He told us that he always
fantasized about young girls in school uniforms when he masturbated.*

*He was most likely to fantasize, masturbate, and indulge in
sexual fondling with schoolgirls when he did not have a continuing
sexual relationship and, during his marriage, had found it difficult
to resist these urges around the birth of their children and when
their relationship was strained and intercourse was infrequent.*

We saw him and his wife together and instituted a sensate focus
programme in an effort to enhance their rather stagnant sexual
life. We instructed him in Orgasmic Reconditioning techniques
which involved him in agreeing to masturbate only while thinking
about adult females and spent five sessions on covert sensitization
which required him to pair fantasies about sexual activity with
schoolgirls with imagery about the consequences of one of his
brothers finding out about his proclivities.

The outcome was that he and his wife started to fully enjoy
intercourse for the first time in years and that he reported a
complete loss of interest in schoolgirls. He is, however, the kind
of person who we would always want to maintain a regular
follow-up with. At three years, things remain stable but we will
continue to see both him and his wife at regular intervals over
the next decade.

Non-Incestuous Homosexual Paedophilia shares much in common with Heterosexual but there are some important differences.
Firstly, reporting rates appear to be much lower and detection
latency considerably longer. One retrospective survey suggested
that the average number of contacts offenders in this category had
with young people before their first arrest was over 300.

Secondly, there is a group of men who are attracted only to
pre-pubertal boys and have never had any adult sexual feelings
or experience, either homosexual or heterosexual. It would appear
that psychological interventions may give them greater control
over their urges but where no adult sexual interest emerges or
was already in existence, the long term prognosis is uncertain.

In contrast, those who do have some adult sexual interest –
and this is the majority – do very well with the combination of
behavioural approaches described above.

The disassociation between homosexual paedophilia and adult
homosexuality is striking and contradicts a still-common prejudice.

Adult homosexuals show less sexual interest, when measured physiologically, in children than do heterosexuals. To put it another way, there is less overlap between adult homosexuals and homosexual paedophiles than there is between adult heterosexuals and heterosexual paedophiles.

Summary

Sexual diversity is, in many of its manifestations, a treatable entity. Some diverse behaviours, particularly paedophilia, arouse such distaste in the population as a whole that rational debate is difficult. However, it is our view that the single step which would reduce the incidence of exploitation and abuse of children would be greater professional and public awareness that effective interventions are available. Whether that can be achieved, remains to be seen.

REFERENCES

Benjamin H. (1954). 'Transexualism and Transvestism as Psychosomatic and Somatopsychic Syndromes.' *American Journal of Psychotherapy*, 8, 219–230.

Erhardt A. A., Baker S. W. (1974). 'Fetal androgens, human central nervous system differentiation and behaviour sex differences.' In *'Sex Differences in Behaviour'*, (Friedman, R. C. ed.) New York: Wiley.

Kinsey A. C., Pomeray W. B., Martin C. E. (1948). *'Sexual Behaviour in the Human Male'*. Philadelphia: W. B. Saunders.

Kinsey A. C., Pomerany W. B., Martin C. F., Gebhard P. H. (1953). *Sexual behaviour in human female*. Philadelphia:, W. B. Saunders.

Lukanowicz N. (1972). 'Incest.' *British Journal of Psychiatry*, 120, 301–313.

McConaghy N., Armstrong M. S., Birrell P. C., Buhrich N. (1979). 'The incidence of bisexual feelings and opposite sex behaviour in medical students.' *Journal of Nervous and Mental Disease*, 167, 685–688.

Rachman S. (1966). Sexual fetishism: an experimental analogue. *Psychological Record*, 16, 293–296.

Reinisch J. (1974). Fetal hormones, the brain and human sex differences. *Archives of Sexual Behaviour*, 3, 51–90.

Chapter 12

Sexual dissatisfaction

Most people consider the enjoyment of a fulfilling sexual life as one of their basic needs and rights. In the way of this, there may be difficulties of opportunity or legality but, very much more commonly, there may be difficulties in functioning which curtail or prevent desired activities. It could be claimed that sexual dysfunction, as it is usually known, is the most common psychological problem since virtually anyone who is sexually active can give instances and times when they were unable to function as usual.

Causes of sexual dysfunction

Sexual dysfunction is one of those areas where it is important to be aware of possible physical causes of difficulty as well as psychological ones. Good practice in sexual therapy involves checking for physical causes. The most common can be grouped into three.

Substance use and abuse
Although moderate acute alcohol consumption can enhance sexual arousal and enjoyment, both acute and chronic excessive consumption have a serious effect on sexual functioning. Acute over-indulgence produces diminished or absent sexual responses in both sexes. Chronic alcohol abuse produces virtually universal sexual problems because of hormonal abnormalities and peripheral neuropathy.

Interestingly, marihuana has been reported as causing sexual dysfunction in male regular users despite its reputation as an aphrodisiac. Opiates certainly lead to sexual dysfunction in both sexes but it is unclear to what extent this is due to specific effects and how much to the generally debilitating effects of uncontrolled dependency.

Many prescribed medications cause lack of sexual interest, ability or enjoyment. The list certainly includes diuretics, anti-hypertensives, antidepressants, phenothiazines and anticonvulsants.

Endocrine disorder

The list is long but the commonest are *Addison's disease, Cushing's syndrome, Diabetes mellitus, Hypopituatarism* and both *Hyper-* and *Hypo-thyroidism*. In particular, diabetes is a common cause of erectile problems in the male and is worth checking for routinely.

Other physical disorders

Essentially, any significant disorder of the cardio-vascular system (e.g. *arteriosclerosis, hypertension*), respiratory system (e.g. *chronic bronchitis* or *asthma*), genito-urinary function (*prostatitis, vaginitis*) or central nervous system (*epilepsy, multiple sclerosis* or *spinal cord lesion*) can give rise to sexual difficulty and treatment of the organic disorder should always, when available, take precedence over psychological intervention.

Psychological causes, although more common, are less certain and consistent in their effects but almost certainly include anxiety about sex or sexual performance, traumatic sexual experiences, lack of sexual knowledge, marital discord, disinterest and infidelity, depression, anxiety and poor self-esteem. Sometimes, an unfortunate series of sexual accidents appears to be the precipitant.

Treatment

The history of treatment of sexual difficulties is an interesting one. For most of this century, very little was available. The medical and allied professions were slow to discard Victorian attitudes towards sexual matters and most sexual dysfunction was untreated. Anorgasmia in women was regarded as normal and premature ejaculation in men as acceptable provided procreation was unimpaired. Psychoanalytically based treatment was available only to a few and, in any case, sexual dysfunction was considered by many psychoanalysts to be untreatable.

There was some behaviour therapy, based on Wolpe's systematic desensitization approach, during the late 1950s and early 1960s but not much, although some successes were reported. The focus in both the psychoanalytic approach and the early behavioural one was always individual therapy.

The publication of 'Human Sexual Inadequacy' by Masters and Johnson in 1970 completely revolutionized and, largely, initiated the field of sex therapy.

Suddenly, the focus was on the couple and treatment approaches were based on symptom removal and stemmed largely from their earlier book 'Human Sexual Response' which was the first scientific account of sexual functioning and which, in itself, moved thinking about sexuality from armchair speculation to consideration of empirical data.

The first accounts of treatment from Masters and Johnson told of astonishingly high success rates which have never been fully replicated. However, their approach was, and remains, so vastly superior to anything that went before that it rapidly achieved virtually complete dominance among practitioners from a variety of theoretical positions. Although Masters and Johnson did not base their approach explicitly on behavioural principles, behavioural psychotherapists have done more than therapists from other orientations to refine and test the basic approach. Where a treatment approach is not specifically attributed in this chapter it can safely be assumed to have been originated by Masters and Johnson.

The general approach of Masters and Johnson involves a series of stages which are general to all disorders. These are:

Non-genital sensate focus

Throughout treatment, couples are instructed that they must put time aside each day in a room where they won't be interrupted in order to carry out homework assignments.

During the Non-Genital Sensate Focus phase, which usually covers the first few sessions, the couple are instructed to refrain from attempts at intercourse and not to touch each others' genitals or the woman's breasts. Instead they have to concentrate on giving and receiving pleasure from touching, caressing and massaging other parts of the body. This stage is important because the ban on intercourse explicitly removes the anxiety about performance which is an issue for most couples. Secondly, physical expressions of affection are often missing from the interaction of couples with a sexual dysfunction because of fears from one or both of them that this might be misinterpreted as an invitation to sexual activity. Most therapists will see the couple every week in order to trouble-shoot any difficulties the couple have during these sessions.

Genital sensate focus

When the couple have reported a number of successful sessions of non-genital activity, they can move to the next stage which allows the genital areas to be touched as well as other parts of the body. The ban on intercourse remains in force and the object is not to achieve orgasm but to experience sexual arousal in a non-threatening context with the emphasis on discovering what gives pleasure to the partner. This will need to last for three to four weeks before most couples are ready to move onto the next stage.

Vaginal containment

When genital sensate focus is regularly found pleasurable, the couple are then instructed to include penetration and vaginal containment in their repertoire. Again, the focus is not on intercourse or the achievement of orgasm but on a non-threatening experience for both partners and the penis being in the vagina. The couple are encouraged to practise this two or three times during a homework session for as long as they find it comfortable. Consideration may need to be given to different sexual positions and the couple may need instruction on these with the aid of drawings or photographs.

Vaginal containment with movement

Most couples will have, by now, broken the ban on intercourse and, if specific treatment exercises have been successful, will have completed the active phase of treatment. However, when this is not the case, containment combined with gradually increasing amounts of movement from whichever partner is most appropriate (usually the woman) provides a smooth and graduated route to this.

This concludes our necessarily brief look at the general principles of the approach which behavioural psychotherapists have taken using Masters and Johnson as a model. We will now consider the various types of sexual dysfunction in turn and say something about possible psychological causes and the special features of their treatment. Despite their emphasis on treating problems as something which exists in a relationship between two people, Masters and Johnson classified dysfunction on an individual basis and that influence largely remains today and we shall, to a large extent, have to follow this. However, we can begin with a couple of problems which are common to both genders.

Lack of sexual interest

Masters and Johnson made no mention of this but it has, in recent years, become regarded as a major sexual problem. It is most common when there is disparity between the sexual drives of the partners or where both lack interest in sex but desire children. Some of this is biological. Men reach their peak of sexual activity in late teenage years whereas women more usually reach their sexual peak in the late thirties. In addition, more men marry younger women than *vice versa* and so this problem is statistically likely. It also occurs in couples who have been together for some time and who have become bored with each other and their regular sexual activity. In some instances, lack of interest extends only to a regular partner and in others it is generalized.

A sensate focus programme is usually helpful, particularly when the therapist emphasizes exploration and novelty. There is no specific intervention which is universally accepted although some workers (e.g. Gillan, 1987) are enthusiastic about the use of erotica, pornography and training in fantasy. It is our experience that a sizeable proportion of people find this unacceptable although some, particularly those who have never experienced average levels of interest, can be helped by such an approach.

Anorgasmia

It is still common for failure to achieve orgasm to be discussed as a problem which only affects women. It is widely assumed that if a man ejaculates, then he is also orgasmic. Indeed, they are often discussed as if synonymous. However, it is our firm clinical experience that, if given the message that it is acceptable to say so, a number of men will say that their enjoyment of ejaculation is absent or diminished. This may be allied to a lack of sexual interest, but not necessarily. Treatment of such individuals is essentially the same as for ejaculatory failure (see below).

The difficulty some women have in achieving orgasm has been widely discussed, both in the academic and clinical press and in more popular media. An important distinction to be made is between situational and non-situational anorgasmia. When orgasms can be achieved during masturbation but not during intercourse (i.e. situational) then it can be very helpful to encourage the woman to teach her partner how to give her pleasure during the phase of genital sensate focus. The simplest way to do this is for her to guide his hand during genital caressing in order to help him replicate her actions during masturbation. When orgasm can be achieved in this way, clitoral stimulation can be applied by either party (aided, in some cases, by a vibrator) during the phase of vaginal containment. Some couples are then able to be routinely orgasmic during intercourse. Some women, because of the variety of human sexual response, will always require clitoral stimulation to achieve orgasm. They should be firmly reassured that this is entirely within normal limits and not a negative reflection on themselves. This cannot be emphasized enough. There is a wide variation in sexual responsivity, just as there is in many attributes, and a fair number of referrals to sexual dysfunction clinics are of individuals (both men and women) with totally unrealistic expectations of the responsivity of themselves and their partners.

When anorgasmia in women is non-situational, then it is usual to start with a masturbation programme which involves examination and exploration of her genitals, the use of guided masturbation techniques and sexual fantasy. If this approach is necessary, it should invariably be carried out by a female therapist. When orgasm is achievable in this way, and it usually is, then the approach outlined above for situational anorgasmia can be followed.

Vaginismus

This refers to an involuntary contraction of the vaginal muscles when penetration of the vagina is anticipated. It renders intercourse painful or impossible and, in severe cases, prevents medical vaginal examination. Although Masters and Johnson recommended the use of graded dilators, this practice is now rare. Most practitioners now encourage genital self-examination, followed by limited vaginal penetration by the women's own finger, gradually increasing the degrees of penetration and moving eventually to two fingers. This would usually be occurring in parallel to sensate focus exercises and, during genital sensate focus, the man should replicate gradual finger penetration. At the vaginal containment stage the woman would begin to guide, under *her* control, her partner's penis into her vagina. Gradually, over several homework sessions they would move to complete penetration. It is particularly important that confidence in vaginal containment is achieved before any movement is attempted. It cannot be emphasized too strongly that, throughout the treatment programme, the woman should feel that she is in complete control. Provided these principles are followed, treatment failures with vaginismus are rare.

Jane

Jane was 25 when we saw her. She was engaged to be married and both she and her fiance, Bill, came to the clinic. They explained that, although they both wanted to, they had been unable to have sexual intercourse and were worried that they should not get married until they had solved this problem.

When seen alone, Jane told us that she had never been able, despite attempts with three previous partners, to allow penetration. She described herself as panicking and 'curling up in a ball' if there was even a remote possibility of penetration taking place. She clearly described involuntary contraction of her vaginal muscles and said she had never been able to insert tampons or have a gynaecological examination.

She was unable to say why she had this problem. There was nothing remarkable about her upbringing or background and her family did not have a particularly negative attitude towards sexual matters. We arranged to have her examined by a female doctor who confirmed our diagnosis of vaginismus and that there was no physical problem.

When we talked to Bill, he confirmed Jane's story and was clearly sympathetic to her anxiety which occurred shortly after the start of any episode of petting. He had enjoyed a satisfactory sex life with both his previous partners.

We were able to move straight to genital sensate focus with them because their current physical contact more or less replicated the non-genital phase.

We firstly asked her to attempt very minor penetration using one finger when she felt maximally aroused but made it clear that she should not attempt anything further. She found it possible to do this and over the next two weeks she became able to fully insert two fingers during sensate focus. We then asked her to guide one of her boyfriend's fingers into her vagina during sensate focus and she, despite initial anxiety, managed to do this on the third attempt. After another two weeks, he was able to insert two fingers fully.

Finally, she was asked to guide Bill's penis into her vagina but not to attempt any movement. However, at this stage they broke the treatment rules and proceeded to intercourse. This went well and they reported that they had enjoyable intercourse each day for the four days preceding their appointment.

They experienced no further problems and we received a piece of wedding cake.

Erectile difficulties

If one wanted an example of how readily anxiety can impair sexual performance then psychogenic erectile failure would be the one to use. Once a man begins, for whatever reason, to worry whether erection will occur, he will inevitably find difficulty in achieving and maintaining one.

Sensate focus provides a very successful platform for demonstrating this. If you combine non-genital sensate focus with the strict instruction that the man should try *not* to have an erection, spontaneous erections invariably occur. However, if the couple attempt to break the ban on intercourse at this point, loss of erection is the usual result.

At the genital stage of sensate focus, a special technique needs to be introduced. This is usually called the 'waxing and waning' technique and consists of instructing the couple to cease all physical contact as soon as a full erection occurs and to wait until it diminishes before resuming caressing. This needs to be repeated three or four times in each session.

This procedure directly contradicts the usual expectation of the man that an erection, once lost, is gone forever.

Vaginal containment should be brief with insertion directed by the woman and needs to follow the 'waxing and waning' principle before containment with movement is attempted.

Treatment is usually successful, although there is a tendency for relapse to occur if a catastrophic view is taken of any minor erectile difficulty. This can be minimized by warnings about the likelihood of recurrence and instructions on how to deal with it if it occurs.

Viraj

Viraj was 42 and had been married for 16 years when he came to the clinic. He was worried that he had been unable to have sexual intercourse with his wife for the past 3 years because he found that he lost his erection as soon as he attempted penetration. Theirs had been an arranged marriage, was a happy one, and they had four children. His wife did not attend and he explained that she spoke little English and, in any case, that it would not be considered culturally appropriate for her to discuss such matters with us. We explained that we felt it diminished his chances of achieving his aim of being able to readily maintain his erection regularly during intercourse if his wife was not involved in treatment but, although accepting this, he was clear that this was not possible.

He was a rather rigid and anxious man who worked as an accountant and liked everything 'black and white'. He wasn't interested in considering how his problem had come about but was adamant that he wanted it 'fixed'.

We therefore asked him to refrain from intercourse until further notice, only engage in non-sexual caressing, and to explain to his wife that he was doing so on our instruction.

We instructed him in 'waxing and waning' in the context of masturbation. He was a bit reluctant to do this regularly because he had masturbated only very infrequently since his marriage. However, he agreed when we said we were 'prescribing' this as a treatment exercise.

He was able to do this and regularly practised gaining and losing an erection although he preferred not to masturbate to ejaculation.

Because we did not have the involvement of his wife, we 'stalled' him at this point until he confessed to us that, after several weeks of this regime, they had resumed intercourse.

He still had occasional difficulty in maintaining erection and continued to do so throughout follow-up but was pleased that he had considerably less difficulty than before.

Premature ejaculation

The specific intervention for this comes in at the genital sensate focus stage. It has much in common with 'waxing and waning' in that the approach, referred to as 'stop-start', asks that the woman stimulates her partner's penis by whatever means they find most acceptable until he signals that any more stimulation will lead inevitably to orgasm. At this point, they stop and wait until this feeling has passed. This is repeated several times during any session, with ejaculation being allowed on the final stimulation.

This approach predates Masters and Johnson who recommended the 'squeeze technique' which involves the woman applying firm pressure to the glans and shaft of the penis (it is much easier to demonstrate this on a model than to describe it) in a way which physiologically inhibits ejaculation. This also is repeated several times a session.

Again, vaginal containment is the next stage and should be confidently manageable before movement during containment takes place. A female superior position is usually recommended initially as this allows the woman to maintain the 'stop-start' principle during this phase.

Outcome is usually good, with compliant people failing very rarely indeed.

Ejaculatory incompetence

One occasionally encounters this problem in a primary form, in the sense that ejaculation has never occurred in that individual either awake or asleep. Our experience of treating such people, by a variety of means which usually begin with individual masturbation programmes, is an unhappy one and a sifting of the literature indicates that this is a fairly universal experience. If it is secondary, in the sense that failure occurs only during attempts at intercourse, then the outlook is much better. The couple are helped to find a way, usually during genital sensate focus, that will induce ejaculation. They will then attempt to ensure that ejaculation occurs closer and closer to the vagina until ejaculation inside the vagina is achieved. Outcome with secondary ejaculatory incompetence seems reasonable, although there are not enough reports to make a definitive statement on this.

Summary

We have deliberately not tried to provide a manual for the treatment of any of the psychological disorders described in this book, although we have attempted to convey the essentials of the therapy process involved. Such manuals do exist, although we would be keen to argue that adequate training and supervision are essential prerequisites for therapy.

This is *certainly* the case for sexual problems. The information provided here is in no way adequate for the inexperienced to contemplate unsupervised treatment of sexual diversity or dysfunction.

However, the intention is that this, and the preceding chapter, will have illustrated that the problems of sexuality are, by and large, treatable entities and that we should be attempting to steer many more people down that path.

REFERENCES

Hawton K. (1985). *Sex Therapy: A Practical Guide*. Oxford: Oxford University Press.
Gillan P. (1987). *Sex Therapy Manual*. Oxford: Blackwells.
Masters W. H., Johnson V. E. (1966) *Human Sexual Response*. Mass. Little Brown.
Masters W. H., Johnson V. E. (1970). *Human Sexual Inadequacy*. Mass. Little Brown.

Part 4

Chapter 13

Innovations in nurse behaviour therapy

Introduction

In the preceding chapters we have described the practice of behavioural psychotherapy and detailed the client groups for whom there is a wealth of evidence that behavioural techniques are effective. However, the behavioural model and the techniques employed within it have a wider application. Many nurses trained in behavioural psychotherapy have used their skills with other groups of clients. Behavioural psychotherapy itself is a rapidly developing area, with the recognition that the approach has so much to give to health care in general. This chapter will look at some of the innovative work that nurses have started or have been involved with.

We hope to develop the idea that the basic skills of problem solving, goal setting and evaluation can be applied to many different areas. The evidence may not be as strong in these other areas, but it might be that if we wrote this book in 10 years time research will have progressed far enough to provide this evidence. Nurses have contributed hugely to the development of the behavioural approach by innovative applications of behavioural techniques with new client groups. Often this work has been done with single or just a few cases. It is from the indications supplied by such work that the impetus to carry out more detailed investigation comes.

We cannot, of course, hope to cover every area in which the behavioural approach has been used. This chapter is a taster in which the reader can sample some examples of different applications of behavioural psychotherapy.

Behavioural approaches to chronic pain

It is now increasingly common to see nurses working in pain clinics and there are many articles in the nursing journals, which discuss pain management and the role of the nurse.

Before considering behavioural approaches to pain management we must first briefly examine different models used to understand pain.

The most common view of pain is the disease model. This tends to see pain as the result of tissue damage leading to peripheral nerve stimulation which is experienced by the brain centrally. Medical procedures aim to discover and treat the damage but, if these are initially unsuccessful, other diagnostic procedures are used which can themselves cause more pain – iatrogenic damage.

Pain, like any other emotional response is more complex than this. Different people respond to identical tissue damage in different ways. An individual's perception and response to pain does not just depend upon the damage itself. Personality, cultural expectations, previous pain experience and the aversive or reinforcing aspects of behaviours associated with pain are all important.

A behavioural model of pain seeks to understand the person's response to pain and determine what makes the experience an individual one. The interaction of *pain behaviours* with the person's environment may reinforce avoidance or confrontation with the pain. If pain behaviours are followed by reinforcing consequences they are more likely to be repeated. This can lead to the continuation of pain behaviour long after the original tissue damage has been repaired.

1 Contingencies

Some examples of this are the prescription of analgesic medication, rest and social attention. If drugs are prescribed to be taken when needed (prn) they are likely to be taken ever more frequently to avoid the chance that pain will occur. People must also communicate suffering to get the drugs so this behaviour is likely to increase. Where rest is prescribed, or reduced exercise, people often let the level of pain be their guide to how much activity they can undertake. If rest is reinforcing, activity is likely to reduce. Social attention will also be reinforcing if emission of pain behaviours is followed by more attention from those around us.

All these factors are called *contingencies*. Medication, social attention and perceived reduction in pain become *contingent* on an increased frequency of pain behaviour, which therefore increases.

2 Fear and avoidance

People may respond to pain in two different ways, by avoiding or confronting it. Many of the factors listed above, such as personality and previous pain experience can decide how a person will respond to pain. The *fear and avoidance* model of pain attempts to explain the effects, not only on the person's psychological response but also on the actual level of pain itself, of confronting or avoiding pain. Figure 13.1 illustrates the fear and avoidance model.

Fear, as with phobias, can lead to avoidance. The more one avoids a feared situation, the more difficult it becomes to confront and the more frightened one becomes then the more one avoids. The same applies to pain. Avoiding pain by reducing activity and taking increasing amounts of pain killers leads to exaggerated perceptions of pain with restricted ability to function normally. The person does not *calibrate* his pain. All pain comes to be seen as possessing the same intensity and is thus to be avoided.

An example is the man suffering from intermittent claudication – a narrowing of the arteries which produces muscular pain on exercise – who knows he gets pain if he walks 50 metres. He fears the pain and so only walks 40 metres. After a while he begins to fear, and perhaps experience, pain at 40 metres so he only walks 30 from then on. Eventually he cannot walk more than a few metres without having to stop and he becomes increasingly handicapped. He has come to perceive the pain after walking just a few metres as equivalent to severe pain on walking longer distances. He has learned that he can avoid pain by stopping and so applies this principle to any occurrence of pain. Because he has not calibrated his pain fears and perceptions against a range of pain experiences he avoids equally all chances of experiencing pain.

A number of nurses trained in behavioural psychotherapy have used techniques derived from such models in order to help people suffering from chronic pain. Contingency management, relaxation, pain focusing and exposure to pain cues are all useful techniques.

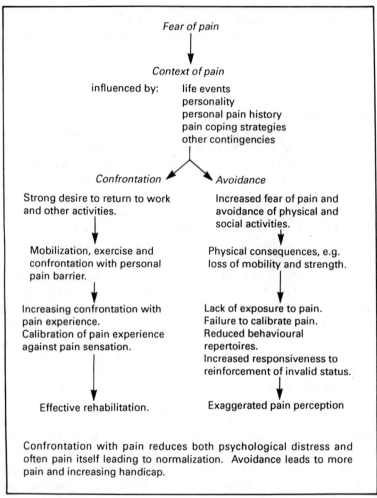

Figure 13.1   The Fear and Avoidance model of pain

1 Contingency management

This aims to help the person replace learnt pain behaviours with behaviours incompatible with a sick role. This obviously requires a change in the contingencies which are reinforcing pain behaviour. To do this we need a detailed assessment of the problem in the form of a behavioural analysis of events surrounding the emission of pain behaviour. Antecedents, behaviour (autonomic, overt behaviour and cognitions) and consequences need to be closely analysed. Identified pain behaviours can then be discussed with the person and his significant relatives, together with what is making them more likely. A programme of increasing activity and self-monitoring of pain is usually devised with the person and his relatives, emphasis being put on positive reinforcement of this programme with lessened reinforcement of pain behaviour.

Exposure

Although contingency management will involve exposure to previously avoided activities, graded exposure to feared activities and situations can be seen as a separate form of treatment. In our previous example, the man who had difficulty walking more than a few metres would be encouraged to undertake a series of graded steps towards longer walks and to repeat this exercise regularly. This would enable him to calibrate his pain as he tested out his self-imposed limits. Pain would not remain an 'all or nothing' experience. Cognitive strategies during therapy would be used to help the person reappraise his thoughts about pain. He may, for example, view any pain as an impending heart attack and regard all exercise as potentially fatal. These thoughts are negative distortions of the real situation and he could be helped to generate alternative cognitive responses to pain.

Pain focusing

A particular form of exposure is pain focusing. This involves systematic exposure in imagination to pain. The person imagines a particularly severe episode of pain in the first person, present tense and includes detailed descriptions of what he is feeling and doing. He concentrates hard on the pain, watches it increase in severity as he does so and is asked to make it worse. After five or ten minutes of this, when he may have been feeling physically in pain, he is asked to notice the pain decreasing. He does not make the pain go away since this may actually increase tension, rather he watches it disappear in the way a pan of boiled water gradually cools naturally. This procedure is repeated regularly.

The rationale for this approach could involve two mechanisms. Because anxiety about pain and anxiety on experiencing pain makes pain worse, exposure to pain in imagination could involve habituation to anxiety and thus lead to reduced pain levels. This can be a useful approach in people who suffer pain that cannot reliably be produced by other, real-life, activities. It may also be that as a person learns to bring on pain and then control it and watch it go away again they feel they are getting control over their pain. Cognitive change of this sort, away from helplessness in the face of pain, improves a person's mood and confidence in dealing with future pain episodes. They are then more likely to confront their pain rather than avoid it.

The behavioural treatment of pain demonstrates the use of behavioural management strategies drawn from learning theory and the empirical behavioural tradition. Contingency management and exposure-based techniques have all been shown to be useful, but there is not enough evidence to point to a definitive treatment of choice. These approaches fall into the general heading of 'behavioural medicine' which is an area of behaviour therapy undergoing an enormous expansion at the moment.

Behavioural medicine was first investigated in angina and primary hypertension, where a person is suffering from raised blood pressure without obvious environmental cues. Behavioural stress management techniques have been shown to reduce blood pressure significantly, familiar techniques such as regular exercise, relaxation training, cognitive restructuring and lifestyle adjustments all playing a part in therapy.

Further work has now made it clear that behaviour therapy has much to offer in the field of physical illness. The next two sections are further examples of this.

Behavioural treatment of irritable bowel syndrome

Irritable bowel syndrome (IBS) is a very common bowel complaint and may account for between 50–75% of attendances at gastroenterology clinics. It is characterized by increased gut motility and pain. The sufferer often goes through a cycle of diarrhoea and constipation with flatulence and severe pain commonly experienced. Bowel habits are irregular and either frequent or delayed.

There is very little evidence that IBS is caused by organic pathology. Although IBS sufferers may have some differences in their bowel physiology and there is also evidence that IBS runs in families. Medical treatment has included minor tranquillizers, laxatives, bulking agents, antispasmodic drugs and high-fibre diets.

Some work has been done by Rob Newell, a nurse therapist, on psychological treatments for IBS. He was involved in a research project which used behavioural methods to help IBS sufferers. The idea of IBS as a psychologically based condition and one which would therefore respond to psychological treatments was being investigated. The major behavioural techniques aim to retrain the bowel and teach people to control pain.

Retraining the bowel

Bowel retraining is used for constipation and diarrhoea. The aim is to establish a regular routine in passing motions. Initially the familiar technique of self-monitoring is used to establish a baseline frequency and help the person develop awareness of his bowel habits. With constipation the client is told to sit on the toilet at the same time every day for half an hour whether or not he passes a motion. Doing this after a meal makes use of the natural gastro-colonic reflex which makes it more likely we will defecate after a meal. The client is told not to strain as this will increase anxiety about whether a motion will be passed and increases discomfort. He should just wait patiently to see if anything happens. This procedure lasts for about three weeks and usually results in the restoration of a normal bowel habit at the end of that time.

Diarrhoea, or frequent bowel motions, requires a different approach but the aim is the same, the establishment of normal and regular bowel functioning. In addition, the procedure aims to break the connection between pain and/or anxiety and passing motions. Often a person will pass a motion in response to anxiety about whether it is necessary to go to the toilet. This in itself can lead to even more frequent bowel motions. A person may also find opening the bowel relieves pain, but the more frequently this happens the more likely the pain will return. A cycle of pain » defecation » pain » defecation builds up.

After self-monitoring the client decides on a certain time to open their bowel daily, using the gastro-colonic reflex to help them decide. They are also instructed to gradually increase the time between experiencing pain and going to the toilet from around initially five minutes. The same rules apply to urgency or anxiety, the time between getting a feeling of urgency and defecation is gradually increased. When actually sat on the toilet they are instructed to tense their buttock and pelvis muscles for

20 seconds to prevent defecation. All these exercises show the person that they are regaining control over their bowel and breaking the rewarding effects of immediate defecation on pain or urgency. The habitual and frequent defecation which is a feature of IBS has been shown to be reduced using exercises such as this.

Coping with pain

We have already discussed pain management strategies. Similar techniques are used with IBS. Newell (1987) reported a single case study where exposure in imagination (or pain focusing) appeared to be the most effective pain management component of his treatment programme for a patient with IBS. Imaginal exposure included pain images and also coping images of the patient continuing with her work whilst experiencing pain. The ability of the patient to bring on pain gave her a sense of controlling it and pain frequency decreased. Other exposure-based techniques have been used with IBS to reduce pain and anxiety. Clients are encouraged to confront situations they previously avoided because of probably random associations with the possibility of experiencing pain in these situations. Breathing control similar to that used to help panic (see Chapter 8) is also used as are more general relaxation techniques.

Behavioural treatments of IBS are showing great promise. They offer a more realistic chance of success than drugs or other medical options. They teach the sufferer to regain control over their bowel habits without relying on ever increasing amounts of chemicals. Once again, because the work is new, much more research is needed before the relative effectiveness of the component parts of the treatment can be assessed.

Neurology

The National Hospital for Nervous Diseases is a world-famous specialist hospital dealing with a wide range of neurological problems. A few years ago a nurse, Steve Shrubb, trained in behavioural psychotherapy was asked to set up a behaviour therapy service for people with neurological problems. This area covers conditions such as Parkinson's disease, multiple sclerosis, epilepsy and many more. Previously there had been no such service at the hospital.

Many people with neurological problems suffer difficulties with anxiety, phobias and difficulty adjusting to the changes in their situation brought about by their condition. In the early days of behaviour therapy at the National Hospital the work was with two types of client.

One part of the work was in helping people come to terms with their illness. For example, the diagnosis of multiple sclerosis (MS) is often a devastating blow to an individual and his or her family. The implications of such a diagnosis are almost impossible to cope with without help.

The second major area of work was an extension of the more usual role of a nurse therapist in dealing with phobias, obsessions, sexual problems, etc. These problems often arise as a consequence of the neurological problem the person is suffering from. It is, therefore, rather an artificial division between the two types of clients, but we will use it for ease of understanding.

Coping with the diagnosis

This process may resemble bereavement. The person and his family have to mourn the loss of health. Denial, anger, depression are all emotions on the path to acceptance of the person's changed health status.

Continuing the example of multiple sclerosis will help to illustrate the type of work needed. There are psychological, physical and social consequences of a diagnosis of MS:

- psychological difficulties include coping with the 'on/off' nature of MS where symptoms may come and go over time, the client remaining symptom free for relatively lengthy periods, only to have recurring periods when symptoms re-emerge. The course of MS can therefore seem very uncertain to clients, who can have unrealistic positive or negative expectations of their future.
- physical effects include decreased mobility, again occurring sporadically and unpredictably. This leads to increased dependence on others and a need to reappraise personal capabilities without becoming too self-restrictive in physical activity.
- social problems may be very handicapping. The problems of the disabled in our society are many and include difficulties such as lack of access ramps to public buildings, few facilities for wheelchairs and a feeling of being a social outcast. This

is particularly true for illnesses with very visible effects and where communication difficulties predominate.

An educational model

In the chapter on the process of therapy, we put particular emphasis on an educational approach to therapy. Helping people to cope with any diagnosis that implies an increasing degree of handicap requires that we put them fully in the picture as to the likely course and outcome of the illness. It is only through education that many myths and fears can be discussed. The family must be made aware of the likely effects, progress and management of the person's illness. For example, a diagnosis of MS does not mean severe disability will immediately follow. This is often the catastrophic interpretation that is given to the diagnosis. An understanding of this may facilitate motivation to adapt which could both prolong independence and maintain a person's quality of life.

Problem solving

Problem solving approaches have been described in this book many times. The framework for problem solving with neurological problems is, however, somewhat different.

Before a diagnosis of MS, for example, a person may be totally unaware of any problems. They will have been living full and varied lives and have had no experience of coping with handicap of this nature. This is in contrast to many people with phobias and obsessions who will have organized their lives increasingly around their problems. Introducing a problem solving strategy may be easier with people who have identified their problems before seeking help than with people for whom the diagnosis of MS has been an unsuspected bombshell. The first stage of the problem solving cycle may, therefore, require more work for these people.

To recap, problem solving consists of four stages:

(i)   Assessment   Identification of the problem(s). Breaking down the problems into manageable units. Defining the impact on family members.

(ii)   Planning   Generation of possible solutions. Selection of one strategy to implement.

| (iii) Implementation | Putting the chosen strategy into action. |
| (iv) Evaluation | Regular monitoring of progress. Modification or choice of another solution where necessary. |

Thus, the person and family are helped to work through their feelings about the person's illness, are educated away from an unrealistic catastrophic model, and are taught to use problem solving techniques to assist them to cope with the new demands likely to be placed on them in the future. As with most behavioural interventions the emphasis is on teaching the people most intimately involved with the problem, ways of coping, practically and psychologically, without long-term professional involvement.

The second part of the work, helping people with neurological problems who also have phobias, obsessions, etc., requires similar adaptations to behavioural interventions. Often phobias arise from the neurological condition itself, for example, a person with epilepsy may fear leaving the house or being alone in case they have a seizure. Most sufferers of epilepsy have this – quite reasonable – fear. However, some people may develop a phobic response to this fearful thought that is out of all proportion to the actual risk. This person may avoid so many situations that he cannot lead a normal life and it is the phobic avoidance rather than the epilepsy that becomes the main problem.

There are several immediately obvious differences between a 'normal' phobia and the example described above. A person with epilepsy has a realistic, physiological basis to his fears. Whereas a person with agoraphobia is not likely to have a heart attack even if he fears he will, the epilepsy sufferer could indeed fit whilst out. In some types of epilepsy, raised anxiety can actually trigger a seizure. The expectation that fear of panic, heart attack, etc., will disappear entirely when treating a person with agoraphobia cannot be applied to epilepsy. People with epilepsy may always remain afraid of fitting.

This implies a lowering of expectations for the nurse as well as the client. However, *calibrating* risk is an important part of therapy. If the person's epilepsy is well controlled, but they still avoid a significant number of situations, they can be taught to assess the risk of a seizure realistically. This may involve such exercises as diary records, behavioural analyses to identify cues and education to differentiate between anxiety symptoms and the aura associated with a pending seizure. This last factor is particularly important where the epilepsy is poorly controlled. The risk in this case is real, but if the person can identify situations where the risk of seizure is greatest, they can be encouraged to enter other, less dangerous situations. They can also learn to anticipate when they might have a seizure following an aura but that this is unlikely to happen following anxiety symptoms.

Some forms of epilepsy are affected greatly by anxiety, raised anxiety actually contributing to an increased frequency of seizures. It has been shown that exposure to feared situations leads to a decrease in anxiety levels as the situations become less feared (just as in phobias). This can then lead to a decrease in seizure frequency. Dahl *et al.*, (1988) emphasizes teaching clients to recognize the particular external cues that precipitate their seizures and then implement appropriate counter measures. This may mean reducing arousal levels, or for some people whose seizures may be associated with reduced arousal levels, actually increasing activity.

Clinical experience using exposure approaches with people who have a genuine neurological base to their fears shows that some modifications are necessary. Exposure has to be generally more frequent and more prolonged. If the time between practice is too long there is a pronounced 'return of fear' which quickly reaches previous levels. The provision of 'safety signals' is also important. These are objects, buildings, people, etc., that have associations of safety for the person and help them remain in feared situations.

Myalgic encephalomyelitis (ME)

We have used the examples of MS and epilepsy to briefly describe the type of work being done with neurology. Since the service was started at the National Hospital it has developed and there are now two nurse behaviour therapists working there. Sue Butler and Trudie Chalder have recently been involved in work on behavioural treatments of myalgic encephalomyelitis (ME).

ME is a newly identified syndrome where the main complaint is of fatigue. This persists for months or years and there is little in the way of clear signs to help diagnose the problem. Often sufferers' complaints are not believed and they may be considered to be malingerers or hypochondriacs. They find it difficult to concentrate or work at the same level they have been used to and have little energy. This can lead to avoidance of many daily activities for fear of exhaustion. The person may consult his GP frequently and become preoccupied with small variations in his health. This can lead to increased anxiety about his health and more frequent visits to the GP.

One point of view put forward is that ME is an atypical depression. The evidence for this is the positive response of some sufferers to antidepressants. However, antidepressants do not merely have an antidepressant function. We know, for example, that some people with panic and anxiety respond well to anti-depressants. Because a particular drug works is no argument for applying a particular diagnostic label.

A different viewpoint is that many of the symptoms are typical of those following a viral infection – post viral fatigue – which may have started the problem off initially. However, the person's response to these fatigue symptoms will determine whether they, and the behaviours associated with them, are reinforced or not.

The model is similar to the psychological model of pain in Figure 13.1. Confrontation or avoidance will produce a different long-term response to the symptoms. A range of factors are involved in determining whether the person confronts or avoids. These include physical fitness, personality, levels of background stress, reinforcement of illness behaviours by significant others, past experience of illness and advice from professionals and self-help groups.

Overlaying the physical symptoms may be a morbid preoccu-pation with health. Worry about physical symptoms may prompt the person to visit his GP for reassurance ever more frequently. The effectiveness of that reassurance diminishes with increasing numbers of visits. Preoccupation, worry, and intrusive thoughts may be a major problem.

Once again, we can offer no definitive treatment plan, but it is obvious from the description above that behavioural techniques used with anxiety could be very helpful. Graded exposure, risk calibration, cue-exposure response prevention, and cognitive restructuring may all have a place. It is these techniques that Butler, Chalder and their colleagues are investigating.

Post-traumatic stress disorder

Recently, the psychological effects of disasters and personal trauma have come under scrutiny. Part of the reason is due to the occurrence of several major disasters in the late 1980s including the Zebrugge ferry capsizal, the Bradford City football club fire, the Piper Alpha oil rig explosion, the Kings Cross fire and the Lockerbie plane crash. Other interest comes from America, where research into the treatment of veterans from the Vietnam war has produced indications that psychological treatments are of use in helping people overcome the after effects of traumatic experiences.

The delayed reaction of traumatic events is termed post-traumatic stress disorder (PTSD). People may not show any effects from a traumatic experience until years later. Then they may experience a number of frightening symptoms.

1 Heightened arousal
This may be experienced as sleep disturbance, hypervigilance, irritability and anger, an exaggerated startle response and physiological arousal in the presence of cues that the person associates with the trauma.

2 Avoidance and dissociation mechanisms
The person may withdraw from others and himself, becoming depressed, with diminished interest in everyday life. He may avoid thoughts, feelings and actual situations that remind him of his trauma. He may not even remember the incident that caused his trauma – an effect known as psychogenic amnesia.

3 Re-experiencing symptoms
Distressing images of his experience may intrude into his consciousness – flashbacks. He may experience frequent and repetitive nightmares and recurrent upsetting recollections of the trauma. These intrusive symptoms are often the most frightening.

Clearly, a person who experiences a traumatic event '... that is outside the range of usual human experience and that would be markedly distressing to almost anyone...' (DSMIII(R)) and who then goes on to develop PTSD, will be extremely distressed and handicapped. Their world is a treacherous place, where seemingly innocuous cues can bring on a terrifying flashback. They are constantly vigilant and jumpy and avoid many ordinary situations which have become too painful for them. Their sleep is disturbed and many resort to drink and drugs to enable them to get through the day.

One of the most obvious sources of traumatic experiences is military service. John Rose, a nurse behaviour therapist in the British army, has worked with many sufferers of PTSD. Years after the Falklands conflict, ex-soldiers still present with typical post-traumatic stress reactions. Their treatment depends on the exact presentation of the problem, particularly how soon the solider presents after the trauma.

The military of most countries stress that soldiers suffering from 'battle shock' be treated near the front line with the expectation that they return to duty as soon as possible. This treatment of the acute stress reaction involves allowing the sufferer to sleep for a couple of days, with or without the aid of drugs. The focus is then on talking through in great detail the soldier's experience. This is one of the main roles for psychiatric nurses in any army in times of conflict. The soldier is helped to process his memories of the experience he has been through until he is able to go back to his unit. This process is designed to take place within 5–9 days.

In peace time the army still experiences incidents which may trigger off traumatic reactions. Terrorists actions or military accidents are regular occurrences. Responding to such incidents is seen as the responsibility of the military unit involved. The same principles of talking through the trauma are employed, but group approaches are used with all the members of the unit involved. The same approach is beginning to be used by police forces where policemen of the same rank are assigned to help the trauma victim deal with his feelings.

Such preventative work should cut down the number of trauma victims who develop PTSD. Where this does happen, and where symptoms have persisted for longer than six months after the trauma experience, professional help is indicated. The principles are the same, however, in that the individual is helped to process the traumatic memories.

There are many ways of doing this and psychodynamic, behavioural and pharmacological methods have been used. American research has identified that:

'... direct therapeutic exposure to the memories of trauma emerged as the treatment technique common to all three theoretical models' (Fairbank and Nicholson, 1987).

Imaginal techniques have been shown to be highly effective in achieving this aim. Imaginal treatments have a long association with behaviour therapy from the days of systematic desensitization. Imaginal exposure is an efficient way of exposing people to situations that they might not otherwise have the opportunity to confront. This certainly applies to memories of trauma.

Both authors of this book have used imaginal exposure to treat people with severe post-traumatic stress reactions. The person is asked to sit and imagine the incident in great detail and recount their experiences in the first person as if they were actually going through it again. They imagine not only what they see and hear, but also what they do in response to this stimuli. We do not need to interfere other than to set the scene and to encourage the person to hold the feared image for as long as possible. Just as with *in-vivo* exposure, the technique can be graded by choosing the least frightening of a number of images, it should be repeated and it should be prolonged for at least an hour. Homework practice can be facilitated by audio-taping the session and asking the person to listen to the tape at home.

A short example may make this more clear.

Andrew was a 29-year-old policeman who was referred for behavioural treatment of agoraphobia. He could not leave his police station and walk down the street without panicking. He was therefore unable to do his job and was in danger of losing it. He was also feeling depressed, generally anxious and was having nightmares.

This problem had started a month earlier when he had been confronted by two drunken and aggressive youths whilst apprehending somebody else for a traffic offence. During the confrontation he had had a flashback of a previous experience which had occurred two years earlier. During this previous incident he had been headbutted unexpectedly whilst arresting someone for shoplifting. The flashback paralysed him with fear and he was unable even to summon help on his radio. Eventually he backed down and left the scene.

Treatment was by one session of imaginal exposure to the headbutting incident. He imagined the scene four times in $1\frac{1}{2}$ hours and rated anxiety levels at 80% of maximum. The session was audio-taped and he continued with the imaginal exposure at home using the tape. Subsequent sessions were spent evaluating his homework diary, which showed a gradual reduction in fear levels. After three weeks he was encouraged to start *in-vivo* exposure to feared situations. This he did in a graded, prolonged and repeated way and was successful in overcoming his fear. He returned to work and after a month was back on his normal duties, avoiding no situations including potential and active conflict situations. His mood improved and his general anxiety reduced. He no longer suffered from nightmares.

The treatment of Andrew illustrates how familiar behavioural strategies based on the principles of exposure were used to help a person with PTSD. A combination of imaginal and *in-vivo* exposure was successful in eliminating not only the phobic element of his problem, but also improved his mood and eliminated his nightmares.

Similar work has been done in the United States with victims of rape. A British study is anticipated in the near future with nurse behaviour therapists involved in the research design and the treatment of rape victims.

One last point to bear in mind may be that where a client presents with an unusual or slightly atypical phobia we should be on the look out for a traumatic onset. If this proves to be the case it is worth considering imaginal exposure to the traumatic incident. However, until controlled research into PTSD is published the optimum treatment strategy remains unclear.

Behavioural psychotherapy in community settings

Several nurses are involved in projects to develop community psychiatric services based on behavioural principles. Two projects are well developed, one in Buckingham and the other in London.

The Buckingham project aims to develop a comprehensive community psychiatric service using some of the techniques developed from work on high expressed emotion. Research in this area has shown that the more 'expressed emotion' in a family where there is a person suffering from schizophrenia, the more likely that person will relapse into florid psychiatric symptoms. Altering the level of expressed emotion in the family, as measured by levels of face-to-face contact, family conflicts, emotionally charged statements, etc., can reduce the probability of relapse for the schizophrenia sufferer.

This can be done in the usual behavioural way using behavioural analyses and problem solving. The family are taught to recognize the signs of high emotion in their system and implement strategies to reduce the stress. This is termed *behavioural family therapy* and involves teaching the family to use more appropriate ways of dealing with conflicts and other family disagreements. High expressed emotion may also involve too much positive emotion, leading to overprotectiveness of the identified patient. Different strategies are involved in this case, the aim being to facilitate independence for the sufferer and reduce anxiety for the other family members, but the basic principles of problem solving difficulties in the here and now remain.

Ian Falloon, a community health physician with much experience in behavioural psychotherapy, has set up the project in Buckingham which aims to use behavioural family therapy to reduce the expressed emotion and general levels of stress for ordinary community psychiatric referrals. Several nurses trained in behavioural skills are involved in the project which provides a comprehensive community psychiatric service to a defined geographical area. The therapy involves an intensive assessment to accurately identify problem areas and communication difficulties. Intervention is then focused on these difficulties, with training in communication skills and problem solving forming two major components of therapy. Their interventions are early and assertive. Whilst beds are available, they hope to reduce admission rates to psychiatric in-patient care.

The London project, a three-year research study, is a more recent attempt to evaluate the effectiveness of a community psychiatric service. This differs from the work in Buckingham in that the aim is to provide a comprehensive community psychiatric service for the severely mentally ill. Called the 'Daily Living Programme' (DLP) at the Maudsley hospital, it is based on work in Wisconsin, America.

When referrals are received at the Maudsley they are randomly assigned to either routine admission to an acute psychiatric ward with traditional follow-up (the control group) or to the DLP (the experimental group). People seen by workers from the DLP are nursed, if at all possible, in their homes rather than on a ward. The rationale is that brief admissions are less intrusive and damaging than long ones and people's recovery will be quicker if they are nursed at home. The DLP, therefore, provides a seven-day, 24 hour service and 40% of its clients suffer from acute psychotic problems.

Whilst therapy is eclectic rather than strictly behavioural, many nurses with behavioural skills – including Gary McNamee the project manager – are involved. Once again the emphasis is on problem solving using a *case-management* approach. The case-management system differs from the more usual key-worker system in that an identified nurse does not necessarily undertake any of the therapeutic activity herself. Instead, it is their defined responsibility to organize all the facets of a person's care directly.

One can see how this differs from the more usual community psychiatric nursing service, where CPNs may offer medication, counselling and supportive psychotherapy, for example, but may pass on the responsibility for housing, DHSS problems, etc., to social services. In contrast, the nurse as case-manager has explicit responsibility for liaising and negotiating with all relevant social agencies directly. Thus, as well as providing therapeutic psychiatric nursing, the nurse functions as direct advocate for the patient, managing his care in all its aspects.

Behaviour therapy skills in this area have been found to be invaluable. Measurements of problem and symptom severity, social and psychological functioning and family burden are all carried out at repeated intervals, including follow-up, to help evaluate the effectiveness of the therapy being offered. In addition, being a research project, McNamee and his colleagues are measuring the efficiency of their project by looking at the frequency of admission and length of stay in acute wards for both the DLP group and the control group. They hypothesize that not only will admission time be reduced in the DLP group, but psychiatric and psychological problem severity will also be less, due to the reduction in disturbance by being nursed at home. Importantly, they are also evaluating the comparative costs of the two types of care.

Both these projects are obviously significant steps in the move from institutional to community care. Behavioural skills have been found to be useful in both schemes. The key principles of problem solving, measurement, evaluation, and short focal interventions in the 'here and now' have been successfully applied to a wide range of clients and their problems. We must await the results of their evaluations to make firm judgements, but the signs are good for the increasing usefulness of behavioural techniques in a general community setting.

Summary

This chapter has been our attempt to widen the scope of the book and help readers appreciate the broad application of behavioural psychotherapy. The examples given are just samples of the sort of lateral thinking that has enabled nurses to apply behavioural principles beyond the normally defined limits. There are many more examples. We have not, for example, described the work by Southern and Henderson on incontinence in the elderly mentally ill, where simple behavioural analysis and problem solving approaches reduced incontinence on four residential wards by 70% and staff time dealing with the consequences of incontinence by 65%. Neither have we strayed into the area of addictions, where evidence is mounting that cue exposure to objects and situations associated with drug or alcohol use can reduce the likelihood of relapse.

This chapter, however, is not intended as a definitive list of the areas of clinical work suitable for behavioural approaches. Rather, we have supplied a sample of what can be done. We hope that it may stimulate readers to consider using the behavioural model in their own areas. It is often innovative practice, usually with one or two clients, measured and evaluated, that provides the indications for future research. For example, such single case studies were the basis for the explosion in research in obsessive-compulsive problems which led to the reversal in prognosis for this group over the last 15 years. Many further groups could benefit from behavioural therapy — it is just a matter of time. As we have seen, nurses can play a major role in researching further applications of behaviour therapy.

REFERENCES

Dahl J., Melin L., Leissner P. (1988). Effects of a behavioural intervention on epileptic seizure behaviour and paroxysmal activity: a systematic replication of three cases of children with intractable epilepsy. *Epilepsia*, **29**, 172–183.

Diagnostic and Statistical Manual of Mental Disorders (revised 3rd edition) (1987). Washington DC: American Psychiatric Association.

Fairbank J. A., Nicholson R. A. (1987). Theoretical and empirical issues in the treatment of post-traumatic stress disorder in Vietnam veterans. *J. Clinical Psychology*, **43**, 44–55.

Lethem J., Slade P. D., Troup J. D. G., Bentley G. (1983). Outline of a fear-avoidance model of exaggerated pain perception – 1. *Behaviour Research and Therapy*, **21**, 401–408.

Newell R. J. (1987). Treatment of irritable bowel syndrome by exposure in fantasy: a case report. *Behavioural Psychotherapy*, **15**, 381–387.

Chapter 14

Behavioural psychotherapy – the future

Throughout this book we have confined ourselves to describing behavioural psychotherapy and tried, as much as is possible within a book, to demonstrate some of the skills necessary in its use. We now turn to the thorny issue of where behavioural psychotherapy should be going and how it should fit in with current nursing developments. There are many debates raging at the moment both, within behavioural circles and nursing itself. In this concluding chapter we will try to draw together the main themes of these debates and see how they relate to the provision of behavioural therapies now and, more importantly, in the future.

Who are the behavioural psychotherapists?

Before looking to the future we must take a baseline of the present. What is the pattern of availability of behavioural psychotherapy in the country now?

Such information is very difficult to collate. There is no registration necessary to practise behaviour therapy, unlike nursing itself or clinical psychology, and many different professionals come to use behavioural methods by a variety of courses, workshops or by just general interest and reading. It is often assumed that, because many behavioural methods come from the work of experimental psychology, clinical psychology and behaviour therapy are synonymous. However, psychology is a broad church and includes many theoretical and clinical schools of thought other than the behavioural one. Clinical psychologists, once employed, may choose from among these ideological orientations in determining their clinical practice. It is, therefore, quite erroneous to assume that psychologists practise behavioural psychotherapy.

The British Association for Behavioural Psychotherapy (BABP) is a multi-disciplinary body that has a varied membership of professions interested in and practising behaviour therapy. It recently staged the highly successful 3rd Behaviour Therapy World Congress in Edinburgh which attracted around 1500 delegates from over 40 countries of the world. The BABP has no statutory function, but its membership may give us a clue as to how many 'behaviour therapists' there are.

Table 14.1 reproduces the membership statistics for 1987–88.

As we can see, clinical psychologists make up the largest group of behavioural psychotherapists. However, there are between 1500–2000 practising clinical psychologists in the country as a whole, so psychologists using behaviour therapy methods are probably less than 50% of the total number of psychologists employed. Quite clearly, psychology does not equal behaviour therapy.

Table 14.1

Profession	Number	Percentage
Clin. Psychology	841	53%
Nursing	260	16%
Psychiatry	99	6%
Social Work	94	6%
Teach. and Lectur.	59	4%
Research	48	3%
Misc. Psychol.	36	2%
Educ. Psychol.	27	1.7%
Psychol. Tech.	25	1.6%
Counselling	14	0.9%
Students	14	0.9%
Occ. Therapy	15	0.9%
General medicine	8	0.5%
Speech Therapy	4	0.3%
Prob. Service	3	0.2%
Miscellaneous	29	1.8%
Unknown	5	0.3%
Total	1581	100%

Nurses are by far and away the next largest group. Of the nursing membership, 50% consists of nurses who have completed or are in training on the ENBCC 650 (Adult Behavioural Psychotherapy). The other 50% comprises some nurses who have completed courses such as the Scottish behaviour therapy course at Dundee, ENBCC 655 (Rehabilitation), ENBCC 705 (Behaviour Modification in Mental Handicap) and others who are practising and interested in behavioural therapies.

The figures also indicate the interest in behavioural methods amongst a wide variety of professions. They do not tell us, however, in which clinical area people work. Members work with anxiety, sexual, rehabilitation, elderly, medical, mental handicap and many other client problems.

Whilst the numbers of psychologists practising behaviour therapy is less than 50%, the numbers of nurses is minute in comparison to the numbers working overall. In another indication of the low level of availability of behavioural psychotherapy, the Community Psychiatric Nurses Association surveyed CPNs and found only 1.3% specialized in behaviour therapy (CPNA, 1985).

Where are the behavioural psychotherapists?

The distribution of nurses trained in behavioural methods is extremely patchy. In a national follow-up study of trained nurse therapists who had completed the ENBCC 650 (Lindley *et al.*, 1985), it was found that nurses tended to concentrate around the centres which trained them. There were, therefore, many in the London area but Wales, Yorkshire and Northern England were all poorly supplied. The BABP membership statistics echo this pattern for all interested professionals. For example, London and the South East has many times the membership of the Northern region.

Barker (1980) followed up 20 nurses who had completed the Committee for Nursing Studies (CNSS) course in behaviour therapy in Scotland. He was interested in the way nurses used the skills gained on this course. His major finding was that:

'the successful implementation of the training is determined largely by the organizational situation to which the student returns, expressed by the attitude of senior managers (especially nursing); the role context delineated for the nurse therapist; and the moral and physical support available for instituting and developing behavioural programmes of nursing care.' (Barker, 1980, p. 69).

So, even trained nurses had difficulty using their behavioural skills where the organization was not supportive, and it was this organization which was the crucial factor in the delivery of behaviour therapy.

This information is far from exhaustive but it does give us a rough guide as to the availability of behaviour therapy nationally. It is clear that behaviour therapy services develop on an *ad hoc*, unplanned basis and have more to do with individual clinical preferences (in the case of psychologists) and a multiplicity of personality, managerial and training factors in the case of nursing. There seems to be no *planned* provision of behaviour therapy. Nationally, there is no recommended number of behaviour therapists per district and no recognition of behaviour therapists as a separate discipline. Mark's (1985) estimate of 1800 nurse therapists being able to meet the needs of primary care patients for behavioural psychotherapy has not been taken up despite the impressive arguments for clinical effectiveness and efficiency. With clinical trials showing behavioural and cognitive-behavioural techniques to be effective in an ever-increasing number of fields there is a need for behavioural psychotherapy to become more widely taught and used. At the moment, however, it seems largely a matter of luck or geographical location whether or not a client has access to a professional skilled in behavioural psychotherapy.

BEHAVIOURAL PSYCHOTHERAPY AND NURSING

We have already summarized some of the main initiatives in training nurses to use behavioural techniques in Chapter 3 and have outlined some writers' ideas about levels of expertise. We will return to the crucial issue of training later but let us first look at some of the issues facing psychiatric nursing at the moment.

Community care

The major emphasis within psychiatry is the closure of the old Victorian institutions where for many years the majority of psychiatric nursing was done. Since 1954 when the first example of nurses visiting patients at home was recorded, the growth of community psychiatric nursing, particularly within the last 10 years, has been phenomenal. Even more recently, government has made the concept of community care a priority. Long-stay clients are being 'resettled' in environments ranging among group homes, sheltered housing, core and cluster developments, individual flats and bed and breakfasts. At the same time the proportion of elderly clients is increasing and, with this, the number of people suffering from dementias. However, new care environments for the elderly are often staffed by social services staff or general nurses. As the traditional domain of the psychiatric nurse gets closed down, anxieties are high about the future.

Management

It often seems to those working at the 'sharp end' of care delivery that the NHS is both constantly underfunded and reorganizing. Traditional nursing hierarchies were swept away by the Griffiths management changes that introduced general management to health care, replacing the existing system of consensus management. Nursing officers had to compete with other professionals for fewer management posts and a secure promotion path within nursing is no longer obvious. This is as true in psychiatry as it is in any other health field. A second report by Griffiths (1988) has suggested new management arrangements for community care, with social services taking over the reins. Whether this is taken up by the government or disappears from sight in the way of the Cumberledge report on 'neighbourhood nursing' teams (1986) remains to be seen. Yet another reorganization, which promises to be as radical as the Griffiths report, is now in progress following the publication of the Health Service Review in February 1989.

Project 2000

A third area of concern to psychiatric nurses, and perhaps the one most feared by us, is the impact of Project 2000. Project 2000 (UKCC, 1985) outlines a new, radical system of nurse training. Its authors suggest a *common foundation programme* (CFP) that all nurses will undertake and which will last up to two years. Following this 'branch programmes' will be available in mental illness, mental handicap, general nursing, children's nursing and midwifery. Nurses will choose which branch they wish to specialize in following the CFP. During training, student nurses will be truly supernumary, in that they will not be included as part of the workforce but will have student status in the true sense of the word. They will gain experience in a variety of nursing environments but will not be relied upon to 'make up the numbers'. The academic part of the course may move to polytechnics, where courses could be based and students will be given grants rather than paid a wage.

That Project 2000 has tremendous implications for the future of psychiatric nursing is immediately obvious. Many fear that the CFP will be general nursing based and psychiatric nursing will, in effect, have to be learnt in a year to eighteen months following the CFP. Altschul makes the point that the CFP must not be interpreted as 'a general training with others also in attendance' (Altschul, 1986) but should include many aspects of psychiatric nurse training such as sociology, psychology and the experience of group work in the development of interpersonal and communication skills. Whether this worthy sentiment is reflected in practice remains to be seen.

Now that the main recommendations of Project 2000 have been accepted in principle by the government, concern is being expressed about manpower levels and who will actually replace the 'lost' students. Nursing unions have had to accept that trainees from youth unemployment schemes (whatever their current title) will be extensively employed in nursing environments. The image of a few highly trained baccalaureate nurses (as in the USA) supervising an army of untrained teenagers is one that must send shudders down the back of any nurse concerned with the quality of care.

Specialists are suggested in the Project 2000 scheme. Health visiting, occupational health nursing, school nursing, district nursing, community psychiatric nursing and community mental handicap nursing being specifically mentioned. Although provision is made for other specialists, no mention is made of nurse behaviour therapists despite the fact that it takes longer to train an ENBCC 650 graduate than a district nurse and such nurses have demonstrated their effectiveness empirically. Altschul (1986) suggests that specialists, perhaps including nurse behaviour therapists, will have to adopt quite different roles under the new scheme. Instead of becoming isolated in their own field of practice they will have to function as consultants and supporters of others. On this point it is interesting to note that most nurse therapists currently spend up to 20% of their time in teaching and supervisory activities.

Post-basic education

Changes are also afoot in the world of post-basic education. A new model of post-registration training is being investigated by educationalists which somewhat resembles the Project 2000 work. It would provide for a core course following on from the basic qualification. This core course, of a few months duration, would involve nurses being released from their work for a few hours a week to look in more depth at some of the basic issues covered in training. Following on from this will be the opportunity to specialize for another few months, perhaps going on further after this to a detailed specialist course. In this way nationally certificated post-registration qualifications such as the 650 or 811/812 certificates may be obtained through a system of locally tiered modules. These suggestions are all very tentative and experimental but there is an English National Board circular (ENB, 1988) that discusses the core course. We will have to await further developments.

Skills mix

Another issue in nursing concerns the problem of who should do what and how many of them there should be — the 'skills mix' issue. A small study by the DHSS found little research evidence to justify the existing staffing levels in a number of varied environments (Moores, 1987). Levels varied greatly, something we have found in our analysis of the provision of behavioural services discussed earlier.

Of relevance to the skills mix issue is the question of what nurses actually do. Altschul (1972) found that unqualified nurses carried out the most interactions with patients on psychiatric wards whilst Cormack (1976) discovered that an average of only 13% of a charge nurse's time was spent talking to patients. This data bodes ill for those who claim that highly trained nurses are value for money. If the quality of the many interactions carried out by unqualified nurses could be improved by specific behavioural training, might this be a profitable group to target, leading to measurable gains in client health? And what about the general public, what is their role? Pembrey (1985) quotes an unpublished study by Alison Kitson which suggests that lay carers and professional nurse carers share many similar qualities, of which commitment, knowledge, skills and respect for persons are the main components. Derek Milne has trained *hairdressers* in simple behavioural skills and demonstrated measurable improvements in their provision of social support to their clients. Who should do what, therefore, is clearly not defined by membership of a particular profession. It is likely to become a political hot-potato as health service policy becomes more of a political, and party political, issue.

QUALITY ASSURANCE

One of the major growth industries in the British health service recently has been the development of methods for ensuring that the service provided is of a high standard. The rise of consumerism, the spiralling costs of health care, tighter financial and professional accountability, have all contributed to this industry. Many quality assurance initiatives have been spawned, including the Kings Fund projects (Shaw, 1986), Monitor (Goldstone *et al.*, 1984), is a system to investigate health care activity, the RCN initiatives on standards of care (Royal College of Nursing, 1980), plus many smaller local attempts to define, set and evaluate the clinical standards deemed desirable.

Quality is normally considered to be a three-cornered concept. Donabedian (1980) divided it into:

- structure variables
- process variables
- outcome variables

Structure refers to the 'nuts and bolts' of the service, nursing activity or other health care activity. Equipment, personnel, skills, knowledge, are all examples of structure criteria that need to be met for the activity to take place. The process refers to the actual job being done and how it is done, the outcome being the finished product. Any assessment of quality should include aspects of all three criteria if the assessment is to be comprehensive. The many different quality assurance approaches tried include large and expensive health authority studies but also ward-based attempts to evaluate quality, identify weaknesses and implement improvements. One of the most positive things about quality assurance is that it can be used by nurses to demonstrate their clinical competence and expertise to managers who often have a non-nursing background. Qualitative data is a better way to evaluate nursing care than quantitative data (such as staffing levels, hours worked, throughput, clients seen per week, etc.).

It can be appreciated that behaviour therapists are particularly well placed to demonstrate the quality of their care. It is part of the fundamental ethic of behaviour therapy that we routinely measure changes in the health status of our clients and evaluate the effectiveness of our procedures using clinical measurement (e.g. McDonald *et al.*, 1988). With the new emphasis on measurable quality, behaviour therapy should benefit as it is shown to be a highly effective and efficient therapy.

Many nurses trained in behaviour therapy are also using their expertise to assist services develop quality assurance strategies. This transfer of behavioural skills from the individual to organizations has been demonstrated successfully by Milne (1988) under the name of 'organizational behaviour management' (OBM). The techniques of assessment, measurement and evaluation are the same, it is merely that the 'client' is not one individual but a group of individuals – the organization.

Behaviour therapy nursing — the future

There are two main challenges that face nurses who believe behavioural techniques offer the best hope to many of our clients. The first of these is to get as many nurses as possible trained in behavioural skills. The second is to convince service planners that behavioural psychotherapy is not an expensive luxury, nor one of a number of equal therapeutic alternatives. The two challenges are closely linked, since training will only be set up with the agreement of managers and it is the trained nurses who can lobby for increased behavioural services.

Training
The history of nurse training in behavioural psychotherapy has been referred to in detail in Chapter 3. We saw how five levels of expertise have been identified ranging from the 'applicator', under the absolute direction of another professional, nurse or otherwise, to the specialist or the nurse therapist, functioning as a totally

autonomous practitioner. Currently, there is a heated debate amongst nurses who train nurse behaviour therapists as to the correct level of training required. One school believes a generalist training will effect greatest change and that we should equip nurses to use behavioural skills in all clinical settings. The other school believes that a more detailed specialist training is better and that greater reliance on research data will make the argument for behavioural treatments eventually unassailable. Whilst the first group believes the behavioural model is applicable to all clinical areas, the second prefers to wait until the evidence is conclusive.

This debate of course is only another manifestation of the specialist/generalist question apparent in many branches of nursing. We believe that both arguments have merit and are not mutually exclusive. Instead, when designing training programmes we should look at several things – the client group we wish to help, the level of expertise needed and the available people best suited to deliver this help.

When training nurses to use behavioural skills we should be looking at who they will be helping when they use these skills. Is the population to be helped wide or narrow? What are the characteristics of the people we are planning to help? We can then make decisions about the level of knowledge and expertise required to carry out this function. Should the people we are training be qualified nurses or not? We need to make value judgements about the competence of various nursing groups and the level of supervision they are likely to need. For example, the nurses we intend to train as independent, autonomous practitioners working without supervision would logically need a more intensive training than nurses who we expect to fit into the applicator role, being supervised by others more skilled in the area. The independent specialist should be a qualified nurse but the applicator function could very well be carried out by untrained nurses.

We have already seen how Kitson identified similar attributes in professional and lay carers (Pembrey, 1985). Might it be the case that it is family members that we should be training? Indeed, Milne makes the point that, 'It is only through the people who provide the context in which problems develop that we can truly expect to have any real influence.' (Milne, 1986, p. 4). This is echoed in much of the practice we have described in this book, particularly the emphasis on involving significant family members – co-therapists – and on the moves to use self-help as a potent form of therapy. Behaviour therapy is often 'behaviour training' so maybe nurses should be trained in this teaching role rather than merely as therapists.

This brings us to another important consideration. Who is available to be trained? In the UK, nurses make up the main body of staff dispensing care directly to patients. However, the proportion of trained staff to unqualified nurses has been falling steadily and, as we discussed earlier in this chapter, is likely to fall still further as a consequence of population and political pressures. On the other hand, highly trained specialists are being seen as a growing part of the nursing picture. It is, however, unlikely that large numbers of trained nurses will ever be taught specialist clinical skills and employed as nurse behaviour therapists. There is only room for a few clinical specialists in each district health authority, their numbers are thus self-limiting and will probably never rise higher than 200–300. The demands for their services are, of course, enormous. We must therefore look again at the layered model of skill-level referred to earlier.

- The nurse therapist
- The generalist
- The specialist
- The technician
- The applicator

The applicator is the deliverer of very specific techniques, heavily supervised and instructed. The technician is also supervised but needs less structure. The specialist is trained in a number of highly specific techniques, but very thoroughly, consequently needing little supervision in his own area. The generalist and the nurse therapist function independently, use their techniques widely and often supervise other staff. The whole system could be seen as a pyramid, with many applicators leading to few specialists and fewer nurse therapists.

We can see that there are likely to be many more people, including relatives, friends and the clients themselves who fit into the first three categories. Many more people are available and could be trained in these groups. The nurse therapists and generalists would be better and more efficiently employed training and supervising these groups. The highly trained nurse specialists would still be needed, but in small numbers and with a different role. Since practically, there are only ever going to be small numbers of these clinical specialists, shorter training programmes should be developed to train nurses and others to the levels of skill needed at less sophisticated levels of the pyramid. This would ensure that behavioural techniques are available to a much larger population than at present.

This changed role for nurse therapists would fit in with the ideas contained within Project 2000 and echoes Altschul's comments (1986), that clinical specialists should concentrate on supporting and training others rather than becoming isolated in their own field of clinical practice.

One group of nurses who are very well placed to use the techniques in this book are community psychiatric nurses (CPNs). Much CPN work has shifted in emphasis from following up and supporting resettled long-stay clients of the large institutions. An increasing number of CPNs now deal with the many mental health problems of a population not previously identified as 'psychiatric'. Sectorized CPN services taking referrals direct from GPs are more likely to see the types of clients for whom behavioural psychotherapy is highly appropriate. In fact, the syllabus for the current CPN course specifically identifies that behavioural techniques be taught. However, some CPN courses spend as little as two days out of a one-year course dealing with the whole field of behavioural psychotherapy. CPNs using behavioural techniques with anxiety problems, for example, could make a significant impact on the mental health of the general population. They should not become specialists, but certainly would need more than two days of instruction to become skilled in behavioural treatments of anxiety.

Basic training

However long it takes to train a CPN to use behavioural psychotherapy with those clients they see who are suitable for this approach, the time could be reduced if basic behavioural skills were taught during RMN training. New syllabuses come and go, but there is no evidence that standards of teaching student nurses behavioural skills have improved. We would like to quote a detailed example.

Briggs and Stewart, both senior members of the board of examiners for mental nursing and responsible for setting RMN papers, include in a recent book (Briggs and Stewart, 1987) a detailed chapter of ideal answers to questions about obsessive-compulsive problems. They suggest that: 'thought stopping, imagery flooding and *in-vivo* flooding' are the most successful therapies available and that 'the nurse should consider techniques such as thought stopping, covert reinforcement and desensitisation' when helping obsessive clients. They also write that:

> 'A process of repression and displacement occurs, producing an apparently unconnected but substitutional behaviour'

and

> 'Care must be taken, for the anxiety and substitutional behaviour may be a protective mechanism which if removed could produce alternative forms of defence'.

This is the language of the 1950s.

Thus, not only do these authors suggest candidates in exams use notions derived from discredited models in their answers, but nowhere do they mention or suggest that the candidate describe the treatment of choice, namely cue-exposure and response prevention. It is these techniques, and these alone, which in the last 20 years have reversed the utterly pessimistic outlook for people suffering from obsessive-compulsive problems, one of the most severely handicapping conditions psychiatric nurses are likely to see.

The above example clearly displays, at the very least, a serious lack of communication between nurses trained in behavioural psychotherapy and those that maintain the educational standards of the profession. If nurses in general, and not just highly trained nurse therapists, are to play a role in treating people with these problems, such misinformation, which extends to the highest level, must be corrected at source.

A new training model

We now come to the point where these varied considerations should be pulled together. Our aim is to provide effective behavioural treatments to as many people as need them, in as efficient manner as possible. The problem is the same today as it was in the early 1970s, when nurses were first trained as specialists in behaviour therapy. There are too many people with problems suitable for a behavioural approach and too few professionals skilled in its application.

Nurses remain the obvious choice to be trained in behavioural psychotherapy since there are many more of us than any other professional group. Moreover, Milne (personal communication) has identified a swing away from 'hard' evidence-based practice in the training of clinical psychologists towards a less validated, less scientific approach. Many psychologists are becoming interested in dynamic approaches again, leaving the field open for nurses to become the major practitioners in behaviour therapy. There is no problem with training nurses to use behavioural methods since it has been demonstrated empirically that it is possible to train nurses to be as effective as any other professional in this field (Marks *et al.*, 1977). However, the training of specialist nurse therapists has not met the needs of our client group. Specialists are still needed, but as supporters, trainers and supervisors as envisaged by the Project 2000 proposals.

We propose that other nurses be systematically trained in behavioural skills, the depth of this training being dependent on the types of problems they are likely to be helping. This training could be shorter and more focused with clinical supervision being carried out locally. The in-service training model — of core course plus intermediate and specialist modules undertaken at local level — would be a more effective and economic model than sending large numbers of nurses away for expensive and lengthy courses. Nurses trained to a certain level of expertise would be expected to teach and supervise those trained to a lesser depth.

It is not unreasonable to expect that at the end of an RMN training (or its equivalent after Project 2000), qualified nurses should at least be able to function at an applicator or technician level in our pyramidal model of behaviour therapy nursing. To do this, schools of nursing would have to cease teaching therapeutic strategies that have been shown to be ineffective, other than in an historical context, and replace them with basic behavioural skills modules.

This is not as radical as it at first seems. For example, would a medical school teach students that Lister's aerial carbolic spray is a viable method of asepsis? Of course not, since it has long ago been replaced by more effective procedures. And yet we have seen that even modern nursing texts reference unhelpful ideas about certain clients (in our earlier example, clients with obsessive problems) and where behavioural methods are cited, these are well out of date. This is as much the fault of nurses trained in behavioural methods as it is the fault of the educators.

We must, however, be realistic. It is suggested by Project 2000 that specialists move away from a mainly therapeutic role and adopt a higher profile of training and supervision role. This is something we would endorse. Whether it is during the common foundation programme for the psychiatric branch or later in-service training modules, student nurses and newly qualified nurses will need greater access to a range of clinical nurse specialists, in our case nurse behaviour therapists. Unfortunately, these specialists are just not there. We have already seen in this chapter how erratic is the distribution of nurse behaviour therapists nationally. Numbers are also quite inadequate to fulfil this new role, which just cannot be accomplished at current levels.

Unlike Marks (1985) we do not suggest a massive number of nurse behaviour therapists to fill the clinical needs. We believe nurses at other levels of a pyramidal model of training could meet the needs of many of the clients for whom behavioural treatment methods are appropriate. However, there does need to be a radical rethink of current ENB training. In 1986 one of the four training centres in England for the ENBCC 650, the course that trains nurses to become nurse behaviour therapists, closed. It has not been replaced and now only about 20 new nurses graduate from this course every 18 months. We deplore the reduction in training places as it is obvious that there needs to be a rather dramatic upsurge in places on the ENBCC 650 course to meet the training needs of the Project 2000 proposals. Without this upsurge, nurses will continue to be denied access to skills and techniques at the important early stages of nurse training.

Thus, the pyramidal model of training would provide qualified trainers and practitioners, trained both nationally and locally. Each layer in the pyramid would be trained less intensively but would be able to supervise the next layer. The presence of nurses at all levels of training possessing behavioural skills would dramatically increase the skills mix of many environments, thus increasing student nurses' opportunity to learn and practise basic behavioural skills.

We must always remember that the only people to benefit from such a change would be the many ordinary people who would finally have access to skilled professionals actually equipped to use appropriate and effective techniques to help them cope better with or overcome their difficulties. The potential that we as nurses have for dramatically reducing the significant levels of distress and handicap suffered by a great many people, as described in some of the case studies presented in earlier chapters, is enormous.

To this end, this book is an attempt to increase the availability of 'how to do it'-type information so that our goal of access to knowledge for some and appropriate therapy for others is brought a step closer. We hope it will be read and its suggestions instituted by the many nurses who wish to help people with the types of problems for which behavioural psychotherapy offers the best hope for an improved quality of life.

REFERENCES

Altschul A. (1972). *Patient–Nurse Interaction*. Edinburgh: Churchill Livingstone.

Altschul A. (1986). Branching out. *Nursing Times*, 82, 31, 47–48.

Barker P. (1980). Behaviour therapy in psychiatric and mental handicap nursing. *J. of Adv. Nursing*, 5, 55–69.

Briggs K., Stewart A. (1987). *Case Studies in Mental Health Nursing – Problems and Approaches*. Edinburgh: Churchill Livingstone.

Community Psychiatric Nursing Association (1985). *The National CPNA Survey Update*, Leeds: CPNA Publications.

Cormack D. (1976). *Psychiatric Nursing Observed*. London: RCN.

Cumberledge J. (1986). *Neighbourhood Nursing*. London: Her Majesty's Stationery Office.

Donabedian A. (1980). *The definition of quality and approaches to its measurement. Explorations in quality assessment and monitoring*. Vol. 1. Health Administration Press, Anne Arbour.

English National Board (1988). Circular 1988/39/APS. p. 7.

Goldstone L. A., Ball J. A., Collier M. M. (1984). *Monitor, an Index of the Quality of Nursing Care on Acute Medical and Surgical Wards*. Newcastle upon Tyne: Newcastle upon Tyne, Polytechnic Productions.

Griffiths R. (1988). *Community Care: Agenda for Action*. London: Her Majesty's Stationery Office.

Lindley P., Marks M., McCaffery F. (1985). National follow up of nurse therapists, In *Psychiatric Nurse Therapists in Primary Care*. Marks I. M., London: Royal College of Nursing.

Marks I. M., Hallam R. S., Connolly J., Philpotts R. (1977). *Nursing in Behavioural Psychotherapy*, London: Royal College of Nursing.

Marks I.M. (1985). *Psychiatric Nurse Therapists in Primary Care*. London: Royal College of Nursing.

McDonald R., Marks I. M., Blizzard R. (1988). Quality assurance of outcome in mental health care: a model for routine use in clinical settings. *Health Trends*, 20, 111–114.

Milne D. (1986). Training Behaviour Therapists. Beckenham: Croom Helm.

Milne D. (1988). Organizational behaviour management in a psychiatric day hospital. *Behavioural Psychotherapy*, 16, 177–188.

Moores B. (1987). Janforum. Comment on 'mix and match': a review of nursing skill mix. *Journal of Advanced Nursing*, 12, 765–767.

Pembrey S. (1985). A framework for care. *Nursing Times*, 81, 47–49, 50.

Royal College of Nursing (1980). Standards of Nursing Care. London: RCN.

Shaw C. (1986). Introducing Quality Assurance. London: Kings Fund Project Paper.

United Kingdom Central Council for Nursing Midwifery and Health Visiting (1985). *Project 2000. A New Preparation for Practice*. London: UKCC.

Appendix A

The following pages contain reproductions of the clinical measures mentioned in the text. They are included in this book with the kind permission of Isaac Marks and are reproduced from Marks, I.M. (1986). *Behavioural Psychotherapy: the Maudsley Pocket Book of Clinical Management*. Wright: Bristol.

Some of the measures are quite specific to certain problems, for example the obsessional checklist should only be used with people who have an obsessional problem. However, 'Problems and Targets', the 'Fear Questionnaire' and 'Work and Social Adjustment' should be used for all clients. Indeed, as we suggested in the text, we believe that 'Problems and Targets' and a 'Work and Social Adjustment' measure could form the basis of a robust outcome measurement package for use in clinical nursing practice generally. We urge readers to experiment with clinical measurement and view it as a useful tool in evaluating nursing practice.

Problems and Targets

Patient: .... Therapist ....
Date ....

PROBLEMS

		Pre	Mid	Post	1 m	3 m	6 m
PROBLEM A	Self						
	Therapist						

		Pre	Mid	Post	1 m	3 m	6 m
PROBLEM B	Self						
	Therapist						

'This problem upsets me and/or interferes with my normal activities'

0	1	2	3	4	5	6	7	8
Does not		Slightly/ sometimes		Definitely/ often		Markedly very often		Very severely/ continuously

TARGETS

		Pre	Mid	Post	1 m	3 m	6 m
A1	Self						
	Therapist						
A2	Self						
	Therapist						
B1	Self						
	Therapist						
B2	Self						
	Therapist						

'My progress towards achieving each target regularly without difficulty'

DISCOMFORT/BEHAVIOUR

0	1	2	3	4	5	6	7	8
None/ complete success		Slight/ 75% success		Definite/ 50% success		Marked/ 25% success		Very severe/ no success

Fear Questionnaire

Choose a number from the scale below to show how much you would avoid each of the situations listed below because of fear or other unpleasant feelings. Then write the number you choose in the box opposite each situation.

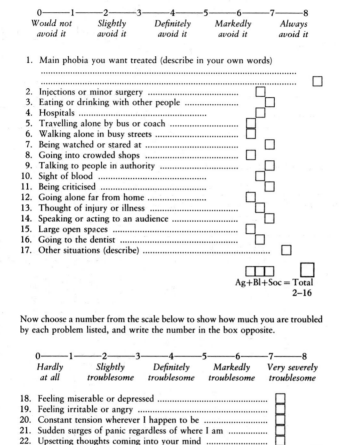

```
0——1——2——3——4——5——6——7——8
Would not    Slightly    Definitely    Markedly    Always
avoid it     avoid it    avoid it      avoid it    avoid it
```

1. Main phobia you want treated (describe in your own words)
   ....
   ....

2. Injections or minor surgery ....
3. Eating or drinking with other people ....
4. Hospitals ....
5. Travelling alone by bus or coach ....
6. Walking alone in busy streets ....
7. Being watched or stared at ....
8. Going into crowded shops ....
9. Talking to people in authority ....
10. Sight of blood ....
11. Being criticised ....
12. Going alone far from home ....
13. Thought of injury or illness ....
14. Speaking or acting to an audience ....
15. Large open spaces ....
16. Going to the dentist ....
17. Other situations (describe) ....

Ag+Bl+Soc = Total
2–16

Now choose a number from the scale below to show how much you are troubled by each problem listed, and write the number in the box opposite.

```
0——1——2——3——4——5——6——7——8
Hardly       Slightly       Definitely     Markedly      Very severely
at all       troublesome    troublesome    troublesome   troublesome
```

18. Feeling miserable or depressed ....
19. Feeling irritable or angry ....
20. Constant tension wherever I happen to be ....
21. Sudden surges of panic regardless of where I am ....
22. Upsetting thoughts coming into your mind ....
23. Other feelings (describe) ....

☐ Total

How would you rate the present state of your phobic symptoms on the scale below?

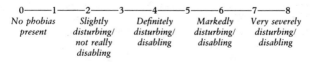

```
0——1——2——3——4——5——6——7——8
No phobias    Slightly      Definitely     Markedly      Very severely
present       disturbing/   disturbing/    disturbing/   disturbing/
              not really    disabling      disabling     disabling
              disabling
```

Please circle one number between 0 and 8.

Work and Social Adjustment

Patient .... Therapist .... Date ....

WORK

BECAUSE OF MY PROBLEMS MY ABILITY TO WORK IS IMPAIRED:

0	1	2	3	4	5	6	7	8	
Not at all		Slightly		Definitely		Markedly		Very severely I cannot work	Self
									Therapist

HOME MANAGEMENT (cleaning, tidying, shopping, cooking, looking after home or children, paying bills)

0	1	2	3	4	5	6	7	8	
Not at all		Slightly		Definitely		Markedly		Very severely I cannot do it	Self
									Therapist

SOCIAL LEISURE ACTIVITIES (with other people, e.g. parties, pubs, clubs outings, visits, dating, home entertainment)

0	1	2	3	4	5	6	7	8	
Not at all		Slightly		Definitely		Markedly		Very severely I never do these	Self
									Therapist

PRIVATE LEISURE ACTIVITIES (done alone, e.g., reading, gardening, collecting, sewing, walking alone)

0	1	2	3	4	5	6	7	8	
Not at all		Slightly		Definitely		Markedly		Very severely I never do these	Self
									Therapist

Columns (right side): PRE date, MID date, POST date, 1MFU date, 3MFU date, 6MFU date

Social Situations Questionnaire

No discomfort	Slight discomfort	Moderate discomfort	Great discomfort	I avoid situation
0	1	2	3	4

	Discomfort	Frequency
1. Walking down the street		
2. Going into shops		
3. Going on public transport		
4. Going into pubs		
5. Going to parties		
6. Mixing with people at work		
7. Making friends of your own age		
8. Going out with someone of the opposite sex		
9. Being with a group of the same sex and roughly the same age as you		
10. Being with a group containing both men and women of roughly the same age as you		
11. Being with a group of the opposite sex of roughly the same age as you		
12. Entertaining people in your home, lodgings, etc.		
13. Going into restaurants or cafes		
14. Going to dances, dance halls or discotheques		
15. Being with older people		
16. Being with younger people		
17. Going into a room full of people		
18. Meeting strangers		
19. Being with people you don't know very well		
20. Being with friends		
21. Approaching others — making the first move in starting up a friendship		
22. Making ordinary decisions affecting others (e.g. what to do together in the evening)		
23. Being with only one other person, rather than a group		
24. Getting to know people in depth		
25. Taking the initiative in keeping a conversation going		
26. Looking at people directly in the eyes		
27. Disagreeing with what other people are saying and putting forward your own views		
28. People standing or sitting very close to you		
29. Talking about yourself and your feelings in conversation		
30. People looking at you		

Appendix A

Compulsions Checklist — Self Rating

Name .... Date ....

INSTRUCTIONS: The following are a list of activities which people with your kind of problem sometimes have difficulty with. Please answer each question by putting a tick under the appropriate number

0 — *I have no problems with activity — takes me about the same time as an average person. I do not need to repeat it or avoid it.*

1 — *This activity takes me about twice as long as most people, or I have to repeat it twice or tend to avoid it.*

2 — *This activity takes me about three times as long as most people, or I have to repeat it three or more times, or I usually avoid it.*

3 — *I am unable to complete or attempt activity.*

				ACTIVITY
				Having a bath or shower
				Washing hands and face
				Care of hair (e.g. washing, combing, brushing)
				Brushing teeth
				Dressing and undressing
				Using toilet to urinate
				Using toilet to defaecate
				Touching people or being touched
				Handling waste or waste bins
				Washing clothes
				Washing dishes
				Handling or cooking food
				Cleaning the house
				Keeping things tidy
				Bed making
				Cleaning shoes
				Touching door handles
				Touching your genitals, petting or sexual intercourse
				Visiting a hospital
				Switching lights and taps on or off
				Locking or closing doors or windows
				Using electrical appliances (e.g. heaters)
				Doing arithmetic or accounts
				Getting to work
				Doing your work
				Writing
				Form filling
				Posting letters
				Reading
				Walking down the street
				Travelling by bus, train or car
				Looking after children
				Eating in restaurants
				Going to public toilets
				Keeping appointments
				Throwing things away
				Buying things in shops
TOTAL				
				Other (fill in)

Obsessive Discomfort, Time, Handicap

PROBLEM A

Patient ....   Therapist ....

PROBLEM B

date	PRE	POST	1MFU	3MFU	6MFU

DISCOMFORT WHEN UNABLE TO PERFORM THIS ACTIVITY IS:

0	1	2	3	4	5	6	7	8
Absent		Slight		Definite		Marked		Extreme → rate here →

A □ A □ A □ A □ A □
B □ B □ B □ B □ B □

TOTAL TIME EACH DAY THIS ACTIVITY TAKES ME:

0	1	2	3	4	5	6	7	8
0–5 mins	5–15 mins	15–45 mins	45–75 mins	1¼–2 hrs	2–3 hrs	3–5 hrs	5–8 hrs	8 hrs + → rate here →

A □ A □ A □ A □ A □
B □ B □ B □ B □ B □

HANDICAP: COMPARED TO MOST PEOPLE THIS ACTIVITY IN MY CASE IS:

0	1	2	3	4	5	6	7	8
No different	Twice as lengthy or frequent/ slightly avoided		3 times as lengthy or frequent/ definitely avoided		4 times as lengthy or frequent/ markedly avoided		5 times as lengthy or totally avoided → rate here →

A □ A □ A □ A □ A □
B □ B □ B □ B □ B □

Conventional Sexual Activity

Rated by self/partner .... Patient .... Therapist ....

	PRE	POST	1MFU	3MFU	6MFU
date	☐	☐	☐	☐	☐
	☐	☐	☐	☐	☐
	☐	☐	☐	☐	☐

I HAVE SEXUAL INTERCOURSE

8	7	6	5	4	3	2	1	0
Not at all		Once a month		Once a week		2–3 times a week		Daily

I HAVE SEX PLAY WITH MY PARTNER
(petting, foreplay)

8	7	6	5	4	3	2	1	0
Not at all, less than once a month		Once a month		Once a week		2–3 times a week		Daily

FOR ME ENJOYMENT DURING THESE SEXUAL ACTIVITIES IS USUALLY

8	7	6	5	4	3	2	1	0
Absent		Slight		Moderate		Marked, but without orgasm		Marked, usually to orgasm

Patient .... Therapist ....

ACTIVITY A

ACTIVITY B

date	PRE	POST	1MFU	3MFU	6MFU
	A ☐ B ☐	A ☐ B ☐	A ☐ B ☐	A ☐ B ☐	A ☐ B ☐
	A ☐ B ☐	A ☐ B ☐	A ☐ B ☐	A ☐ B ☐	A ☐ B ☐
	A ☐ B ☐	A ☐ B ☐	A ☐ B ☐	A ☐ B ☐	A ☐ B ☐

I GET URGES TO DO THIS:

0	1	2	3	4	5	6	7	8
Less than once a month		*Once a month*		*Once a week*		*Once a day*		*3 times daily or more*

rate here →
rate here →

I MASTURBATE OR HAVE SEX WHILE THINKING ABOUT THIS:

0	1	2	3	4	5	6	7	8
Less than once a month		*Once a month*		*Once a week*		*Once a day*		*3 times daily or more*

rate here →

I CARRY OUT THIS ACTIVITY:

0	1	2	3	4	5	6	7	8
Less than twice a year		*Every 3 months*		*Once a month*		*Once a week*		*Daily*

rate here →

Hyperventilation and Panic

This questionnaire — a physical symptom checklist — is given to the client to fill in at two points during the hyperventilation 'provocation test' described in Chapter 8.

1. Before the test when the client is asked to rate the severity of the symptoms he experiences during a panic.
2. After voluntary hyperventilating when the client is asked to rate the severity of the symptoms he just experienced.

The two questionnaires are then compared and contrasted as described in the text in Chapter 8.

	Not at all	Slight	Moderate	Severe	Very severe
MUSCLE PAIN					
WEAKNESS					
SWEATING					
CATARRH					
TREMOR					
DROWSINESS					
NUMBNESS OF EXTREMITIES					
DRY MOUTH					
FEELINGS OF UNREALITY					
HEART RACING					
NAUSEA					
STINGING					
APPREHENSION					
UNHAPPINESS					
SHAKINESS					
EARACHE					
ANXIOUSNESS					
CHOKING					
HEADACHE					
HEART POUNDING					
FAINTNESS					
TENSION					
TINGLING					
PINS AND NEEDLES					
COLDNESS OF EXTREMITIES					
DIZZINESS					
TIGHT MUSCLES					
BREATHLESSNESS					

Adapted from Clark, D. M. and Hemsley, D. R. (1982). The effects of hyperventilation; individual variability and its relation to personality. *Journal of Behaviour Therapy and Experimental Psychiatry*, **13**: 41–47.

Index